MUSICAL STUDIES

MUSICAL STUDIES
By ERNEST NEWMAN

HASKELL HOUSE PUBLISHERS Ltd.
Publishers of Scarce Scholarly Books
NEW YORK, N. Y. 10012
1969

First Published 1905

HASKELL HOUSE PUBLISHERS Ltd.
Publishers of Scarce Scholarly Books
280 LAFAYETTE STREET
NEW YORK, N. Y. 10012

Library of Congress Catalog Card Number: 68-25297

Standard Book Number 8383-0309-9

Printed in the United States of America

PREFACE
TO THE FIRST EDITION (1905)

THE greater part of the following matter has already appeared in various periodicals—the *Fortnightly Review*, the *Contemporary Review*, the *Speaker*, the *Chord*, the New York *Musical Courier*, the *Atlantic Monthly*, the *Weekly Critical Review*, the *Monthly Musical Record*, and the *Daily Mail*. All have been greatly altered, however—some practically rewritten. The larger articles—those on Programme Music, Strauss, and Berlioz —have been made up from sundry articles that appeared at different times and in different journals ; any one who has tried to weld heterogeneous material of this kind into one mass will appreciate the difficulty of the work, and will, I trust, make allowances for whatever awkwardness of form the essays may show here and there.

I must apologise for the fact that occasionally one essay touches slightly upon ground that has already been more fully treated in another. It sometimes happens that two quite different lines of thought, starting from widely separated points, will converge and meet; or, on the other hand, that the one æsthetic principle will prove applicable to different phenomena. I am conscious of this occasional overlapping in the essays, but there seemed no way of avoiding it; if an argument was to have its proper force it had to be given in full, even if for a page or so it duplicated what had already been said elsewhere.

My thanks are due to the Editors of the journals I have named for their permission to reprint.

E. N.

PREFACE
TO THE SECOND EDITION

AS this Second Edition is printed from moulds, no alteration of or addition to the text of the First Edition has been possible. I should have liked to expand one or two of the essays at various points and to revise them at others. There is always something new to be said, for example, about programme music, while any article on a living subject, such as that on Strauss, is bound to contain many things that are not so apposite now as when they were first written. But even these may have a value as pictures of a bygone state of things ; and in this way such matter as that relating to the earlier attitude of the critics and the public towards Strauss may be of some historical interest. The Strauss article obviously needs bringing up to date. But even if that were done, the new article would in turn be behind the times in another year or two ; while the reader will find a further discussion of Strauss, and a consideration of the trend of his art since the *Symphonia Domestica*, in my little book on him in the series of "Living Masters of Music." The Appendix to the present volume is wholly new.

E. N.

CONTENTS

To JAMES HUNEKER

A

MUSICAL STUDIES

BERLIOZ, ROMANTIC
AND CLASSIC

I

IT is fairly safe to say that—with the possible
exception of Liszt—there is no musician
about whom people differ so strongly as
about Berlioz. His case is, indeed, unique.
We are pretty well agreed as to the relative
positions of the other men; roughly speaking,
all cultivated musicians would put Wagner and
Brahms and Beethoven in the first rank of
composers, and Mendelssohn, Grieg, and Dvořàk
in the second or third. Even in the case of
a disputed problem like Strauss, the argument
among those who know his work is not, I take
it, as to his being a musician of the first rank,
but as to the precise position he occupies among
the others of that limited regiment. Upon
Berlioz, however, the world seems unable to
make up its mind. The dispute here is not as
to where he stands among the great ones, but
whether he really belongs to the great ones at
all. Though there is no absolute unanimity of
opinion upon the total work of, say, Wagner or
Beethoven — no complete agreement as to the

amount of weakness that is bound up with their strength—there is at all events perfect unanimity of opinion that Wagner and Beethoven are of the royal line. But we have Berlioz extolled to the skies by one section of competent musicians, while another section can scarcely speak of him politely; he really seems to create a kind of physical nausea in them; and some of them even deny his temperament to have been really musical. There is surely nothing in the history of music to parallel the situation. The difference of opinion upon him, be it observed, is quite another thing from the frequent and quite excusable perplexity that men feel over a *contemporary* composer. Men drift widely apart over Wagner while he is alive; but the next generation, at all events, sees him practically through the same eyes. The quarrel over Berlioz is not a contemporary quarrel; the bulk of his most significant work had all appeared before 1850, and yet here we are, half a century after that time, still debating whether he is really one of the immortals. For many people Schumann's old question, "Are we to regard him as a genius, or only a musical adventurer?" still remains unanswered.

On the whole—looking for a moment only at the external aspect of the case—the current is now flowing not from but towards him. Even putting aside the exceptional spasm of 1903, the centenary of his birth, he probably gets more performances now than he ever did. Messrs. Breitkopf and Härtel are bringing out a magnificent complete edition of his works in score, superbly edited by Weingartner, the great conductor, and Charles Malherbe, Archivist of the Paris Opera ; while in the admirable little Donajowski editions the full scores of the *Symphonie fantastique, Harold en Italie, Roméo et Juliette*, and half-a-dozen of the overtures, can now be had for a total expenditure of a few shillings. Publishers do not generally take to bringing out full scores, particularly at very low prices, unless there is some demand for the works ; and I think we may take it that just now there is a quickening interest in Berlioz. Yet all the while the critical war goes on, without signs of compromise on either side. The attitude of a great many people is of course to be explained partly by imperfect acquaintance with Berlioz's work, partly by their having revolted against him at the outset and never settled down to ask themselves whether their first impressions did not need revising. It is not every one who has either the candour or the capacity for hard and patient work of Weingartner, who has placed on record his own progress from the traditional view of Berlioz as "a great colourist, the founder of modern orchestration, a brilliant writer, and, in fact, almost everything else except a composer of inspiration and melody," to the view that Berlioz is one of the great masters, rich in feeling, in beauty, in inventiveness. Many worthy people no doubt took their cue from Wagner, who, besides giving a nonsensical pseudo-analysis of Berlioz in *Opera and Drama*, referred to him disparagingly in a well-known letter to Liszt. It is tolerably clear, however, that Wagner knew comparatively little of Berlioz at that time, and that in running down *Benvenuto Cellini* and *La Damnation de Faust* he was only indulging that unfortunate habit of his of expressing himself very positively upon subjects he knew nothing about.[1] But put aside all the criticism of him that comes from imperfect knowledge — and it must be remembered that up to quite recently it was not easy to get a perfect knowledge of him, for his scores were rather scarce, and so badly printed as to make the reading of them a trial—

[1] The reader who is interested in the matter may turn to Wagner's letters to Liszt of 1852. Here he speaks slightingly of Berlioz's *Cellini*, and alludes to "the platitudes of his Faust *Symphony* (!)" The last phrase alone is sufficient to show that Wagner was completely ignorant of the work he had the impertinence to decry—for every one knows that Berlioz's *Faust* is not a symphony. In a recent article in *The Speaker* on "The Relations of Wagner and Berlioz," I have, I think, shown that Wagner could not have known a note either of the *Faust* or the *Cellini;* the dates of performance and of publication put any such knowledge on his part out of the question. It is necessary, however, to warn the reader that in both the English translation of the Wagner-Liszt letters (by Dr. Hueffer, revised by Mr. Ashton Ellis), and the big Glasenapp-Ellis *Life of Wagner*, the real facts are kept from the English public. The incriminating phrase, "Faust Symphony," is quietly abbreviated to "Faust," so that there is nothing to rouse the reader's suspicions and make him look further into the matter. In the big *Life*, again, now in course of publication, Mr. Ellis, though he has thousands of pages at his disposal—though, indeed, he can devote a whole volume of five hundred pages to two years of Wagner's life—still cannot find room for the brief line or two from the 1852 letter that would put the real facts before the reader ; discreet and silent dots take their place. The British public is apparently to be treated like a child, and told only so much of the truth about Wagner as is thought to be good for it—or at any rate good for Wagner.

and we are still left face to face with a certain amount of good critical intelligence that cannot, do what it will, take to Berlioz's music. And since criticism is, or ought to be, concerned not only with the psychological processes that go to make a work of art, but also with the psychological processes that make us judge it in this way or that—it is worth while trying to discover what it is in Berlioz that makes so many worthy people quite unsympathetic towards him.

II

Let us first of all look at him biographically and historically, as he was in himself and in his relations to his contemporaries. His is perhaps the strangest story in all the records of music. In contrast to musicians like Bach, Beethoven, Mozart, Wagner, and a score of others, who grew up from childhood in an atmosphere saturated with music, Berlioz is born in a country town that is practically destitute of musical life. Even the piano is not cultivated there, the harp and guitar being almost the sole instruments known; in 1808—five years after the birth of Berlioz—there is still only one piano in the Department. There is no teacher of music in the place; Berlioz's father ultimately combines with other residents to bring over for this purpose a second violinist from the theatre at Lyons. Although the music in the boy cannot quite be kept down, for nearly the first twenty years of his life he is, to all intents

and purposes, ignorant of the elements of technique, and never hears a bar of first-rate music.
"When I arrived in Paris in 1820,"[1] he says, " I
had never yet set foot in a theatre ; all I knew of
instrumental music was the quartetts of Pleyel
with which the four amateurs composing the
Philharmonic Society of my native town used to
regale me each Sunday after mass ; and I had no
other idea of dramatic music than what I had
been able to get in running through a collection
of old operatic airs arranged with an accompaniment for the guitar." Yet, untutored as he was,
and practically ignorant of even the elements of
harmony, he had from his boyhood been writing
music. The opening melody of the *Symphonie
fantastique* was really written by Berlioz in his
twelve year, to some verses from Florian's *Estelle;*[2]
and we know of other boyish compositions, fragments of which have been conserved in some of
his later works. It may not be absolutely true,
as M. Edmond Hippeau says, that until the age
of twenty-three he was "ignorant of the most
elementary principles of music"; but at all events
he was just beginning to learn these principles at
an age when nine other composers out of ten have
left far behind them all the drudgery of the
apprentice. In Paris he does indeed study after
a fashion ; but it is characteristic of him that he
gets most of his musical experience from the per-

---

[1] This is an error ; he arrived in Paris in 1821.
[2] See Julien Tiersot's *Hector Berlioz et la société de son temps*
(1904)—an excellent book that is indispensable to every student of
Berlioz.

formances at the Opera, and from a diligent reading of the scores of Gluck in the library of the Conservatoire.

Even in Paris, at that time, there was little to call out the best there was in such a man as Berlioz—little that could teach him the proper use of his own strange faculties, or by whose standard he could test the worth of his own inspiration. He did indeed hear a little Gluck occasionally, and a travesty of Weber; but it was not until 1828 that Beethoven made any impression on Paris. Orchestras were generally incompetent and audiences ignorant. The calibre of the average French orchestra of the time may be gauged from the fact that even the more reputable bands found Mozart's symphonies by no means easy. One shudders to think what the ordinary orchestras must have been like, and what was the quality of music to which they had grown accustomed. As for the audiences, where they were not extremely uneducated they were extremely prejudiced, clinging blindly to the remains of the pseudo-classical principles that had been bequeathed to them by their fathers. An audience that could be worked into a perfect frenzy of rage because an actor, outraging all the proprieties of the time, actually referred in *Othello* to something so vulgar as a handkerchief, would hardly look with favour on anything revolutionary either in idea or technique. At the opera the Italians were most in vogue. The French public knew little of instrumental music pure and simple, and were almost entirely ignorant of the huge developments of German music. Cherubini, of course, was a stately and impressive figure, a serious thinker of the same breed as the great Germans ; but apart from him, there were no Parisian composers who could by any stretch of the imagination be called modern, or could do anything to teach a man like Berlioz. Lesueur, the favourite master of Berlioz, seems to have been progressive—indeed, revolutionary—in some of his theories of music and poetry ; but his theory was better than his practice. From such a type as the amiable and ineffectual Boïeldieu nothing new could possibly come. He frankly avowed his inability to understand Beethoven, and declared to Berlioz his preference for " la musique qui me berce." Yet this young musician from the country, with years of lost time to regret, with little musical education, with the very slightest of stimuli from the great music of the past, and with little encouragement in his own surroundings, produces in quick succession a number of works of the most startling originality—original in every way, in the turn of their melodies, in their harmonic *facture*, in their orchestration, in their rhythm, in their view of men and things. Now that the complete Berlioz is being printed, we know a good deal more of him than was possible even a few years ago. We do not now commence our study of him with the *Symphonie fantastique ;* we can watch the workings of his brain in the two early cantatas—*Herminie* and *Cléopâtre* —that in the eyes of two sapient juries of the time were insufficient to win him the *Prix de*

Rome. Here we see a freshness of outlook and of style—particularly in the matter of rhythm—that is one of the most remarkable phenomena in the history of music. In his earliest years, as in his latest, Berlioz was himself, a solitary figure owing practically nothing to other people's music, an artist, we may almost say, without ancestry and without posterity. Mozart builds upon Haydn and influences Beethoven ; Beethoven imitates Mozart and in turn influences the practice of all later symphonists ; Wagner learns from Weber and gives birth to a host of imitators. But with Berlioz—and it is a point to be insisted on—there is no one whose speech he tried to copy in his early years, and there is no one since who speaks with *his* voice. How many things in the early Beethoven were made in the factory of Mozart ; how many times does the early Wagner speak with the voice of Weber ! But who can turn over the scores of Berlioz's early works and find a single phrase that can be fathered upon any previous or contemporary writer ? There was never any one, before his time or since, who thought and wrote just like him ; his musical style especially is absolutely his own. Now and then in *L'Enfance du Christ* he suggests Gluck—not in the turn of his phrases but in the general atmosphere of an aria ; but apart from this it is the rarest thing for him to remind us of any other composer. His melody, his harmony, his rhythm, are absolutely his own.

III

We are face to face, then, with a personality which, whether we like it or not, is of extraordinary strength and originality. If we are to realise what kind of force he was, and how he came to do the work he did, we must study him both from the standpoint of history and from that of physiological and psychological science. Musical criticism is apt to become too much a mere matter of wine-tasting, a bare statement of a preference of this vintage or a decided dislike for that. We need to study musicians as a whole, as complete organisms hanging together by virtue of certain peculiarities of structure. If a man does not like Liszt's music he compares it disparagingly with Wagner's—as if this placing of people on the higher or lower rungs of a ladder were the be-all and the end-all of criticism. Shakespeare is the greatest figure of the Elizabethan literary world; but what critic thinks of disposing of Ford and Massinger and Jonson and Webster and Marlowe and Tourneur with the offhand remark that not one of them was a Shakespeare? In the same way it is not sufficient to write down Berlioz as a purveyor of extravagant ideas clothed sometimes in ugly and unpleasing forms; it is much more profitable to set ourselves to find out why he came to have such a bias in art, and what were his relations to the general intellectual movements of his time. It is only when we study him from the historical standpoint that we can understand many of his ideals; and to understand them is more important than to rail at them. The criticism that rejects the less beautiful specimens of an art because they are not perfect is like the natural history that would take account only of the typical organisms, passing over the many instructive variations from the type. In the long run human folly and human failure are just as interesting to the student of humanity as its wisdom and its triumphs; and the critic should always aim at being an impartial student of humanity, not a mere wine-taster or a magistrate.

As we have seen, whatever other qualities we may deny to Berlioz, we cannot at any rate refuse his claim to originality. Readers of Théophile Gautier's *Histoire du Romantisme,* in which the cool, objective poet and critic reviews all the leading figures of the Romantic movement—Victor Hugo, Gérard de Nerval, Alfred de Vigny, Delacroix, and a score or so of lesser lights—will remember that Berlioz is the only musician admitted to that brilliant company. It was not due to any personal preference on Gautier's part, or to his ignorance of the other Romantic musicians; there simply were no others. So far as music was concerned, the whole Romantic movement began and ended with Berlioz. When we are tempted to feel annoyed at some of his extravagances or banalities we should remember that he had to conquer a new world unaided. He was not only without colleagues but without progenitors. When he arrived in Paris in 1821, at the age of eighteen, what was the position of music in France? Gluck's epoch-making work had terminated in 1779 with *Iphigenia in Tauris;* the dramatic school of which he was the leader made something like its last effort in Sacchini's *Œdipe à Colone* in 1789. The often charming but flimsy work of Dauvergne, Duni, Monsigny, Dalayrac and Grétry was without any importance for the opera of the future. Two musicians alone commanded serious respect — the great Cherubini, who, however, was neither typically French nor very revolutionary, and Méhul, whose *Joseph* appeared in 1807. Lesueur and Berton do not count; while Hérold, strong man as he was in some ways, was not strikingly original either in form or in expression. The French music produced during the years of Berlioz's early manhood was of the type of Boïeldieu's *La Dame Blanche* (1828), Auber's *Masaniello* (1828) and *Fra Diavolo* (1830), or Adam's *Postillon de Longjumeau* (1836). Neither Spontini in the first decade of the century, nor Rossini in later years, was a necessary link in the chain of development of French music. In fact, of almost all the music heard in Paris between 1790 and 1830 we may say that whenever it was great it was not French, and whenever it was French it was not great. Above all it was scarcely ever *contemporary* music; it rarely showed any trace of having assimilated the life and art of its own day. Especially was it unaffected by the hot young Romantic blood that in the second and third decades of the century was transforming both French poetry and French painting. Think of the artists and poets, and then think of the musicians, and you seem to enter another and inferior world of thought.

It was Berlioz, and Berlioz alone, who brought French music into line with the activities of intelligent men in other departments. He put into it a ferocity and turbulence of imagination and an audacity of style to which it had hitherto been a stranger. Often when I listen to him now I feel that we do not even yet quite appreciate his originality. Even after the lapse of so many years the music sometimes strikes us, in spite of all the enormous development of the art between his day and ours, as startlingly new and unconventional. What then must it have sounded like in the ears of those who heard it for the first time? Imagine the bourgeois audience of those days suddenly assailed by the March to the Scaffold, or the Witches' Sabbath, in the *Symphonie fantastique !* There was here as violent a rupture with the staid formulas of the classic and the pseudo-classic as anything achieved by Victor Hugo or Delacroix or Gros or Géricault.

The springs that moved Berlioz, in fact, were just the springs that moved his great contemporaries. The essence of their revolt was an insistence upon the truth that beauty is co-extensive almost with life itself. The nerves of the younger men were sharper than their fathers'; their ears were more acute, their eyes more observant. They saw and felt more of life, and tried to express in art what they had seen and felt; which could not be done without not only breaking the mould of the pseudo-classic technique, but also finding voice for a lot of sensations and ideas to which the men of the previous generation had been impervious. Recent French critics have noticed, as one evidence of the more sensitive nerves of the early Romanticists, the fineness and variety of their perceptions of colour. To the literary man of the eighteenth century an object is merely blue or red; the new writers perceive a dozen shades of blue and red, and ransack the whole vocabulary to find the right discriminating word.[1] There was a general effort to escape from the conventions that had fast-bound poetry, painting, the drama, and the opera. The dress of the actors and singers now aimed at some correspondence with that of the epoch of the play, instead of making the vain attempt to produce an historical illusion with the costume of their own time. The subjects of dramas, novels, poems, and operas, instead of being exclusively classic, were now sought in contemporary manners or in earlier European history; and with the change of matter there necessarily came a change of style. At the same time there sprang up an intellectual intimacy, previously

---

[1] It is interesting to note that Alfred de Musset anticipated Arthur Rimbaud and the modern symbolists in having coloured audition. He once maintained that the note F was yellow, G red, a soprano voice blond, a contralto voice brown. See Arvède Barine's *Alfred de Musset* (in *Les Grands Écrivains Français*), p. 115.

unknown, between all classes of artists. The poet and the musician hung about the studio of the painter; the painter and the poet sang the songs of the musician, or attended the performances of his opera, to criticise it from the point of view of men who themselves were used to thinking in art. The imagination of each was stimulated and enriched by the ideas and sensations of the others. The new achievements of line or colour or language or sound prompted the devotee of each art to fresh experiments in his own medium. This in turn led to another new phenomenon, of particular importance in the history of music. There came to the front an original type—the literary musician, who made a practice, and sometimes a profession, of writing about his art, of educating the public at the same time as he clarified his own ideas and tested his own powers. This type was accompanied by yet another new product—the literary man or poet who wrote on music, not as a professor or a pedant, and not after the manner of the Rousseaus and Suards of the eighteenth century, but with dynamic force and directness, correlating music with life and thought, estimating it by its actual meaning to living men. There was nothing in the eighteenth century to correspond to the prose writings of musicians like Berlioz and Schumann, nothing to compare with the treatment of musical subjects by literary men such as Hoffmann and Baudelaire.[1] And yet, while there was in this

[1] Hoffmann was, of course, a musician as well; but he is more truly the novelist who wrote about music than the musician who wrote fiction.

way a greater actual expenditure of brain-power upon music and art generally, the men themselves were not such solid types as the men of the eighteenth century. Neither Hugo, nor Gautier, nor Delacroix, nor Berlioz had the intellectual weight and fixity of Diderot, or Condorcet, or David, or Gluck. The reason of the eighteenth century was transformed into sentiment, its activity into reflection, its repose into enthusiasm, its sobriety into passion.

Against this spirit the now anæmic idealism of pseudo-classical art could not stand for long. If artists had taught the public to believe that whatever tasted of real life was vulgar or barbaric, the public must now be disabused of that notion. All life was claimed as the province of the artist; he claimed also the right to draw it as he had seen it. "There are no good subjects or bad subjects," said Victor Hugo; "there are only good poets and bad poets." Expression—vital expression, biting to the very heart of the theme —was now the ideal; beauty, in the limited sense that had been given to it by the false classics, was only a formula more or less platitudinous. "The realisation of beauty by the expression of character" was the avowed purpose of the Romanticists. M. Brunetière aptly contrasts with this the classic theorem of Winckelmann, that the ideal beauty was "like pure water, having no particular savour." "We must say it and repeat it," cries Hugo in the preface of 1824 to the *Odes et Ballades;* "it is not the need for novelty that torments our minds ; it is the need for truth—and

that need is immense." Delacroix summed up
the general falsity of the conventional attitude
towards art when he wrote: "In order to make
an ideal head of a negro, our teachers make him
resemble as far as possible the profile of Antinous,
and then say, 'We have done our utmost; if he is,
nevertheless, not beautiful, we must abstain altogether from this freak of nature, this squat nose
and thick lips, which are so unendurable to the
eyes.'" A journalist of 1826 (cited by M. Gus-
tave Lanson in his admirable *Histoire de la
Littérature française*) cried, "Vive la nature
brute et sauvage qui revit si bien dans les vers de
M. de Vigny, Jules Lefèvre, Victor Hugo!" It
was not that they worshipped ugliness and
violence in themselves, but that they felt there
are certain occasions when truth can be reached
only through the repellent and the extravagant,
which, however, may be bent by a wise eclecticism
to the purposes of the ideal. There is scarcely
anything in the imagination of Berlioz that is not
paralleled in the imaginations of the contemporary
poets and painters; there is no leap of theirs
towards freer verse or more expressive colour
that was not also taken by the musician. Only
while they had at least some roots in the past,
not only in their own country but in England
and Germany, and while they were many and
could support and purify each other by mutual
criticism, Berlioz stood by himself, without any
musician, dead or living, being of any practical
value to him in the course he took.

IV

Few literary and artistic movements have their social and physical roots laid as clearly open to us as the Romantic. The most astonishing thing in connection with this chain of causes and results is that there should be only the solitary figure of Berlioz to represent the musical side of it. One would have thought that the vast liberation of nervous energy effected by the Revolution and the Napoleonic period would have been too great to be confined to literature and the plastic arts —that a really French school of music would have arisen, interwoven with the past and the present of French history and social life, and as typical of contemporary French culture in its own way as the poetry, drama, and painting of the time were in theirs. That this did not happen was in all probability due to the confirmed hold which the theatre had upon music-lovers in France. To nine men out of ten there music was synonymous with opera ; and opera meant a spectacle in which only the greatest pleasure of the greatest number had to be consulted. It was an art-form in which compromise was carried to its highest points ; the audience was cosmopolitan and not too critical, and the composers, whether native or foreign, had to think only in the second place of art, and in the first place of speaking a musical language that would be intelligible and acceptable to all. No independent, contemporary expression of culture could be expected in opera, for no one, composer or spectator, took it quite seriously enough for that.

On the other hand, there was no purely instrumental form existing that could serve as a vehicle for such revolutionary modes of feeling as found expression in the literature and painting of the day. Finally, there was no public with sufficient musical training to demand a new revelation in music, or to comprehend it if it came. The French orchestras of the time, as we have seen, were almost uniformly inefficient, incapable of playing great music with any intelligence. It was impossible, then, for the public to be as alive, as up-to-date, in music as it was in other things; and music, more than any other art, is dependent upon collective as distinguished from individual patronage. Perhaps, also, the language of French music was as yet not sufficiently developed to fit it to answer the needs of the young generation of Romanticists. It was not real enough, not close enough to actual life to spur the energies of men either into approval or disgust. There was no mistaking the angry flare of the new spirit in other fields. The realism of Gros or of Delacroix was patent to every eye; the mere change in the choice of subjects was a challenge and a provocation. So again in poetry, one could not fail to be agitated by the incessant whipping of the language to new feats of technique, the perpetual evocation of new forms of expression, new vibrations of verbal colour. All this was on very much the same plane as the everyday life of men. It was something they could feel a fighting interest in. But no one took music so seriously. It was long before it lost the grand manner, the trick of wig and sword, of the eighteenth century ; and when it did there was nothing of equal grandeur to take its place. Where it was great, and had the large stride and the flowing cloak, it breathed of the psychology of the past ; where it took part in the lives of the men of its own day it attacked them only on their more sensuous, more frankly epicurean side. It was a mistress, not a wife.

In Berlioz alone, then, the Romantic movement expended its musical energies. He alone among French musicians of the time shows the same characteristics of body and mind as went to the making of the art or literature of his contemporaries. With him, as with them, the physiological structure counts for very much. No doubt a good deal of the motive-power came from the great awakening of the Napoleonic era. The nation that had been wrestling for a generation with every country in Europe necessarily touched life on more sides than it had ever done before. The old formalities no longer sufficed ; indeed, the mere antiquity of any thought or any practice was no recommendation of it in the eyes of this people, to whom the strange kaleidoscopic present was a spectacle of ever-changing interest. It was this aspect of the situation to which Stendhal gave expression when he compared his own century with the eighteenth, the classic nutriment with the romantic. "The classic pieces are like religions—the time for creating them has gone by. They are like a clock that points to midday when it is four in the afternoon. This kind of poetry was all right for the people who, at Fontenoy, raised their hats and said to the English column, 'Gentlemen, be good enough to fire first.' And it is expected that this poetry should satisfy a Frenchman who took part in the retreat from Moscow!" When the Napoleonic empire had fallen, a new motive-power of great literary value was discovered in the intense melancholy which, according to Musset, seized upon the younger spirits at the sudden limitation of the nation's activities. "A feeling of inexpressible *malaise* commenced to ferment in every young heart. Condemned to inaction by the sovereigns of the world, given up to indolence, to *ennui*, the young men . . . experienced, at the foundation of their souls, a misery that was insupportable."

The physiological causes, however, of this nervous irritability, this dissatisfaction with existing things, which is as strongly marked in Berlioz as in Musset or Delacroix, were probably more important than the moral ones. The majority of the artists and literary men of this epoch had a poor, neurotic physique. In almost all of them there was a tendency to nervous derangement, or some weakness of the heart or lungs that would predispose them to melancholy. Maxime du Camp bore strong testimony to the physical lassitude that characterised this epoch. "The artistic and literary generation that preceded me," he wrote, "that to which I belonged, had a youth of artistic sadness, inherent in the constitution of men or in the epoch." Again, speaking of the proclivity to suicide among the young men of the time, he says, "It was not merely a fashion, as one might believe ; it was a kind of general debility that made the heart sad and the mind gloomy, and caused death to be looked upon as a deliverance."

This *défaillance générale*, this *tristesse sans cause comme sans objet, tristesse abstraite*, must have had its roots in something deeper than the mere psychological outlook of the youth of the period. It seems probable that there was a general physical exhaustion, a widespread undermining of physique. The children born about the beginning of the century must have had for their parents, in many cases, people who had lived in an atmosphere of intense social and political excitement, and had probably undergone a considerable amount of actual physical hardship. The Napoleonic wars can hardly have failed to leave their mark upon the physiological constitution of the French race. If it be true that the fine nervous quality of the Irish comes in part from the centuries of troubled life through which the race has passed, there must certainly have been some impression left upon the physique of France by the lurid, swiftly changing episodes of the Revolution and the Empire. The mere loss of young blood must have counted for a good deal. De Musset, indeed, in his *Confession d'un enfant du siècle*, bears testimony to the melancholy of the young generation—"une génération ardente, pâle, nerveuse," "conceived between two battles," and born of "les mères inquiètes."[1]   Maxime Du

---

[1] Buckle (note 316 to Chap. VII. of the *History of Civilisation*) remarks that "All great revolutions have a direct tendency to in-

Camp too suggests this explanation of the morbidity of the time, and adds to it another. "Often I have asked myself whether this depression may not have been the outcome of physiological causes. The nation was exhausted by the wars of the empire, and the children had inherited their fathers' weakness. Besides, the system of medicine and hygiene then prevalent was disastrous. Broussais was the leader of thought, and doctors went everywhere lancet in hand. At school they bled us for a headache. When I had typhoid fever I was bled three times in one week, sixty leeches were applied, and I could only have recovered by a miracle. The doctrines preached by Molière's Diafoiruses had lasted on to our day, and resulted in the anæmic constitution so frequently met with. Poverty of blood combined with the nervous temperament makes a man melancholy and depressed."

One consequence of this flawed physique was that the young men of the time not only had extravagant conceptions, but that they took these and themselves with enormous seriousness. The majority of them posed unconscionably at times. They could not be unhappy without playing upon their own sensations for the benefit of an audience; there was something of the actor in

crease insanity, as long as they last, and probably for some time afterwards; but in this as in other respects the French Revolution stands alone in the number of its victims." See the references he gives, bearing upon "the horrible but curious subject of madness caused by the excitement of the events which occurred in France late in the eighteenth century." Buckle speaks only of the Revolution, but of course the subsequent wars must have operated in much the same way.

almost all of them. Each was a Werther in his own eyes, a person towards whom the cosmos had behaved with a special and quite unpardonable malevolence. Listen, for example, to the declamation of Chateaubriand: "I have never been happy, I have never attained happiness though I have pursued it with a perseverance corresponding with the natural ardour of my soul; no one knows what the happiness was that I sought, no one has fully known the depths of my heart; the majority of my sentiments have remained immured there, or have only appeared in my works as applied to imaginary beings. To-day, when I still regret my chimæras without however pursuing them, when, having reached the summit of life, I descend towards the tomb, I wish, before dying, to revert to those precious years, *to explain my inexplicable heart*, to see, in short, what I can say when my pen abandons itself unconstrainedly to all my recollections."[1] One detects a little note of insincerity in it all. The gentleman doth protest too much; he is wearing his heart too visibly on his coat-sleeve, trafficking in melancholy as a man traffics in cotton or steel, simply because there is a market for that kind of thing. We need to read Berlioz's letters with this suspicion always before us if we are to take them at their real value. A fair summary of the half-sincere, half-posing mood that was prevalent among the young men of genius of the time is to be had in Géricault's portrait of himself, in the

---

[1] Chateaubriand, *Souvenirs d'enfance et de jeunesse*, p. 2.

Louvre, with the forced melodrama of the skull
on the shelf intruding itself upon the real earnest-
ness of the picture as a whole. We get plenty
of this somewhat far-fetched and too conscious
diablerie in some of the early work of Berlioz;
and there is no need to be more contemptuous of
it there than when we meet with it in the poets
or the painters who were his contemporaries.
To say nothing of the grandiloquent Hugo and
his youthful followers, even so strong and philosophical a type as Flaubert was decoyed now
and then into the same kind of pose of exaggeration. His early letters have their full share of
sentimentality, of talk about man being as a frail
skiff in the tempest, and all the other formulas
of the school,[1] although Flaubert expressly
dissociated himself from the more lymphatic
specimens of Romanticism. " Do you know," he
wrote, " that the new generation of the schools
is extremely stupid ; formerly it had more sense ;
it occupied itself with women, sword-thrusts,
orgies; now it apes Byron. . . . It is who shall
have the palest face and say in the best manner
' I am *blasé, blasé !* ' What a pity! *blasé* at
eighteen ! "

V

If ever the physiological structure of a man
had to be taken into account in trying to explain

---

[1] In his letter of March 18, 1839, he gives Ernest Chevalier the
plan of a work that is curiously like that of Berlioz mentioned on
page 38, in its preposterous fantasies and its over-emphasis of
form and colour.

the nature of his work, it is surely when we are dealing with Berlioz. We have only to look at his portrait to see how highly strung he was, how prone he must have been to disorders of the nervous system. There is a passage in one of his letters that seems to indicate an anxiety for his health on the part of his father, who, being a doctor, would probably understand his son's bias towards nervous troubles: "Je suis vos instructions quant au régime," writes Hector; "je mange ordinairement peu et ne bois presque plus de thé." His early life, after he left the paternal home, was certainly one of great privation. He moreover seems to have been exceedingly careless of his health, indulging in long walks without a proper supply of food—presuming upon a nervous energy that to him no doubt seemed like a solid physical constitution. Worse even than this was his occasional deliberate resort to starvation, as one of his friends tells us, "pour connaître les maux par lesquels le génie pouvait passer." The wonder is not that he should always have been a prey to some trouble or other of the nerves, or that in middle age he should have been attacked by a frightful intestinal disorder, but that he should have lived as long as he did, and found strength enough for such work as he has bequeathed to us. "How unhappily I am put together," he once wrote to his friend Ferrand—"a veritable barometer, now up, now down, always susceptible to the changes of the atmosphere—bright or sombre—of my consuming thoughts." As it was, the nerves plainly underwent a gradual deterioration. There are the same general mental characteristics in his later work as in his earlier, but the music of the last fifteen years of his life will as a whole hardly bear comparison with that written between the ages of twenty-five and forty. The fine bloom seemed to have been rubbed off his spirit; even where the music still has the nervous energy of former years it is almost entirely an external thing—a mere tendency to break out into the unexpected because of the impossibility of continuing for long on the one level path; while too often there is a sheer dulness that evidently comes from the long-continued stilling of his pains with opium. But until his system wore itself out in this way through every kind of over-strain, it was clearly one of extraordinary sensitivity, susceptible to a hundred impressions that must have remained a sealed book to every other French musician of the time.

This was the keynote to his mental life and to the world which he tried to reproduce in art; and if we study his physical organisation he becomes far more typical of the Romantic movement than the most brilliant of his contemporaries. If their distinguishing mark was the extraordinary seriousness with which they took their artistic impressions, the strange convulsions produced in them by the sight of a beautiful thing or by the mere rapturous act of composition, it must be said that not one of them can compare with Berlioz in this respect. A hundred passages, in his *Memoirs*, his letters, and his prose works, reveal his temperament as perhaps the most extraordinarily volcanic thing in the history of music.   Musicians as a whole have an unenviable notoriety for not being as other men are ; they surpass even the poets in the fineness of their nerves and the tendency of these to evade the control of the higher centres.   But surely, outside the history of religious mania or the ecstasy of the mystics, there is nothing to parallel the abnormal state into which Berlioz was thrown by music.   " When I hear certain pieces of music, my vital forces at first seem to be doubled. I feel a delicious pleasure, in which reason has no part ; the habit of analysis comes afterwards to give birth to admiration ; the emotion, increasing in proportion to the energy or the grandeur of the ideas of the composer, soon produces a strange agitation in the circulation of the blood ; tears, which generally indicate the end of the paroxysm, often indicate only a progressive state of it, leading to something still more intense.   In this case I have spasmodic contractions of the muscles, a trembling in all my limbs, a complete torpor of the feet and the hands, a partial paralysis of the nerves of sight and hearing ; I no longer see, I scarcely hear : vertigo . . . a semi-swoon."   Still more curious is the effect created on him by music he does not like.   " One can imagine," he says, " that sensations carried to this degree of violence are rather rare, and that there is a vigorous contrast to them, namely *the painful musical effect,* producing the contrary of admiration and pleasure.

No music acts more strongly in this respect than that whose principal fault seems to me to be platitude plus falsity of expression. Then I redden as if with shame ; a veritable anger takes possession of me ; to look at me, you would think I had just received an unpardonable insult ; to get rid of the impression I have received, there is a general upheaval of my being, an effort of expulsion in the whole organism, analogous to the effort of vomiting, when the stomach wishes to reject a nauseous liquor. It is disgust and hatred carried to their extreme limit ; this music exasperates me, and I vomit it through all my pores."

This is not a piece of merely literary exaggeration, for time after time in his letters we come across corroborative evidence that Berlioz was really affected by music in this way. He thus surpasses in nervous extravagance the most abnormal of the young poets and painters of his time. And as with them the susceptibility of their physical organisms led to a new sympathy with things, a new tenderness, a new pity, so did the weakness of Berlioz lead him to the discovery of shades of emotion that had never before found expression in music. Madame de Staël's remark, that "la littérature romantique . . . se sert de nos impressions personnelles pour nous émouvoir," had a wider application than she imagined. The French Romantic was a new type in art ; in most cases a nervous sufferer himself, he had glimpses of a whole world of human pain and pathos that were denied his forerunners. The great figures of the eighteenth century are for the most part objective, travelling by the way of reason rather than that of emotion, philosophers rather than artists, living in the central stream of things, and with a broad, clear outlook on the actual affairs of their own day. Their very sentiment is a different thing from the sentiment of the later generation; it is more under control, has less heart and more brain in it, is less suggestive of an overwhelming surge along the nerves. Only now and again in the literature of the eighteenth century do we catch a foreshadowing of that species of quivering emotion which found, sometimes only too easily, expression in the Romantics. We have it in a noteworthy passage of Diderot: "Le premier serment que se firent deux êtres de chair, ce fut au pied d'un rocher qui tombait en poussière; ils attestèrent de leur constance un ciel qui n'est pas un instant le même; tout passait en eux, autour d'eux, et ils croyaient leurs cœurs affranchis de vicissitudes. O enfants! toujours enfants!" This, in the literature of its time, is like a lyric of Heine appearing among the pages of Lessing, a song of Schumann in the middle of a score of Gluck. We have something of the same tone again, a similar adumbration of the romantic spirit, here and there in the *Rêveries* of Rousseau. But it is in the Romantics that we first find the full expression of that new tremor of feeling that comes from the sense of the weakness of our poor flesh, the sense of the mortality of our clay, our hourly nearness to corruption, our community with everything that suffers and perishes.

VI

Before coming to consider his music, let us complete the study of Berlioz as an organism by examining his prose, where we shall find many things that throw light on his structure. The assistance given to the student of musical psychology by the prose writings of musicians is so great, that one could almost wish that every composer of any note had left the world a volume or two of criticism or of autobiography. They would not necessarily have added very much to our positive knowledge of life or art ; but a book is such an unconscious revelation of its writer, he shows himself in it so faithfully and so completely, no matter how much he may desire to pose or deceive, that the psychologist is able to reconstruct the man's mind from it as the scientist can reconstruct in imagination the body of an animal from a few of its bones. One does not lay much store, for example, by the actual contents of the volumes of prose which Wagner was unkind enough to bequeath to us ; but after all one would not willingly let them die, for they are of the utmost help to the study of Wagner, indirectly, if not directly, throwing sidelights on him of which he was quite unconscious. The prose of Berlioz has greater intrinsic interest. Deeply as he said he loathed his journalistic work, he was after all a born journalist, a fluent writer, a cynical wit, an accomplished story-teller in certain *genres*, a master of polished and mordant irony.

C

My present purpose, however, is not to attempt
an appreciation of Berlioz's prose as a whole, but
to call attention to certain curious elements in it
that have not, so far as I am aware, been pointed
out before, and that are extremely interesting to
the student of so strange and complex a personality as Berlioz.

Readers of Hennequin's fine, if not quite convincing, essay on Flaubert in *Quelques Écrivains
Français*, will remember the attempt to exhibit
the structure and functioning of the novelist's
brain by dissection of his prose. Flaubert, he
shows, tends always to write thus and thus; he
has a vocabulary of such and such a kind, and he
tends to build up words in such and such a way.
Proceeding from this basis, Hennequin goes on
to examine Flaubert's construction of his sentences, then of his paragraphs, then of his
chapters, then of his novels, and thus to explain
the final form of the books in terms of a fundamental intellectual structure that has been con-
ditioned by a certain verbal faculty.   Hennequin,
I think, pushes his method rather too far here,
making blindly for his thesis regardless of all that
may be urged against it; but on the whole the
essay is a novel and valuable contribution to a
neglected science—the study of a man's brain
through the medium of his forms of expression.
Now any one who reads critically through the
prose works of Berlioz must be struck by certain
elements in the prose that seem to give the key
to much that is almost inexplicable in his music
and his character.   " Extravagant," "theatrical,"

" bizarre "—these are the terms that have always
been used of Berlioz. Sir Hubert Parry takes
the easy course of attributing his theatricalism
to his being a Frenchman, oblivious of the fact
that the French disliked it and ridiculed it more
than any other nation. The early prose of Berlioz indicates that he was a man of a cerebral
structure that tended always to express itself
extravagantly ; a man who did not see things
upon the ordinary level of earth quite so clearly
as shapes in cloud and on mountain-top.

The big effects at which he aimed in music
were, indeed, only one form of manifestation of
a curious faculty that was always leading him
to the grandiose. The ordinary orchestra, the
ordinary chorus, the ordinary concert-room would
never do for him ; everything must be magnified,
as it were, beyond life-size. Similarly in his
prose, the ordinary similes, the ordinary metaphors rarely occur to him ; the dilated brain can
only express itself in a dilation of language.
Thus one adjective is rarely enough for Berlioz ;
there must generally be at least three, and these
of the most exaggerated kind. A thing is never
beautiful or ugly for Berlioz ; it is either divine
or horrible. A scene in his early work, where
Cleopatra reflects on the welcome to be given her
by the Pharaohs entombed in the pyramids, is
"terrible, frightful." His *Francs Juges* overture
in one place is described as " monstrous, colossal,
horrible." On another occasion he writes, " There
is nothing so terribly frightful as my overture. . .
It is a hymn to despair, but the most despairing

despair one can imagine—horrible and tender."
Everywhere there is the same tumefaction of
language. When he ponders over the memory
of his first wife and her sufferings, he is overcome
by "an immense, frightful, incommensurable,
infinite pity." Towards the end of his life he is
seized by "the furious desire for immense affec-
tions." He can hardly speak of anything that
has moved him without this piling-up of the most
tremendous adjectives in the language.

As might be expected, his imagery is of the
same order; the very largest things in the universe are impressed into the service of his similes
and metaphors. He speaks in one place of
"those superhuman adagios, where the genius
of Beethoven soars aloft, immense and solitary,
like the colossal bird above the snowy summit
of Chimborazo." He had never seen the bird
above the summit of Chimborazo, but his brain
reverts spontaneously to this conception in the
effort to express the sensation of immensity and
solitude given him by Beethoven's music. The
pyramids, being conveniently large, frequently
enter into his similes. "It needs a very rare
order of genius to create the things that both
artists and public can take to at once—things
whose simplicity is in direct proportion to their
mass, like the pyramids of Djizeh." "Yesterday," he writes after a certain performance of his
works, "I had a pyramidal success." When the
pyramids fail him he falls back on Ossian, or on
Babylon and Nineveh. After having heard 6500
children's voices in St. Paul's, he writes, "It was,

without comparison, the most imposing, the most
Babylonian ceremony I had ever beheld." The
"Tibi omnes" and the "Judex" of his *Te Deum*
are "Babylonian, Ninivitish pieces." One night
he hears the north wind "lament, moan, and
howl like several generations in agony. My
chimney resounds cavernously like a sixty-four
feet organ-pipe. I have never been able to resist
these Ossianic noises."

Occasionally the heaping of Pelion on Ossa
becomes necessary in order to enable him to
give the reader a faint impression of what he
feels. Beethoven is "a Titan, an Archangel,
a Throne, a Domination." When he is writing
his hated feuilletons, "the lobes of my brain
seem ready to crack asunder. I seem to have
burning cinders in my veins." The scene of the
benediction of the poniards in the *Huguenots*
is a terrible piece, "written as it were in electric
fluid by a gigantic Voltaic pile ; it seems to be
accompanied by the bursting of thunderbolts and
sung by the tempests." A reminiscence of some
incident in his career brings out this ejaculation
—"Destruction, fire and thunder, blood and
tears ! my brain shrivels up in my skull as I
think of these horrors!" His second love, he tells
us, "appeared to me with Shakespeare, in the
age of my virility, in the burning bush of a Sinai,
in the midst of the clouds, the thunders, the
lightnings of a poetry that was new to me."

All his youthful conceptions and desires were
of this extravagant order. He writes in a letter
of 1831, from Florence, "I should like to have

gone into Calabria or Sicily, and enlisted in the ranks of some chief of *bravi*, even if I were to be no more than a mere brigand. Then at least I should have seen magnificent crimes, robberies, assassinations, rapes, conflagrations, instead of all these miserable little crimes, these mean perfidies that make one sick at heart. Yes, yes, that is the world for me: a volcano, rocks, rich spoils heaped up in caverns, a concert of cries of horror accompanied by an orchestra of pistols and carbines; blood and lacryma christi: a bed of lava rocked by earthquakes; come now, that's life!"[1] In the same year he has the idea of a colossal oratorio on the subject of "The Last Day of the World." There are to be three or four soloists, choruses, and two orchestras, one of sixty, the other of two or three hundred executants. This is the plan of the work: "Mankind having reached the ultimate degree of corruption, give themselves up to every kind of infamy; a sort of Antichrist governs them despotically. A few just men, directed by a prophet, are found amid the general depravation. The despot tortures them, steals their virgins, insults their beliefs, and commands their sacred books to be burnt in the midst of an orgy. The prophet comes to reproach him for his crimes, and announces the end of the world and the Last Judgment. The irritated despot has him thrown into prison, and, delivering himself up again to his impious pleasures, is surprised in the midst of a feast

[1] He puts the same rhodomontade into the mouth of his Lélio.

by the terrible trumpets of the Resurrection; the dead come out of their graves, the doomed living utter cries of horror, the worlds are shattered, the angels thunder in the clouds — that is the end of this musical drama."

These examples will be sufficient to show the peculiarity of mind to which I have referred. The early ideas of Berlioz seem to bear the same relation to those of ordinary men as a gas does to a solid or a liquid; the moment they are liberated they try to diffuse themselves through as much space as they can. In this connection it is interesting to note that from his earliest years he had a love for books of travel and for pondering dreamily over maps of the world; he sought the remoter conceptions that were not limited by any narrow boundary. One gets a curious sensation, after reading much of his prose, that the things of the world have lost their ordinary proportions and perspectives; the adjectives are so big and so numerous that one begins to take this inflated diction as the normal speech of men. Occasionally a truly superb effect of vastness, of distance, is produced, an effect we also get sometimes in Berlioz's music. It has always seemed to me, for example, that the opening of his song " Reviens, reviens," gave the most perfect suggestion of some one being recalled from a great distance; the whole atmosphere seems to be attenuated, rarefied almost away; the melancholy is the melancholy of a regret that sweeps the ocean to the horizon and fails to find what the eyes hunger for.

VII

It is time, however, to remind ourselves that the picture painted so far does not represent the complete Berlioz.   It is all the more necessary to give ourselves this reminder because the only Berlioz known to most people is this being of wild excitement and frenzied exaggeration, with a dash in him here and there of pose.   There is a "legend" of each great composer—a kind of half-true, half-false conception of him that gradually settles into people's minds and prevents them, as a rule, from thinking out the man's character and achievement for themselves.   There is the Mozart legend, the Beethoven legend, the Liszt legend, the authenticity of which not one amateur in a thousand thinks of questioning.   There is the Berlioz legend, too, the causes of the growth of which, in this country especially, are not far to seek.   We really know very little of him over here.   The *Carnaval romain* overture and the *Faust* are heard occasionally ; but the average English amateur, when he thinks of Berlioz, has chiefly in mind the *Symphonie fantastique* and the *Harold en Italie*—particularly the final movements with their orgies of brigands, witches, and what not.   Industrious compilers of biographies and of programme notes do their best to keep this side of Berlioz uppermost in the public mind, by always harping upon the eccentricities of his youth.   One needs to remember that Berlioz died in 1869, and that from, say,

1835 to 1869 he was a very different man, both
in his music and in his prose, from what he was
between 1821 and 1835. His letters to the
Princess Sayn-Wittgenstein hardly suggest for
a moment the Berlioz of the earlier letters to
Humbert Ferrand and others. And as for his
music, the British public that winks and leers
knowingly at the mention of his name, thinking
all the time of the *Symphonie fantastique* and
the *Harold en Italie*, would do well to reflect
that it knows nothing, or next to nothing, of the
Waverley, *Francs Juges*, *Le Roi Lear* and other
overtures, of *Lélio*, of the *Tristia*, of *Le Cinq
Mai*, of the *Messe des Morts*, of the operas
—*Benvenuto Cellini*, *Béatrice et Benedict*, *La
Prise de Troie*, and *Les Troyens à Carthage*—
of the *Symphonie funèbre et triomphale*, of the
Roméo et Juliette, of *L'Enfance du Christ*,
of the *Te Deum*, and of other works, to say
nothing of the score or so of songs. In the
whole history of music, there is probably no
musician about whose merit the average man
is so sublimely confident on the basis of so
sublime an ignorance of his work.

VIII

Bearing in mind, then, that the Berlioz whom
we have hitherto been discussing is mostly the
youthful Berlioz—the writer of mad letters, the
actor of extravagant parts, the composer of the
Symphonie fantastique (1829–1830), and *Lélio*

(1831–1832)—let us look for a moment at his art as it was then, and afterwards trace it through its later and more sober manifestations.

In trying to follow him historically we meet with this difficulty, that it is impossible to say exactly when some of his conceptions first saw the light. He was in the habit of using up an early piece of material in a later work, especially if the early work was one that had been tried and had failed. We know, as I have already said, that the theme of the opening of the *Symphonie fantastique* is taken from a boyish composition. A phrase from another boyish work—a quintett —is used again in the *Francs Juges* overture. Parts of the early cantata *La Mort d'Orphée* become the *Chant d'amour* and *La harpe éolienne* in *Lélio*. The *Chœur d'ombres* in *Lélio* is a re-production of an aria in the scena *Cléopâtre*— one of his unsuccessful *Prix de Rome* essays. Part of the *Messe solennelle* (1824) goes into *Benvenuto Cellini* (1835–1837). The *Marche au supplice* in the *Symphonie fantastique* is taken from his youth-ful opera *Les Francs Juges*. The fantasia on *The Tempest* goes into *Lélio*. I strongly suspect, indeed, that more of his work dates from the first ten years of his artistic life (1824–1834) than we have ever imagined. My theory is that he was overflowing with ideas in his younger days, and that there was a gradual failure of them in his latest years, owing to the terrible physical tortures he endured, and the large quantities of morphia he had to take to still his pangs. At first he turns out work after work with great rapidity. Taking the larger ones alone, we have in 1826[1] *La révolution grecque*, in 1827 or 1828 the *Waverley* and *Francs Juges* overtures, in 1828–1829 the eight *Faust* scenes, in 1829 the *Irish Melodies*, in 1829–1830 the *Symphonie fantastique*, in 1830 the *Sardanapalus* and the *Tempête*, in 1831 the *Corsair* and *Le Roi Lear* overtures, in 1831–1832 the *Rob Roy* overture, *Le Cinq Mai*, *Lélio* and part of the *Tristia*, in 1832–1833 various songs, in 1834 the *Harold en Italie*, and the *Nuits d'Été*, in 1835–1837 *Benvenuto Cellini* and the *Messe des Morts*, in 1838 the *Roméo et Juliette*. This is a good output for some twelve years of a busy and struggling man's life, during the earlier part of which he was little more than an apprentice in his art. Berlioz lived another thirty-one years, but in that time did surprisingly little. Again keeping to the larger works, we have in 1840 the *Symphonie funèbre et triomphale*, in 1843 the *Carnaval romain* overture, in 1844 the *Hymne à la France*, in 1846 the completion of *Faust*, in 1848 the remainder of the *Tristia*, in 1851 *La Menace des Francs*, in 1850–1854 the *Enfance du Christ*, in 1849–1854 the *Te Deum*, in 1855 *L'Impériale*, in 1860–1862 *Béatrice et Benedict*, in 1856–1863 the double opera *La Prise de Troie* and *Les Troyens à Carthage*. Even allowing for the facts that in his middle and later periods he spent a good deal of time in foreign tours and in literary work, we shall still, I think, be forced to conclude that his ideas flowed

---

[1] One or two of these dates can only be looked upon as approximative, but if wrong at all, they are so only to the extent of a year or two, which does not affect the question.

more slowly in his later days, while they were certainly of an inferior quality at times. We must remember, too, that some of his works were written long before their production, and that there is sometimes reason to believe this to have been the case even where we have no positive testimony on the point. The *idée fixe* theme of the *Symphonie fantastique* first appeared in *Herminie* (1828); the "Harold" theme in the *Harold en Italie* had already figured on the *cor anglais* in the *Rob Roy* overture. It is probable that the *Roméo et Juliette* was not all written in 1838 as a consequence of Paganini's gift, as every one was led to believe; Berlioz had the idea of the work in 1829, and perhaps conceived some of the music then.[1] The *Symphonie funèbre et triomphale*, produced in 1840, was to a great extent written in 1835. The stirring phrases that are the life and soul of the *Carnaval romain* overture (1843) are taken from *Benvenuto Cellini* (1835–1837); while the theme of the love-episode in the overture had already appeared in *Cléopâtre* (1829). It is, indeed, impossible to say how much of the music of what I have called Berlioz's second epoch really dates from his first, thus still further diminishing the quantity belonging to the years after 1838. I think, if the truth were known, it would be found that one or two of the themes of *Béatrice et*

---

[1] It appears from the Sayn-Wittgenstein letters that the beautiful theme of the love-scene in *Roméo et Juliette* was inspired by the youthful love for Estelle that also produced the opening theme of the *Symphonie fantastique*. It must, therefore, have been quite a boyish invention, though no doubt its development and general treatment really belong to 1838.

Benedict, ostensibly written between 1860 and 1862, belong to 1828, when Berlioz first resolved to make an opera out of Shakespeare's play. It is incontestable that the ten years from 1828 to 1838 were years of inexhaustible musical inspiration. At times, he himself has told us, he thought his head would have burst under the peremptory pressure of his ideas; so rapidly did they flow, indeed, that he had to invent a kind of musical shorthand to help his pen to keep pace with them. There was, I take it, very little of this in the last two or three decades of his life. Make what allowances we will for other demands upon his time, it seems undeniable that his brain then worked less eagerly and less easily in musical things. Had the ideas been there in full vigour they would have come out in spite of all other occupations; and that they were not there as they were in his youth can only be explained, I think on physiological grounds.[1]

[1] M. Julien Tiersot, in his admirable *Berlioz et la société de son temps*, divides the life of Berlioz into five epochs—1803–1827 (his childhood, youth, and apprenticeship), 1827–1842 (the epoch of his greatest activity), 1843–1854 (in which he does little except *Faust*, which in reality, perhaps, dates from an earlier time), 1854–1865 (the epoch of *L'Enfance du Christ, Béatrice et Benedict*, and *Les Troyens*), and 1865–1869 (barren of works). The discussion in the text will make it clear why I have substituted my own classification for that of M. Tiersot, and will, I hope, be convincing. One other point deserves noting. Towards the end of his *Mémoires* Berlioz tells us that he had dreamed a symphony one night, but deliberately refrained from writing it because of the expense of producing and printing it. Such a reason may have weighed a little with him; but no one who knows anything of artistic psychology can regard it as the total explanation. If the dream-work had really sunk into Berlioz's soul and he had felt that he had full command of it, he could not have rested until he had it down on paper, if only for his own gratification. It is far more probable that he felt himself unequal

The latter aspect of the case, however, will be dealt with more fully later on. Here we may just note that Berlioz's early life was in every way calculated to produce both the inflation of the prose style that we see in his letters and the eccentricity and exaggeration that we see in some of his early music. His friend Daniel Bertrand tells us that "in his youth he sometimes amused himself by deliberately starving, in order to know what evils genius could surmount; later on his stomach had to pay for these expensive fantasies." At the time of his infatuation with Henrietta Smithson, he used to play the maddest pranks with his already over-excited brain and body; he would take long night-walks without food, and sink into the sleep of utter exhaustion in the fields. His body, like his brain, could not be kept at rest; he had a mania for tramping and climbing that invariably carried him far beyond his powers of endurance.[1] In 1830 the veteran Rouget de l'Isle, without having seen the youthful musician, diagnosed him excellently from his correspondence — "Your head," he wrote, "seems to be a volcano perpetually in eruption." We may smile at his antics all through this epoch, especially in *l'affaire Smithson*. But though there may have been a little conscious pose in it all, it is

to the mental strain of thinking out his vision and forcing the stubborn material into a plastic piece of art. There was, I take it, a lassitude of tissue in him at this time that made protracted musical thinking a burden to him.

[1] On the whole question see the chapter on "Le Tempérament" in Edmond Hippeau's *Berlioz Intime*.

unquestionable that in the bulk of it he was in deadly earnest. Twice he tried to commit suicide—once at Genoa, and again in the presence of Henrietta. Nor were they merely stage performances, mere efforts at effect; it was not his fault that they did not turn out successfully.

IX

Roughly speaking, it will be found that the Berlioz I have so far depicted comes into view about 1827. It was about that date, apparently, that youthful enthusiasm, combined with starvation and folly, gave his system that lurid incandescence that people always think of when they hear the name of Berlioz. It is about that date that his letters begin to show the inflation of style to which I have referred, and his music begins to acquire force and penetration and expressiveness, together with a tincture of the abnormal. Previously to 1827 he had presumably not written very much, or if he had it has not survived. What has remained is now accessible to us in the new complete edition of his works. There we can see some songs that, whatever their precise date may be, clearly belong to his earliest period. One of the very earliest—*Le Dépit de la Bergère*—shows a quite inexperienced brain and hand. *Amitié, reprends ton empire* is of much the same order; it looks, indeed, like a pot-boiler, an attempt to meet the contemporary demand for this kind of thing. Nor does the

little cantata *La révolution grecque* come to anything. But negative and futile as much of this
early work is, it shows one thing quite clearly—
that individuality of manner that accounts at once
for the successes and the failures of Berlioz. As
I have already pointed out, his type of melody is
something peculiarly his own. The same may
be said of his harmony, which moves about in a
way so different from everything we are accustomed to that often we are quite unable to see
the *raison d'être* of it. The popular judgment is
that his melody is ugly and his harmony shows a
want of musical education. This, however, is
rather a hasty verdict. Nothing is more certain
than that our first impression of many a Berlioz
melody is one of disgust—unless it be that the
second impression is one of pleasure. What
Schumann noticed long ago in connection with
the *Waverley* overture is still quite true, that
closer acquaintance with a Berlioz melody shows
a beauty in it that was unsuspected at first. I can
answer for it in my own experience, for some of
the things that move me most deeply now were
simply inexpressive or repellent to me at one time ;
and I fancy every one who will not be satisfied
with the first impression of his palate, but will
work patiently at Berlioz, will have the same experience. The truth seems to be that many of
his conceptions were of an order quite unlike anything else we meet with in music, and hence we
have some difficulty in putting ourselves at his
point of view and seeing the world as he saw it.
And occasionally this individuality of thought de-

generates into sheer incomprehensibility. Some of his melodies, play and sing them as often as we will, never come to mean anything to us. It is not that they are ugly or commonplace, not that they are cheap or platitudinous, but simply that they convey nothing ; they stand like something opaque between us and the emotion that prompted them ; instead of being the medium for the revelation of the composer's thought they are a medium for the concealment of it. In cases like these the explanation seems to be that his mental processes, always rather different from ours, are here so very different that the chain of communication snaps between us ; what was a difference of degree now becomes a difference of kind ; he speaks another language than ours ; the thought, as it were, lives in a space of other dimensions than ours. We may find a rough-and-ready analogy in a writer like Mallarmé, where the general strangeness of thought and style becomes now and then downright unintelligibility. In the one case as in the other, we are dealing with a type of brain so far removed from the normal that the normal brain occasionally finds it simply impossible to follow it.

So again with the harmony of Berlioz. Here the peculiarity of his style has often been commented on, with its odd way of getting from one chord to another, its curious trick of conceiving the harmony in solid blocks, that succeed one another without flowing into one another—much as in certain modern Dutch pictures the colours stand away from each other as if a rigid line

D

always lay between them and prevented their being blended by the atmosphere. The general explanation of this peculiarity of Berlioz's harmony is the easiest one—that it comes from his imperfect technical education. There may be something in this, but a little reflection will show that it is a long way from being the complete explanation. In the first place, one needs scarcely any "training" to avoid some of the progressions that Berlioz constantly uses; the mere hearing of other music would be sufficient to establish unconsciously the routine way of getting from one chord to another; and if Berlioz always takes another way, it can only be because the peculiarity of his diction has its root in a peculiarity of thought. In the second place, the harmonic oddities are really not so numerous in his earliest as in his later works. The melodies of the *Waverley, Francs Juges,* and *King Lear* overtures and of many of the earlier songs are usually harmonised more in the ordinary manner than the melodies of the works of his middle and last epochs; which seems to show again that his harmonic style was rooted in his way of thinking, and became more pronounced as he grew older and more individual. In the third place, if the peculiarities of his harmony had been due to lack of education, one would have expected him, when in more mature years he revised an early work, to correct some of the so-called faults to which a wider experience must have opened his eyes. But it is quite clear that the matter never struck him in this way.

In the new edition of his works we have some instructive examples. In 1850, for example, he revised one of his songs, *Adieu, Bessy*, which he had written in 1830. He has altered it in many ways, and made many improvements in the melody, in the phrasing, and in the accompaniment; but the sometimes odd harmonic sequences of the original version remain unchanged in the later. It clearly never struck him that there was anything odd about them; he had really seen his picture in that particular way; it was a question not so much of mere technique as of fundamental conception. In the fourth place, we must always remember that whatever Berlioz thought he thought in terms of the orchestra. He neither played nor understood the piano, and his writing is not piano writing. Now every one knows that many effects that seem strange or ugly on the piano are perfectly pleasurable on the orchestra, where they are set not in the one plane, as it were, but in different planes and different focuses. I fancy that when Berlioz imagined a melodic line or a harmonic combination he saw it not merely as a melody or a harmony but as a piece of colour as well; and the movement of the parts was not only a shifting of lines but a weaving of colours. Many things of his that are ugly or meaningless on the piano have a beauty of their own when heard, as he conceived them, on the orchestra, set in different depths, as it were, with the toning effect of atmosphere between them; not all standing in the same line in the foreground, with the one white light of the piano making confusion among their colour-values.

There is good reason for believing, then, that much of Berlioz's peculiarity of style is far less the result of lack of education than is generally believed, and that more of it must be attributed to a peculiar constitution of brain that made him really see things just in the way he has depicted them.

Among these early songs and other works there are some that show great strength and charm and originality of expression, such as *Toi qui l'aimas, verse des pleurs, La belle voyageuse, Le coucher du soleil,* and *Le pêcheur* (that was afterwards incorporated in *Lélio*). His two youthful overtures, the *Waverley* and the *Francs Juges,* though relatively unsubtle in their working-out —for he had little feeling for the symphonic form pure and simple—are yet very individual, while parts of the *Francs Juges* in particular are exceedingly strong. Then the apprentice makes rapid strides on to mastery. The year 1828 may be taken as the turning-point in his career. His unsuccessful scena for the *Prix de Rome—Herminie*—exhibits remarkable ardour of conception. There is much that is very youthful in it ; but it is decidedly individual, and above all it shows a feeling for rhythm to which there had been no parallel in French music up to that date. The next year saw another *Prix de Rome* scena— *Cléopâtre*—of which the same description will mostly hold good. The rhythmic scene is just as delicate, the melody is becoming purer and stronger, and we have in the aria *Grands Pharaons* a really fine piece of dramatic writing. About the same time he wrote the original eight scenes from *Faust*, containing such gems as the chorus of sylphs, the song of the rat, the song of the flea, Margaret's ballad of the King of Thule, her "Romance," and the serenade of Mephistopheles. Berlioz's musical genius was now entering upon its happiest phase; never, perhaps, did it work so easily and so joyously as in 1829 and the next seven or eight years. It was about 1829, too, that his orchestration began to be so distinctive; one can see him reaching out to new effects in the *Cléopâtre*, the chorus of the sylphs, the ballad of the King of Thule, the *Ballet des Ombres* and the fantasia on *The Tempest*.

This increasing mastery of his thoughts coincided with the epoch of his most intense nervous excitement, in which Henrietta Smithson played the part of the match to the gunpowder. So there came about the typical Romantic Berlioz of the *Symphonie fantastique* and *Lélio*, moving about in the world with abnormally heightened senses, his brain on fire, turning waking life into a nightmare, dreaming of blood and fantastic horrors. He exploited this mad psychology to its fullest in the last two movements of the symphony; after that the volcano lost a good deal of its lurid grandeur, and in *Lélio* we get rather less molten lava and rather more ashes than we want. Some of the music of *Lélio*—the ballad of the fisher, the *Chœur des ombres*, the *Chant de bonheur*, the *Harpe éolienne*—is among the finest Berlioz ever wrote; but the scheme as a whole, with its extraordinary prose tirades, is surely the maddest thing ever projected by a musician. Here was the young Romantic in all his imbecile, flamboyant glory, longing to be a brigand, to indulge in orgies of blood and tears, to drink his mistress' health out of the skull of his rival, and all the rest of it. But after all there is very little of this in Berlioz's music. We meet with it again in the "orgy of brigands" in the *Harold en Italie;* and whether that really belongs to 1834 or was written two or three years earlier, at the time when the hyperæmic brain was working at its wildest in the *Symphonie fantastique* and *Lélio,*[1] matters comparatively little. In any case, the madness ends in 1834 with *Harold.*

And then, with almost startling suddenness, a new Berlioz comes into view. We first see the change in the scena *Le Cinq Mai*—a song on the death of the Emperor Napoleon, to words by Béranger—which is dated 1834 by M. Adolphe Jullien and 1832 by Herr Weingartner and M. Malherbe. The precise date is unimportant. The essential fact is that Berlioz's brain was now acquiring what it had hitherto lacked—it was beginning to be touched with a philosophic sense of the reality of things. He had, of course, in much of his earlier work, written seriously and

[1] The date of *Lélio* is 1831–1832, but the most absurd thing in it, the *Chanson de brigands*, was written in January 1830—at the same epoch, therefore, as the *Symphonie fantastique.* It is fairly clear that 1829-1830 marked the climax of Berlioz's eccentricity, and that his passion for Henrietta Smithson had much to do with it.

beautifully ; but *Le Cinq Mai* has qualities beyond these.   His songs *La captive* (1832) and *Sara la baigneuse* (1833 ?) carry on the line from the earlier songs and overtures ; what we get in addition, in *Le Cinq Mai*, is a gravity and ordered intensity of conception that as a whole are absent from the earlier works.   He is becoming less of an egoist, more capable of voicing the thought of humanity as a whole ; the Romanticist is making way for the complete human being.   In the *Nuits d'Été* (1834) there is a larger spirit than in any of his previous songs.   Between 1835 and 1838 we have three noble works — *Benvenuto Cellini*, the *Requiem*, and *Roméo et Juliette* ; and to no previous work of Berlioz would the epithet " noble " be really applicable   The change is not so much a musical as an intellectual—we may almost say ethical—one.   Look at him, for example, in the opening of the *Requiem*.   All the madness, the pose, the egoism of the *Symphonie fantastique* and its brethren have disappeared.   Berlioz now has an eye for something more in life than his own unshorn locks and his sultry amours.   He no longer thinks himself the centre of the universe ; he no longer believes in the Berliozcentric theory, and does not write with one eye on the mirror half the time.   In place of all this we have a Berlioz who has sunk his aggressive subjectivity and learned to regard life objectively.   His spirit touched to finer issues, he sings, not Berlioz, but humanity as a whole.   He is now what every great artist is instinctively—a philosopher as well as a singer ; by the *Requiem* he earns his right to stand among the serious, brooding spirits of the earth. So again in the final scene of *Roméo et Juliette*, where he rises to loftier heights than he could ever have attained while he was in the throes of his egoistic Romanticism. Here again, as in the *Requiem*, he speaks with the authority of the seer as well as the voice of the orator; there is the thrill of profound conviction in the music, the note of inspired comprehension of men and nature as a whole. In a word, the old Berlioz has gone; a new Berlioz stands in his place, wiser than of old, purified and chastened by his experiences, artist and thinker in one.

X

In 1838, then, everything seemed of the happiest promise for his art. But that promise, alas, was not fulfilled so amply as might have been hoped for. Whatever the real cause may have been, Berlioz, as we have seen, now slackened greatly in his musical production. It could not have been wholly due to his *feuilleton* writing, for he was never so busy with this as in the seven years onward from 1833 (the year in which he married Henrietta Smithson, and had to earn money in some way or other). He complains to Humbert Ferrand that his journalism leaves him little time to write music, but the facts are that he was really keeping up a very good output. At the end of what I have called his first epoch he received some large sums of money—4000 francs for the *Requiem* (1837), 20,000 francs from Paganini for *Harold en Italie* (1838), and 10,000 francs for the *Symphonie funèbre et triomphale* (1840)—enabling him to give up journalism and to travel. He was away frequently between 1841 and 1855, but not enough to account for the singularly small amount of music he wrote—an amount that becomes still smaller in the later years.

We cannot, I think, resist the conclusion that even between 1840 and 1855 the seeds of his illness were in him and affecting his powers of work. So far as can be ascertained from his letters, he became aware of his malady about 1855, but there is no warrant for thinking it actually began then ; his father had suffered from the same complaint, and the son was evidently a doomed man. It is about 1855 that his letters begin to show what ravages his awful malady—a neuralgia of the intestines, he calls it—was making in him. The atrocious pain weakened him through and through ; then the springs of energy within him were still further relaxed by the quantities of opium he had to take. He lost, at times, even his interest in art. In November 1856 he speaks to the Princess Sayn-Wittgenstein of " the horrible moments of disgust with which my illness inspires me," during which " I find everything I have written " (he is working at *Les Troyens*) " cold, dull, stupid, tasteless ; I have a great mind to burn it all." A month later he writes that he has been so ill that he could not go on with his score. Thus the melancholy record continues in letter after letter : he is ill " in soul, in body, in heart,

in head ; " an access of his " damned neuralgia "
keeps him on his back for sixteen hours ; "I cannot walk, I only drag myself along ; I cannot
think, I only ruminate ; " "I live in an absolute
isolation of soul ; I do nothing but suffer eight or
nine hours a day, without hope of any kind, want-
ing only to sleep, and appreciating the truth of
the Chinese proverb—it is better to be sitting
than standing, lying than sitting, asleep than
awake, and dead than asleep ; " " my neurosis
grows and has now settled in the head ; sometimes
I stagger like a drunken man and dare not go out
alone ; " " these obstinate sufferings enervate me,
brutalise me ; I become more and more like an
animal, indifferent to everything, or almost everything ; " his doctors tell him he has " a general
inflammation of the nervous system," and that he
must "live like an oyster, without thought and
without sensation ; " some days he has "attacks
of hysteria like a young girl ; " " Mon Dieu, que
je suis triste !" ; "I suffer each day so terribly, from
seven in the morning till four in the afternoon,
that during such crises my thoughts are completely
confused ; " he takes so long over the writing of
Béatrice et Benedict because, owing to his illness,
his musical ideas come to him with extreme slow-
ness—while after he has written it he forgets it,
and when he hears it it sounds quite new to him.
To his other correspondents it is always the same
pitiful story : "On certain days I cannot write ten
consecutive lines ; it takes me sometimes four
days to finish an article."

It is impossible to believe that so serious a dis-

order began only in 1855, when Berlioz first became
fully conscious of it; it must have been in him
years before, and must even then have affected his
powers of work.[1]   But such music as he did find
energy to write is eloquent of the new condition
of his being.   Not only bodily but mentally Berlioz was a changed man—a point that should be
insisted on in view of the traditional misunderstanding of him.   I have already remarked upon
the Berlioz "legend" that is generally accepted,
a legend founded solely on the Berlioz of twenty-
five or thirty.   Heine gave perhaps the finest
expression to this aspect of him in the passage in
which he speaks of him as "a colossal nightingale,
a lark the size of an eagle, such as once existed,
they say, in the primitive world.   Yes, the music
of Berlioz, in general, has for me something
primitive, almost antediluvian; it sets me dreaming of gigantic species of extinct animals, of
mammoths, of fabulous empires with fabulous
sins, of all kinds of impossibilities piled one on
top of the other; these magic accents recall to us
Babylon, the hanging gardens of Semiramis,
the marvels of Nineveh, the audacious edifices
of Mizraim, such as we see them in the pictures
of the English painter Martin."   That is not a
bad description, in spite of its verbal fantasy, of
the Berlioz of the last two movements of the
Symphonie fantastique, the orgy of brigands in
Harold en Italie, the ride to the abyss in *Faust*,
and, let us even say, the "Tuba mirum" of the

[1] Jullien (p. 241) says "it was about this time that the neuralgia
to which he had always been subject settled in the intestines. . . ."

Requiem. But it is only a quarter, a tenth, of the real Berlioz. Yet the old legend still goes on ; even so careful a student as Mr. W. H. Hadow has just said, in his article in the new " Grove's Dictionary," that " his imagination seems always at white heat ; his eloquence pours forth in a turbid, impetuous torrent which levels all obstacles and overpowers all restraint. It is the fashion to compare him with Victor Hugo, and on one side at any rate the comparison is just. Both were artists of immense creative power, both were endowed with an exceptional gift of oratory, both ranged at will over the entire gamut of human passion. But here resemblance ends. Beside the extravagance of Berlioz, Hugo is reticent ; beside the technical errors of the musician the verse of the poet is as faultless as a Greek statue."

One really gets rather tired of this perpetual harping upon the extravagance of Berlioz. The picture is pure caricature, not a portrait ; one or two features in the physiognomy are selected and exaggerated, posed in the strongest light, and factitiously made to appear as the essential points of the man. Yet a baby with any knowledge of Berlioz could demonstrate the falsity of the picture. Where is the " extravagance," the want of "reticence," in the *Waverley* overture, the *Roi Lear* overture, the first three movements of the *Symphonie fantastique*, the twenty or thirty songs, the bulk of *Faust*, the bulk of *Harold en Italie*, the bulk of *Lélio*, the three fine pieces that make up the *Tristia*, the *Cinq Mai*, the bulk of the

Requiem, Benvenuto Cellini, Roméo et Juliette,
the noble *Symphonie funèbre et triomphale,* the
Carnaval romain overture, the *Enfance du Christ,
Béatrice et Benedict,* or *Les Troyens?* Out of
all these thousands of pages, how ridiculously
few of them deserve the epithet of "extravagance"; of how many of them is it true that
Berlioz's "eloquence pours forth in a turbid,
impetuous torrent which levels all obstacles and
overpowers all restraint"?

The truth is that even in the youthful Berlioz
there was considerable "reticence," considerable
power to sympathise with and express not only
the flamboyant but the tender, the pathetic, the
delicate. We have already seen that his intellectual and moral powers came to their climax
about 1838, at which time he was singing with
enormous passion, but also with perfect restraint
and impressive nobility. Both the music and the
prose of his later years show how greatly his
character was altering; it is simply ludicrous to
attempt to describe *this* Berlioz in the language
that was applicable only to the worst of the Berlioz of twenty years before. Physical and mental
suffering, trials in private and perpetual disap-
pointment in public life, chastened the man's soul,
brought out the finer elements of it. He fought
the powers of evil calmly and steadily with that
admirable weapon of irony of his. Once he forgot himself, in the Wagner affair of 1861; but
one can forgive, or at any rate understand, the
momentary wave of malevolence that surged up in
him then, if one thinks of the grievous illness

that racked the poor frame, and the unending insults that had been his own lot as an opera composer. Apart from this episode, Berlioz always commands our respect in his later years. Always the brain, the spirit, were uppermost; where other men would have become abusive he only became more mordantly witty; where the passion of defeat would have obscured the eyes of other men he only saw the more clearly and penetratingly. Look at him in his later portraits, with that fine intellectual mouth, full of a strength that is not contradicted, but reinforced, by the ironic humour that plays over it. Yes, he met the shocks of fortune well, and they were many and rude. If we want a summary contrast of the later and the earlier Berlioz, we have only to compare the ebullient letters of his youth with the letters written to the Princess Sayn-Wittgenstein between 1852 and 1867. The very style is altered; the later letters read easily and beautifully, without any of those abrupt distortions and exaggerations that pull us up with a shock in the earlier ones. When he has to castigate, he does it like a gentleman, with the rapier, not the bludgeon. And how perfectly does he maintain the essential dignity of the artist against this well-meaning but inquisitive and slightly vulgar aristocrat; with what fine breeding, what exquisite use of the iron hand within the glove, does he repel her interferences with matters that concern only himself, conveying to her that there are precincts within his soul to which neither her friendship nor her position give her the right of entry!

No, the cheap literary oleographs that do duty
for the portraits of Berlioz are ludicrously insug-
gestive of what Berlioz really was. His fever
had all died down even by 1846—supposing the
ride to the abyss in *Faust* really to belong to that
and not an earlier date; and everything after then
speaks of a vastly altered being. Had he only
kept his health up to this stage of his career, who
knows to what sunlit heights he might not have
attained? In spirit, in experience of life, in
moral balance, in the technique of his art, he had
now enormously improved; but set against all
this was that insidious disease that so woefully
hindered the free working of what had once been
so eager and keen a brain. It diminished the
quantity of work he could do; it spoiled some of
it altogether—the cantata *L'Impériale*, for example, where the unimpressive writing is throughout that of a mentally exhausted man. Yet a
sure instinct seems often to have guided him
even in this epoch of distress and frustration.
He could write only a few hours each week;
but as a rule he seems to have chosen happily
his times for work, seizing the rare and fleeting
moments when the poor brain and body were
held together in a temporary harmony. The
best of his later work need not fear comparison
with the best of his earlier periods. And how
changed in mood and outlook it all is! All his
old Romanticism is gone, not only from his music
but from the basis of his music. Instead of the
old violent literary themes, with their clangorous
rhetoric and their purple colouring, he now loves

to dwell among themes of classic purity of outline, and to lavish upon them an infinite delicacy of treatment. His musical style becomes at times extraordinarily beautiful and supple; without losing any of the essential strength of his earlier manner, he confutes, by the exquisite, pearly delicacy of *L'Enfance du Christ* and *Béatrice et Benedict*, the ignoramuses who then, as now, saw nothing in him but a master of the *baroque* and grotesque. His subjects are simple; he draws and colours them, as in *Béatrice and Benedict*, with the rarest and brightest grace,[1] or, as in *L'Enfance du Christ*, with a curiously engaging simplicity of manner that suggests Puvis de Chavannes or the *primitifs*. And his strength, where he chooses to let it show, is now so finely controlled, so thoroughly and masterfully bent to the creation of beauty. In the great *Te Deum* we see his style at something like its finest; all the coarseness and clumsiness that clung to his earlier strength have gone; the muscle shows none of the raw vigour of the early days, but plays easily and flexibly under the velvet skin; while in his softer moments there is a new and extraordinary sweetness, a honeying of the voice that yet sacrifices none of its old virility. And for his last work he draws not upon any of the Romantic contemporaries of his youth, not even upon that other Romanticist—Shakespeare—to whom he was always so closely drawn, but upon

---

[1] He himself describes it as "a caprice written with the point of a needle, and demanding excessive delicacy of execution." Yet this is the man for whom the world can find only the one epithet of "extravagant"!

his beloved Virgil ; it is with a classic subject, set
with classic sobriety of manner and amplitude of
feeling, that he chooses to end his career. What
that work meant for him only those can realise
who study his letters during the seven years in
which he was engaged upon it. It was his refuge,
his method of escape from the world ; it was for
him that "tower of ivory" of which Flaubert
speaks, into which the artist can mount, there to
dream of the ideal that is unrealisable in life.
He was a dying man all these years, and in much
of the music of *Les Troyens* there are only too
many signs of physical and mental exhaustion.
But it has its extraordinarily fine moments, and
the general conception is grander than anything
Berlioz had attempted since the *Requiem.* There
is something strangely moving in this reversion
of the old musician, in his latest years, to the
passions and the ideals of his youth. Fiction
could not invent anything more touchingly beautiful than that final meeting with the Estelle he
had loved as a boy of ten or twelve, and the
resurgence of all the old romantic feeling for his
Stella montis—that curious blinding of the fleshly
eye that permitted him to see in the woman of
sixty-seven only the winsome girl he had loved
half-a-century before. In his art there was a
similar atavism ; the old fighter puts away, with
a sadly ironic smile, the red flag under which he
had once fought so fiercely, and seeks companion-
ship among the great calm figures of the past.
There may have been a deliberate intention of
separating himself quite pointedly from Wagner,

E

which may account for something at least of his later clinging to Gluck and the classics. But on the whole it seems more probable that the reversion to these less fevered, more spacious spirits was just the spontaneous sinking of the weary soul into the arms that were most ready to receive it. He knew he was a beaten man ; he knew that during his lifetime at any rate his star was doomed to suffer eclipse ; whatever chance he might have had of fighting his way through the clouds again, of overcoming the Parisian ignorance of and prejudice against him, was shattered by the disease that broke him, body and soul. So he retired into himself and waited, as calmly and philosophically as might be, for the end.

To us his situation seems even more tragic than it must have seemed to himself. Knowing what extraordinary promise he was giving in 1838, we can only regard the last thirty years of his life as a failure to redeem that promise, at all events in its entirety. In both fields—the vocal and the instrumental—he seems to halt uncertainly, not quite knowing how to carry on the work he had begun. The later music, as I have tried to show, is generally beautiful enough ; the fault does not lie there. But Berlioz failed to beat out for himself the new forms that might reasonably have been expected from him by those who had followed his career from the first. All his life he longed ardently to be an opera composer. But the failure of *Benvenuto Cellini* in 1837, combined with the intrigues of his enemies, shuts him out of the Opera for twenty-five years ;

in 1846, again, the failure of *Faust* gives him another crushing blow. When he resumes his operatic writing, the capacity and the desire to strike out new forms seem to have gone; he is content to work within the limits of the frame that Gluck bequeathed to him. All this time he practically neglects purely instrumental music, thus failing to work out the conclusions towards which he seemed to have been feeling his way in his earlier works. Nothing in him comes to its full fruition; each branch is lopped off almost as soon as it leaves the trunk. He is a pathetic monument of incompleteness; his disease and the ignorant public between them slew his art. But the work he actually did seems on this account only the more wonderful. He was a genius of the first rank; and there is little doubt that the better his music is known the more respectful and the more sympathetic will be the tone of criticism towards him.

To MRS. ROSA NEWMARCH

"FAUST" IN MUSIC

THE musical settings of *Faust*, in one form or another, now number, I believe, something like thirty or thirty-five. It is perhaps the most popular of all subjects with musicians, far outdistancing in favour the Hamlets and Othellos and Romeo-and-Juliets and all the other lay figures which composers are fond of using to show off their own garments. It cannot be said that they have added very much, on the whole, to our comprehension of the drama; indeed, with half-a-dozen exceptions the Faust-symphonies and Faust-operas and Faust-scenes have quite failed to justify their existence. One of the main difficulties in the way of the musician—even supposing him to have the brain capacity to rise to the height of the psychology of the thing—is the enormous range and wealth of material of the drama itself. The First Part of Goethe's work alone, or the Second Part, is quite sufficient to tax the constructive powers of any composer to the uttermost; but to reshape the whole of *Faust* in music is a desperate undertaking. Since Goethe's day we are bound to see the Faust picture through *his* eyes; any harking back to earlier forms of it is quite out of the question. And Goethe, while he has enormously extended and deepened the spiritual elements of the story, has by this very means set the musician a problem of discouraging difficulty. No musical

version of the play, in the first place, can be
adequate unless it embraces Goethe's Second
Part as well as the First. Due opportunity,
again, must be given for the exposition of all the
essential, the seminal "motives" of the drama,
and they are many indeed. The composer is
thus on the horns of a dilemma. If he wants his
work to stand in the same gallery with Goethe's,
he has to run a line through Faust's soul long
enough and sinuous enough to touch upon all its
secret places ; but any one who tries to do this
soon perceives how hard it is to focus so vast a
scene and to keep the picture within one frame
of reasonable size. An opera or a symphony
that should attempt to cover all the psychological
ground of the drama would take at least ten or
twelve hours in performance. Apparently the
only rational course for the future composer who
may think of setting the Faust subject is to take
two or three evenings over it, after the manner
of Wagner's *Ring of the Nibelung;* and until
this is done we shall have to rest satisfied with
the more or less inadequate versions we have at
present.

The cosmic quality of the subject, one would
think, should have attracted more of the first-
rank men, considering how many of the second
and third rank it has tempted to self-destruction.
One wonders, for example, why it should have
fallen to the lot of Gounod to give so many
honest but uninstructed people their first, perhaps their only, idea of *Faust*—an experience
something like getting one's first notions of

Hamlet from the country booth. We can understand their taking the thing seriously, for I fancy
we all took it seriously at one time—in the callow
stage of our musical culture—and many quite
respectable musicians do so still. Yet we have
only to come back to it one day, after dropping
acquaintance with it for many years, to see what
a laughter-moving monstrosity the thing is. The
book gets as near the inane at times as anything
founded on Goethe could do, though the music
has its good points, of course. In the overture
and opening scene there really is some suggestion of the gravity and the spirituality of the
problems of Faust's soul; but from the time
Margaret and Mephistopheles appear upon the
scene the thing becomes for the most part mere
opera, and Faust just the ordinary amorist—
l'homme moyen sensuel. The melodrama, *quâ*
melodrama, is sometimes good of its kind; the
Valentine scenes generally ring true, and now
and then they become really impressive. There
is plenty of lovely music, too, in the opera, which
may suffice you if you are not very critical as to
the poetic basis—if you do not attempt, that is,
to get below the ear-tickling sounds and to see
the characters as Goethe has drawn them. But
once you begin to think of these matters you can
only smile at Gounod and his fellow-criminals
who concocted the libretto.

Look at the Gounod overture, for example.
For a couple of minutes it is worthy of almost
the loftiest subject or of the best man who has
taken up the *Faust* theme; and then how woe-

fully it fizzles out, drifting back into its native
habitat of banality, where the air is more congenial to it—for all the world like a man who
goes to an Ibsen play, sternly resolved to be a
serious moralist for one evening at least, but at
the end of the first act makes for the nearest
music-hall or *café chantant.* One can see where
it is all tending; Faust the philosopher has
already, at this early stage of his career, become
Faust the *boulevardier.* So with the opening
scene, wherein we just catch the accent of
Goethe for a breath or two, but never longer.
And then that absurd devil Mephistopheles, with
his stage strut, his stage idiom, his stage brain!
"Are you afraid?" he asks Faust at his first
red-fire appearance, when "Are you amused?"
would be more appropriate. There is a touch of
the genuine sardonic quality in his serenade; but
on the whole he suggests not so much the spirit
of denial as the spirit of the pantomime rally.
Nor, till you quietly think about the structure
of the libretto, do you realise how exceedingly
funny it all is. In the drinking-scene it is
Wagner who gets up to sing the song of the
rat; Wagner! who by no process of shuffling of
names can be got out of our heads as the pupil
and companion of Faust. It is true he does
not go very far with the ballad, Mephistopheles
interrupting him after the first line or two—for
which Gounod, remembering that Berlioz had set
the same song once for all—was no doubt duly
grateful to the devil. Then Mephistopheles
sings his fatuous air about the Calf of Gold, and

quarrels with Valentine—who, oddly enough, is also of the party—about his sister. So the opera goes on—very charming where it has least to do with the subject, but merely feeble or ludicrous when it comes near enough to Goethe to suggest a comparison. For Gounod, whose own religion was merely Catholicism *sucré*, not only lacked the brain to grasp the austere philosophy of a subject of this kind ; his musical faculty was not deep enough nor strong enough to save him from aiming perpetually at drama and achieving only melodrama. Watch him, for example, in the scenes where he is trying to carry on a dramatic dialogue, and see to what straits he is put in the effort to make the orchestra do something expressive in between the actors' speeches. See the catchpenny trade he drives in those stale operatic formulas for whose poetic equivalent we have to go to the country booth ; see him capering about with his fussy little runs and twiddles, and striking all kinds of pompous musical poses, that really signify nothing at all, and only remind us of the conventional up-down-right-left-cut-thrust of stage-fencing. And this banal thing, this cheap vulgarisation of Goethe, this blend of the pantomime, the novelette and the Christmas card, still represents *Faust* in the minds of nine musical amateurs out of ten ! It is no more the real Faust than Sardou's *Robespierre*, for example, is the real Robespierre ; in each case a portentous name has simply been tacked on to a piece of very ordinary melodrama. The most pleasing elements in Gounod's work—the really lovely, if not always profound, love-music—are precisely those that withdraw it furthest from Goethe ; for here it is clearly not Faust speaking to Margaret, but any man to any woman, any Edwin to any Angelina. Gounod's Margaret alone suggests dimly the drama of Goethe ; but that is because she is the easiest of all the characters to represent in music. In most of the settings of *Faust*, indeed, the portrait of Margaret carries a kind of conviction even when the other two characters have nothing more in common with Faust and Mephistopheles than the names. He must be a very inferior musician who could fail here. The essence of Margaret's character is simplicity, innocence, the absence of all complicating elements ; and accordingly we find that all the settings of her have a strong family resemblance to each other. Schumann's Margaret is very German, Liszt's very German but at the same time quite cosmopolitan, Berlioz's curiously *moyen-âge*, Gounod's decidedly modern and town-bred, but all have the same fundamental qualities ; none does violence to our conception of the real Margaret. Faust, however, has to be something more than the seducer of Margaret ; we want to see some traces in his music of the weariness of life, the disgust with knowledge, that distinguish him at the beginning of the drama ; we want to see him growing at once stronger and weaker as he develops, his character being purged of its dross, his soul's insight into the world of real things becoming prophetically clear just as he is bidden to leave it. Unless some elements at least of this picture are given us, the composer has no right to attach to his painting the title of *Faust*.

One wonders, again, why a musician like Boïto should ever have thought himself fit company for Marlowe and Goethe. Here is a poet—one can cheerfully pay a tribute to his general culture if not to his musicianship—with a semi-musical gift that rarely rises above the mediocre and generally dips a point or two below it, who not only fancies he can throw new light on Faust's soul through his music, but serenely undertakes a reconstruction of the drama that Goethe gave him. Boïto made such a really good libretto for Verdi out of *Othello* that it is rather surprising what an abject mess he has made of *Faust*. His hash of the great drama is really deplorable. His superior culture and his finer literary palate put him above the commonplace Gounod conception of the play as a melodramatic story of a man, a maid, and a devil. He knows there is a "problem," a "world-view," in it that really makes it what it is. But as soon as he begins to set the play to music he seems to forget what the problem is, where it begins and where it ends. The result is that he is not content to write a piece of plain, straightforward music of the ordinary operatic type, but must needs drag in just enough of Goethe's great plan to make the whole thing preposterous. I say nothing of his musical deficiencies—of his incurable old-Italian-opera tricks of style, his lame, blind, and halt melody,

the monotonous tenuity of his harmony, the odd
jumble of Wagner and Rossini in his idiom, his
notion that the terrible is adequately expressed
in five-finger exercises, and the horrible by a
reproduction of the noises made when the bow
is drawn across all four strings of the violin at
once. These are mere details, as is also the
fact that his powers of dramatic characterisation
are very limited, or that his choruses of angels
would be more suitable to *contadini*, or that his
Mephistopheles is transported bodily and mentally from the *buffo* stage. What is most
awesome in Boïto's opera is the pseudo-philo-
sophical scheme of the libretto. He begins with
a Prologue in Heaven that is almost entirely
superfluous, not one-fifth of it being concerned
with Faust. The first half of the first Act might
also be dispensed with entirely, for all it has to do
with the problem of Faust's soul. The second
half of this Act, and the first half of the next, are,
in the main, essential to the drama, though there
is no need for musical composers to retain, in the
garden scene, the episodes between Mephistopheles and Martha, that are right enough in the
play, but mar the more ideal atmosphere of music.
The descent into the *buffo* is perilously easy here ;
and it is much better to omit all this, as Schumann
does, and concentrate the whole of the light on
Faust and Margaret.

Boïto's next scene, however—the Walpurgis
night—is pure waste of time and space ; there
is a great deal too much of Mephistopheles and
the chorus, and not half enough of Faust to let

us grasp the bearing of the scene upon the
evolution of his soul. The whole of the third
Act helps to carry on the story; but the fourth
Act—the Classical Walpurgis Night—becomes
pure nonsense in Boïto's handling of it. Whatever meaning there may be in the Helena episode
in Goethe's long allegory, there can be no sense
at all in simply pushing her on the operatic stage
in order to sing a duet with Faust, the pair
having incontinently fallen in love at first sight
—presumably behind the scenes. Finally, the
Epilogue—the Death of Faust—ends the work
only in an operatic, not a spiritual, sense; there
being no spiritual connection between the earlier
and the later Faust, no reason why he should die
just then, no hint of the bearing of his death upon
his life. And why in the name of common sense
should Boïto have permitted himself to rewrite
the final Act, the crowning pinnacle of the whole
mighty structure that Goethe has so slowly, so
painfully reared? In place of the great motives
and profoundly moving scenes of the poetic drama
—Faust's schemes for human happiness, the poor
old couple and their little house on the shore, the
conversation with the four gray women, the
blinding and death of Faust, the coming of
Mephistopheles with the Lemures to dig the
grave, the pathetic death-scene, the transpor-
tation of the purified Faust into that diviner
air where he meets the purified Margaret—instead
of all this we have Faust back again in the old
laboratory of the first Act, Mephistopheles holding
out banal operatic temptations to him, after the

manner of Gounod, and Faust clinging for salvation to the Bible and going straight off to
heaven on his knees, all in the most approved
fashion of the Stratford-on-Avon novelette.[1]
Yet, bad as it is, Boïto's *Mefistofele* is not the
worst that might be done with the drama.   His
musical faculties may be of the kind that move
us to more laughter than is good for us; but
he certainly had some understanding of the
inner spirit as well as of the external action of
Goethe's poem; and the very extent of his
failure serves to show how difficult it is to
mould the play to musical requirements.   The
difficulty lies not so much in finding appropriate
musical episodes as in dealing with such a multiplicity of them as there is.   The drama, indeed,
is amazingly rich in musical "stuff"—as Wagner

[1] The reader may need to be reminded that the published score
of *Mefistofele* is an abbreviation of the opera as it was originally
given. The opening scene of the first Act and the Walpurgis
Night scene in the second have been cut down (see Mazzucato's
article on Boïto in "Grove's Dictionary"). "The grand scene at the
Emperor's Palace," says Signor Mazzucato, is "entirely aban-
doned." "A strikingly original *intermezzo sinfonico* . . . stood
between the fourth and fifth Acts; it was meant to illustrate the
battle of the Emperor against the pseudo-Emperor, supported by
the infernal legions led by Faust and Mephistopheles—the incident
which in Goethe's poem leads to the last period of Faust's life.
The three themes—that is, the *Fanfare* of the Emperor, the
Fanfare of the pseudo-Emperor, and the *Fanfare infernale*—were
beautiful in conception and interwoven in a masterly manner, and
the scene was brought to a close by Mephistopheles leading off
with 'Te Deum laudamus' after the victory." As to the beautiful
conception and the masterly interweaving I am inclined to be
sceptical; but in any case the inclusion of this scene simply puts
Boïto in a worse light than ever. The whole episode is practically
without significance as far as regards Faust's spiritual evolution.
So far as music is concerned, it merely gives the opportunity for a
clap-trap battle-piece.

would have put it—of the first order ; as Berlioz
expressed it in connection with Gounod's *Faust*,
"the librettists have passed over some admir-
ably musical situations that it would have been
necessary to invent if Goethe had not already
done so."

There is a vast quantity of the poem, of course,
that is as alien to the spirit of music as it is to
that of literature.   But there is a certain irre-
ducible minimum that *must* be dealt with, if the
musical setting is to aim at reproducing the
spiritual problem of Goethe with anything like
completeness.   The Prelude and the Prologue
in Heaven may, in case of need, be dispensed
with ; but almost all the First Part ought to be
utilised, not following Goethe word for word,
of course, but taking the pith of each scene.
Here and there we come across sections that
either defy musical treatment or are comparatively unimportant episodes in the poem.   But
the main psychological moments must all be
dealt with ; and the omission of any one of these
cuts a piece out of the intellectual interest, breaks
the subtle line of development, and makes all
that comes after it seem insufficiently led up to.
The First Part of Goethe's *Faust*, in fact, is in
itself a masterpiece of construction, holding the
balance most carefully and skilfully between
dramatic action and philosophical reflection.   Omit
any of the steps by which the characters have been
brought to the dramatic completeness in which
we see them at the end of the First Part, and
you break the spell that makes them real to us.

F

There is, then, in the First Part alone, more than enough to constitute the poetical material of at least two operas. Many composers have chosen to end their labours here, with the death of Margaret and the flight of Mephistopheles with Faust; and from the purely operatic point of view there is much to be said for such a course. The First Part does at least run on the lines that are common to a philosophical drama and an opera; whereas the Second Part deliberately flouts the musical sense at point after point. In the First Part the poetry marches hand-in-hand with the ethical conception; in the Second Part the poetry has often to be dug out of the jungle of prosaic diffuseness in which Goethe has hidden it. Nevertheless one great purpose runs like a fine, continuous thread through all the seemingly unrelated incidents of the drama; and this line at least must be followed by the musician, though he may disregard the excursions from its direct course which Goethe so often permits himself. The poet's purpose, of course, was not complete, could not possibly be complete, without the Second Part. From the very beginning we feel that the vast issues must end, full-orbed, in something like the remote, non-earthly atmosphere of the opening; and we keep in our memory the words of the Prologue in Heaven—

> " A good man, through obscurest aspiration,
> Has still an instinct of the one true way "—

waiting for the ultimate gleam that shall make the darkness of Faust's first perplexed flight quite clear to us. Plainly one-half only of the problem had been stated in the First Part; and though comparatively few people read the Second Part, and few of those who have read it once read it twice, it is really the rounding-off of the philosophical conception here that gives the First Part its proper meaning. The human striving of the earlier poem demanded the later episodes, both 'as poetical completion and ethical solution. Without the Second Part, the First Part is a broken cadence, a discord only half resolved. Goethe himself, we are told, "compared the Prologue in Heaven to the overture to Mozart's *Don Giovanni*, in which a certain musical phrase occurs which is not repeated until the finale." A musical setting can be adequate only if it really deals with the central spiritual forces of *Faust*, not only as they affect the protagonist up to the death of Margaret, but in the crowded after-years. Life was wider than art to Goethe; and the vastness and unwieldiness of the scheme of the play are mostly due to his attempt to embrace so much of life in it. The trouble with the average musical setting is that it fails to rise to the level of Goethe's own lofty humanism. The theatrical is there in plenty; but there is little that brings home to us the grave philosophy of the drama, little that speaks of that great, moving, human figure of the Second Part, beating his way painfully through the darkness to the light. Above all, one cannot spare the ethical elevation of that final scene, with its supremely pathetic picture of the man's defeat in the very moment of victory, and its mystical suggestion of this material defeat being in reality a spiritual triumph. Goethe, in fact, made the subject an essentially modern one—put into it the fever and the fret, the finer joys and finer despairs, the deepened philosophy and the more impassioned spiritual aspirations, of the generations that succeeded the great upheaval of the eighteenth century. In Marlowe's *Faustus* we feel that, powerful as the wings of the poet are, there still clings to them something of the grossness of the Middle Ages, and the grossness, only more superficially refined, of the Renaissance. The thick breath of materiality hangs like a cloud over Marlowe's drama. Faustus himself has in him much of the coarseness of tissue of the Elizabethan age. On the purely human side, especially in the later scenes, he does indeed touch and move us ; but in the mainsprings of his being, in the limitations of his desire—

> " Sweet Mephistopheles, thou pleasest me ;
> Whilst I am here on earth, let me be cloyed
> With all things that delight the heart of man.
> My four-and-twenty years of liberty
> I'll spend in pleasure and in dalliance,
> That Faustus' name, whilst this bright frame doth
> stand,
> May be admired through the furthest land "—

how immeasurably does he fall short of the philosophic Faust of Goethe—

> " Two souls, alas ! reside within my breast,
> And each withdraws from, and repels, its brother.

> One with tenacious organs holds in love
> And clinging lust the world in its embraces;
> The other strongly sweeps, this dust above,
> Into the high ancestral spaces."

The mere magic-working Mephistopheles of Marlowe, again, takes on, in the modern poet, something of the terrifying grandeur of one of the essential forces of the universe. How subtle is Goethe's insight into him, and how one longs to get something of that subtlety in his music—

> " Part of that Power, not always understood,
> Which always wills the Bad, and always works the Good."
> .   .   .   .   .   .
> " Part of the Part am I, once all, in primal Night—
> Part of the Darkness which brought forth the Light,
> The haughty Light, which now disputes the space,
> And claims of Mother Night her ancient place."

He is the element of destruction that is the other half of being; not a mere tempting devil, the crude beguiler of the theological fancy, but simply the evil side of Faust becoming self-conscious. See, for example, in the eleventh scene of the First Part, and again in the fourteenth scene, how he probes to the very depth of Faust's soul, dragging into the light the true motives that sway him, which Faust himself is incompetent to analyse. His taunt in the seventeenth scene, again, "Thou, full of sensual, super-sensual desire," is a stroke of which Marlowe was incapable.

There are one or two scenes in the Second Part which lend themselves to music, but have been curiously neglected—it being strange, for ex-

ample, that no musician of the first rank has set
the scene of Faust's discovery of ideal beauty
(Act i., Scene 7). But on the whole the Second
Part is uncongenial to music, until we come to
the gravely passionate human element at the end.
Even to poetry Goethe's plan is somewhat unpropitious, as Schiller pointed out to him. " A
source of anxiety to me," he wrote in 1797, " is
that *Faust*, according to your design, seems to
require such a great amount of material, if the
idea is finally to appear complete ; and I find no
poetical hoop which can encircle such a cumulative
mass. . . . For example, Faust must necessarily,
to my thinking, be conducted into the active life
of the world, and whatever part of it you may
choose out of the great whole, the very nature of
it seems to require too much particularity and
diffuseness." If the "poetical hoop" was so
hard to find, a musical hoop to contain such
wildly-mixed material is beyond the power of
man to cast. All the musician can do is to make
sure of the final scenes (from Act vii. Scene 4
onwards) ; though even then—and this is the
perpetual dilemma—one feels the need of some
connecting link between the Faust whose life is
drawing so near to the end, and the Faust whom
we saw being torn away by Mephistopheles from
Margaret and the prison. As Schiller said, Faust
must go "into the active life of the world" before that stupendous cadence can have its true
significance ; yet most of the intermediate scenes
into which Goethe has put him can never be
caught up into the being of music. As one looks

at the poem itself, one admits despairingly that it would be impossible to build the first four Acts into any operatic structure. But one broad purpose of spiritual development runs through even this desert of apparently endless aridity ; and surely this might be treated by the musician, if not in operatic, at least in symphonic form. That is, between the stage of Faust's life that ends with the death of Margaret and the awakening of Faust to a new joy in earth and a resolution to seek the highest good, and the stage where his own death puts the seal on the drama, we might have a symphonic interlude that would make the transition less abrupt for us. The comparative vagueness of the music in this form would match the increased indefiniteness of the poetical handling ; while the more positive operatic form could be resumed in the Fifth Act, where the closeness of the association with actual life demands the continuous use of words. It is not an ideal device, perhaps, but it is the only adequate one. Only in some such manner as this can we hope to get the real *Faust* translated into music. As it is, the composers who have grasped the philosophy of the work have been restricted to a canvas far too small for the whole subject, while those who have not laid stress on the philosophy have simply not dealt with the Faust drama at all.

Men like Wagner and Rubinstein, again, who have really had the thinker's appreciation of the deeper currents of the theme, and have tried to express these in the single-movement form, have been woefully hampered by the limited space in which they have been compelled to work. Wagner, of course, never meant his *Faust Overture* to be a complete treatment of the subject ; it was intended merely as one section of a large Faust Symphony. The general excellence and the one defect of the work inspire us with regret that the scheme as a whole was never carried out. Its one shortcoming is that it deals only with the melancholy, brooding, world-weary Faust of the opening of Goethe's poem, the egoistic Faust on whom the larger world-issues have not yet dawned. We should like to have had Wagner's treatment of the final and complete Faust, taken out of himself, touched with sublimer sorrows and compassions, pouring out his soul upon the greater interests of humanity. As it is, however, we have in the *Faust Overture* the veritable Faust of the opening of Goethe's poem. No attempt is made at the portraiture of Margaret—the beautiful theme in the middle section simply representing the " ever-womanly " floating before Faust's eye in vague suggestion—nor is there any Mephistopheles in the work. But in regard to the special task Wagner seems to have set himself, the translation into music of the first scene of Goethe's First Part, nothing more perfect could well be imagined. There are few more convincing pieces of musical portraiture than this great grey head, with the look of the weary Titan in the eyes, that looms out in heroic proportions from Wagner's score.

One of the least known of the settings of *Faust* —or at any rate of the fine settings of it—is that of Henri Hugo Pierson.[1] Though he was an Englishman, his music is practically unknown in England, for which his residence in Germany is no doubt mainly responsible. It is a pity such a man could not have found in his own country the conditions under which his talents could thrive and expand ; for when one realises how much strength and originality there is in his music, one feels that had he worked in England he might have helped to found a native school, and so brought our musical Renaissance to birth at any rate a generation earlier than it has come. His music is always that of a musician who is at the same time poet and thinker. The very plan of his *Faust* is original. As its title indicates, it deals only with the Second Part of Goethe's play. This in itself is a slight fault, for it brings before us that tremendous drama of regeneration without having prepared us for it by the previous drama of struggle and error. Starting with Ariel and the Chorus of Fairies singing round the sleeping Faust, Pierson takes us through the scene in the Emperor's Castle, the calling up of the apparitions of Paris and Helena, and the attempt of Faust to seize the Grecian beauty—all from Act i. From the second Act we have Wagner and the birth of the Homunculus, and

---

[1] Henry Hugh Pearson was born at Oxford in 1815. He settled in Germany, where he found a more congenial musical atmosphere than was to be had at that time in England. After writing for a little while under the pseudonym of "Edgar Mansfeldt," he reverted to his own name, but metamorphosed it into Henri Hugo Pierson. His "Music to the Second Part of Goethe's *Faust*" was brought out at Hamburg in 1854. Pierson died in 1873.

the journey of Faust, Mephistopheles, and the Homunculus through the air. From the third Act we have the scene before the Palace of Menelaus (Helen and the Chorus of captive Trojan women), the coming of Faust as a knight of the Middle Ages, his dialogue with Helena, the appearance and death of Euphorion; from the fourth Act, the battle between the Emperor and his enemies; from the fifth Act, the song of Lynceus the warder, the entry of the four Grey Women—Want, Guilt, Care, and Need—and the blinding of Faust; the digging of the grave by the Lemures, the death of Faust, the choruses of the spirits and the anchorites, the chorus of the younger seraphs and angels ascending with the spirit of Faust, the scene in the empyrean, and the final "Chorus Mysticus"—*Alles Vergängliche ist nur ein Gleichniss.*

The scheme, it will be seen at once, is not an ideal one. It achieves comprehensiveness at the expense of organic unity. It keeps too strictly to the letter and the order of Goethe's scenes; episodes like the battle, that are of the very slightest significance, are needlessly included; other and more essential episodes are so lightly dwelt upon that their full value can hardly be brought out; and others are omitted altogether. As a mere piece of architecture the thing is extremely imperfect. Too much use, again, is made of the melodrama—*i.e.* the union of the reciting voice with the orchestra—one of the least justifiable and most trying forms of art ever invented. But with all its faults of structure it is a notable

work; the music redeems all its errors. The
opening scene, with Ariel and the spirits, is exquisitely fresh and sunny ; the death of Euphorion
and the death of Faust are both very moving,
and there are some fine choruses in the work,
notably the " Heilige Poesie." Pierson re-creates
for us the philosophic atmosphere of the Second
Part of *Faust*, and gives us the same impression
of the largeness of the issues at work ; which is
no small achievement. It is a pity one of our
Festival Committees could not be prevailed upon
to let us hear the score, or at any rate a portion
of it.

Unduly neglected, again, is Henry Litolff's
setting of certain scenes from Goethe (op. 103).
Like Pierson, he adopts occasionally the unplea-
sant form of declamation with orchestral accompaniment. This spoils an otherwise fine treatment
of the first scene (in Faust's study). It is really a
symphonic poem with a vocal element here and
there ; and paradoxically enough, though Faust
is restricted to declamation, the Earth-Spirit sings
his part to a melodic and very expressive *quasi
recitativo*. The movement has the prevailing
fault of all Litolff's writing—a certain slackness
and want of resource in the development ; but the
ideas themselves are often most striking. The
first scene concludes with a fine setting of the
Easter Hymn. The second scene, before the City
Gate, is exceedingly fresh and charming ; while the
seventh, the scene in the Cathedral (No. 20 of
Goethe's First Part) is a masterly piece of work—
finer even, perhaps, than Schumann's version of

the same scene. If Goethe's drama has moved many of the second-rate musicians only to show how very second-rate they are, it has at all events stimulated others to efforts that at times put them very nearly in the ranks of the first-rate.

Rubinstein's orchestral poem *Faust* — which the composer styles simply " Ein musikalisches Charakterbild "—is not altogether easy to understand, in its literary intentions, in the absence of a guide. It is in one movement only, and contains apparently no allusion to Mephistopheles, nor, as far as can be gathered beyond doubt from the music itself, to Margaret—for the suave melodies that are interposed as a contrast to the more passionate and more reflective utterances of Faust are not distinctively feminine in nature. They may have nothing at all to do with Margaret, or they may represent Faust's attempt to resolve his philosophic doubts by a contemplation of the simpler and more constant elements of human nature—just as Wagner, in his *Faust Overture*, does not so much limn an actual Margaret as suggest the consolation which the thought of womanly love can bring to the soul of Faust. Rubinstein's work, though not quite on the same plane as Wagner's, is yet exceedingly sincere. What it lacks is sufficient definiteness to make us refer it to Faust and to Faust only. It is clearly a strenuous picture of a lofty and noble soul, striving in its own way to read "the riddle of the painful earth," and mournfully acknowledging, at the last, that its only portion is defeat and disillusion. But this is a psychological frame that might be

made to fit a score of pictures ; and one misses, in
Rubinstein's piece, the conclusive sense of congruence with Faust as we know him in Goethe's
poem. There is nothing in it to clash with the
poet's conception ; the emotional atmosphere is
the same in both ; but in spite of the title the
musician has put upon his work, it is less a study
of individual character than a description of a
type. Rubinstein's Faust is the least definite and
the most symbolical of them all.

Rubinstein's tone-poem and every other purely
orchestral setting of the subject, however, pale
before the magnificence of Liszt's *Faust Symphony.* Liszt writes three movements—entitled
respectively " Faust," " Margaret," " Mephistopheles "—and then sums up the whole work in
a choral setting of Goethe's final lines, " Alles
Vergängliche ist nur ein Gleichniss," etc. Here
the larger scale on which the picture is painted
permits Liszt both a breadth and an intimacy
of psychology which are impossible in the one-
movement overtures. In the long first movement
(taking about twenty-five minutes in performance),
we really do feel that Faust is being analysed
with something of the same elaboration and the
same insight as in Goethe's poem. The handling
is a trifle loose here and there, owing to Liszt
repeating his material from time to time in
obedience to literary rather than to musical necessities ; but apart from this the " Faust " movement
is extraordinarily fine character-drawing, and certainly the only instrumental Faust study that
strikes one as being complete. In the " Mar-

garet" movement he incorporates very suggestively a reference here and there to the phrases of the " Faust," thus not only sketching Margaret herself but giving the love-scenes in a form of the highest concentration. This section is surpassingly beautiful throughout ; in face of this divine piece of music alone the present neglect of Liszt's work in England is something inexplicable. Almost the whole Margaret is there, with her curious blend of sweetness, timidity, and passion ; while Faust's interpositions are exceedingly noble. All that one misses in Liszt, I think, is the tragic Margaret of the scene in the Cathedral and the prayer to the Mater Dolorosa. The " Mephistopheles " section is particularly ingenious. It consists, for the most part, of a kind of burlesque upon the subjects of the " Faust," which are here passed, as it were, through a continuous fire of irony and ridicule. This is a far more effective way of depicting " the spirit of denial " than making him mouth a farrago of pantomime bombast, in the manner of Boïto. The being who exists, for the purposes of the drama, only in antagonism to Faust, whose main activity consists only in endeavouring to frustrate every good impulse of Faust's soul, is really best dealt with, in music, not as a positive individuality, but as the embodiment of negation—a malicious, saturnine parody of all the good that has gone to the making of Faust. The " Mephistopheles " is not only a piece of diabolically clever music, but the best picture we have of a character that in the hands of the average musician becomes either stupid, or vulgar, or both. As we listen to Liszt's music, we feel that we really have the Mephistopheles of Goethe's drama.

The Mephistopheles of Berlioz's *Faust* is interesting in another way. Berlioz, of course, played fast and loose in the most serene way with the drama as a whole, accepting, rejecting, or altering it just as it suited his musical scheme. He blandly avows, for example, that he takes Faust, in one scene, into Hungary, simply because he wants to insert in the score his arrangement of a celebrated Hungarian march! Moral criticism would be wasted on one so naked and unashamed as this—though perhaps after all it is only pedantry that would regard most of Berlioz's alterations of Goethe's drama as very serious perversions of the main Faust legend. So long as the central problems of the character are seen and stated, it matters very little through what incidents the composer chooses to bring them home to us. And Berlioz really has a very strong grip upon the inner meaning of the legend. His success, indeed, is somewhat surprising when we consider how he approached the work. He had been greatly impressed, in his youth, by Gérard de Nerval's translation of Goethe's poem ; but instead of attempting a continuous setting of the work at this time (1829), he aimed only at setting eight disconnected scenes. These were (1) " The Easter Scene " ; (2) " The Peasants' Dance " ; (3) " The Chorus of Sylphs "; (4) " The Song of the Rat "; (5) "The Song of the Flea"; (6) " The Ballad of the King of Thule "; (7) "Margaret's Romance and the Soldiers' Chorus "; (8) " Mephistopheles' Serenade." Faust, therefore, had practically no part in this selection; and it was not till seventeen years later that Berlioz brought out his complete "dramatic legend." It looks as if his early interest in the work were more pictorial than philosophical, for the two songs of Margaret alone suggest the deeper emotional currents of the drama. Mephistopheles, however, seems to have captivated his young Romantic imagination from the first, and, in the ironic serenade to Margaret, the character as he conceived it is already fully sketched. Berlioz's devil is, perhaps, the only operatic Mephistopheles that carries anything like conviction; he never, even for a moment, suggests the inanely grotesque figure of the pantomime. Of malicious, saturnine devilry there is plenty in him; no one, except Liszt, could compete with Berlioz on this ground. But there is more than this in the character. In such scenes as that on the banks of the Elbe, where he lulls Faust to sleep, there is a real suggestion of power, of dominion over ordinary things, that takes Mephistopheles out of the category of the merely theatrical and puts him in that of the philosophical.

Nor, in sheer character-drawing, can any other operatic Faust and Margaret compare with the figures of Berlioz; and when we consider the piecemeal manner in which the work was built up, it is astonishing how just, how sure, how incisive this portraiture is. It may not be precisely

Goethe; but it is a magnificent translation of Goethe into French. Faust, of course, is the Romantic Faust, with his passionate intimacy with nature. We miss in Berlioz what we get in Schumann, for example—the close following of Goethe's philosophical plan. Berlioz is not greatly interested in Faust's schemes for the regeneration of mankind; his own culture had not brought him into contact with Louis Blanc and Proudhon and Saint-Simon. But of its kind it is all amazingly fine. No other Margaret, except Liszt's and perhaps Schumann's, can compare with Berlioz's for pure pathos—the sensuous simplicity of soul that wrings the heart with compassion. Altogether, though the opera of Berlioz deals only with the more primordial passions of the drama, and ends in a manner rather too suggestive of a Christmas card conceived in a nightmare, it is more subtle, more profound, than almost any other work of the same order.

Only one setting surpasses it—that of Schumann; not because it achieves a finer individual portraiture than Berlioz's work, but because, on the whole, it stirs us more deeply in precisely the way we are stirred by Goethe's poem. Schumann's plan is peculiar and original. Whereas most other composers who have employed the operatic or cantata form have drawn largely on Goethe's First Part and almost ignored the Second, it is from the Second Part that two-thirds of Schumann's work are taken. Out of the First Part we have only the garden scene, Margaret before the image of the Mater Dolorosa, and the

G

scene in the cathedral. Faust, therefore, does
not so far appear at all, except in the tiny garden
scene; and the sole structural fault of the work
is that something of the earlier Faust should
have been shown to us, before he appears, in the
next section, as the refined and vigorous humanist
of Goethe's Second Part. Setting this defect
aside, however, the remainder of the work gives
us the quintessence of Goethe's drama. We
have first the scene, at the opening of Goethe's
Second Part, where Ariel and his fellow-spirits
sing round the sleeping Faust; then Faust's
return to mental health and energy, and his
resolve to devote himself henceforth to the
highest activities of human life. Upon this
scene there follows the visit of the four grey-
haired women—Want, Guilt, Need, and Care—
the blinding of Faust by the breath of Care, the
last outburst of his passionate zeal for life and
freedom, and his death. The remainder of the
work is devoted to a textual setting, line for line,
of the final scene of Goethe's poem—the hermits,
the choruses of angels, the three women, the
penitent (formerly Margaret), the Mater Gloriosa,
and the "Chorus Mysticus."

Schumann's scheme is thus in the highest
degree philosophical. It austerely disregards
the conventional elements that enter into the
usual operatic *Faust*, and concentrates itself on
the essential spiritual factors of the poem. Mephistopheles appears only for a moment in the
garden duet, and again in Faust's death-scene,
so that there is no attempt at full portraiture of

him. Schumann's Margaret really suggests the
Margaret of Goethe. The same mediæval atmosphere seems to environ her, both in the garden
and in the cathedral. She is naïve in the scene
with Faust as Goethe's Margaret is naïve ; and
in the scene where she bends before the Mater
Dolorosa, and again when the evil spirit, in the
cathedral, harries her with his taunts, everything
is set in the right key and the right colour. In
the portrait of Faust it is the thinker, the philosopher, that is uppermost throughout. All
through Schumann's Second Part, indeed, we
feel this constant preoccupation of the musician
with the great human elements of the drama ;
while in the exquisite, subtilised mysticism of the
Third Part these elements glow with a purer and
rarer light. The work is uneven in its musical
inspiration ; but on the whole we can say that
Schumann's is the real *German* Faust, the Faust
of Goethe. Writing in his eightieth year, the
old poet pointed out one of the main reasons for
the enduring interest in his work : " The com-
mendation which the work has received, far and
near, may perhaps be owing to this quality—that
it permanently preserves the period of a development of a human soul, which is tormented by all
that afflicts mankind, shaken also by all that disturbs it, repelled by all that it finds repellent, and
made happy by all that which it desires. The
author is at present far removed from such conditions : the world, likewise, has to some extent
other struggles to undergo : nevertheless, the
state of men, in joy and sorrow, remains very

much the same ; and the latest born will still find cause to acquaint himself with what has been enjoyed and suffered before him, in order to adapt himself to that which awaits him." It is this grave note, this width of outlook upon man and the world, that we have in Schumann's work in fuller quantity and richer quality than in any other setting of *Faust*. His is really the spirit of the *Faust* conceived by the great poet—full of a passionate reflection upon life, an uplifted, philosophical sense of tragedy, a mellow sympathy with and pity for the troubled heart of man. From first to last he has made his emotions out of the deeper, not out of the more superficial, passions of the play.

To GRANVILLE BANTOCK

PROGRAMME MUSIC

I

THERE are three stages in the history of every new truth. Take, as an example, the Darwinian theory. First of all it is assailed with tooth and claw by a thousand people who know nothing about it and have never given ten minutes' consecutive thought to it, but who hate it simply because it disturbs their long mental inertia. Then, when its truth becomes more and more evident, and too many clear-headed people believe in it for it to be laughed down, and too many strong people adopt it for it to be howled down, the partisans of the older school become obnoxiously polite to it; they no longer call it a mass of error, but they graciously permit it to take rank, after their own particular theory, as a secondary and imperfect kind of truth. Finally, it is universally accepted, purged of its admixture of error, and both it and its predecessors are then seen to be just inevitable stages in the development of the human mind, the second having no more title than the first to be considered the end of the story. At first Darwin's theory of development is thought to be crushed by the mere flinging at it of citations from the Bible; then the professional theologians try to impress it into their own service; finally its victory over misunderstanding and ignorance and prejudice is complete, but by this time it is no longer the ultimate theory of things, but only a stepping-stone to other theories. Something of the same kind has happened, or is in process of happening, with programme music. Formerly the dear old virginal academics shuddered if the foul word polluted their chaste ears; now they condescend to discuss it, more or less temperately, but always with the idea that it is merely an inferior branch of the great music-family—a kind of poor relation of absolute music; in a little while the rationality of the thing will be beyond question, but by that time it will probably be making way for something still newer than itself—though what that may be we have at present no means of knowing. Just now we are in the second stage of the controversy upon the subject. The advocate of programme music, it should be said at once, is not necessarily a hater of absolute music, nor is the lover of absolute music necessarily an enemy of programme music. One can like Wagner and Strauss and Liszt and Berlioz and still appreciate to the full the Bach fugue or the Mozart or Beethoven or Brahms symphony. Still it is an unfortunate fact that too often a liking for the one kind of art goes along with an abhorrence of the other. Any narrowness of this kind is to be regretted on either side; but if one partisan exhibits more of it than the other, I should say it is the absolutist, who is usually much less fair towards programme music, and less open to conviction, than the programmist is to absolute music. And since the contest between the two schools is very strenuous just now, and as one of the services of the critic is to give an art room to breathe and grow by clearing away dead traditions from around it, some good may be done to the creative musician, as well as to the ordinary concert-goer, by a review of the field of dispute between the antagonists.

II

Just as the average programmist is, on the whole, more generous in his appreciations than the average absolutist, so he has done more to clear up the darkness that envelops too much of the subject. From this side there has come some good æsthetic discussion; from the other side there has come little but dogged and tiresome repetition of old catch-words, without any serious attempt to grapple with the psychology of the question as a whole. In the latest edition of Grove's Dictionary of Music, Mr. Fuller Maitland gives us an example of this method of "killing Kruger with your mouth." "It is only natural," he says, "that programme music should for the time being be more popular with the masses than absolute music, since the majority of people like having something else to think of while they are listening to music." The last clause I take to be purely random assertion; there are millions of people—even among the masses—who prefer abstract ear-tickling that saves them the trouble of thinking of anything

else while they are listening. Nay, one of the
complaints of the untutored amateur against programme music is that it is so hard to follow—
that he cannot sit quietly in his seat and just
listen to the music as it comes, but must needs
first read and pre-digest a long story out of the
analytical programme. Minds of this kind—and
I have met with many of them—protest simply
because they *have* to think of something else
while the notes are being poured into their ears.
This rather lame device is one way of disparaging
programme music—the device of implying that
it is most popular with the "masses," with people,
that is, of limited musical culture—which is of
course not true. The other way of denigrating
it is the time-honoured one of an appeal to the
past; it is the æsthetic equivalent of the frequent
appeal to the Agnostic to remember what he
"learned at his mother's knee." "In the great
line of the classic composers," Mr. Maitland tells
us, "programme music holds the very slightest
place; an occasional *jeu d'esprit*, like Bach's
Capriccio on the Departure of a Brother, or
Haydn's 'Farewell' Symphony, may occur in
their works, but we cannot imagine these men,
or the others of the great line, seriously undertaking, as the business of their lives, the composition of works intended to illustrate a definite
programme. Beethoven is sometimes quoted as
the great introducer of illustrative music, in virtue
of the Pastoral Symphony, and of a few other
specimens of what, by a stretch of terms, may be
called programme music. But the value he set

upon it as compared with absolute music may be
fairly gauged by seeing what relation his 'illustrative' works bear to the others. Of the nine
symphonies, only one has anything like a programme; and the master is careful to guard
against misconceptions even here, since he super-
scribes the whole symphony, 'More the expression of feeling than painting.' Of the pianoforte
sonatas, op. 90 alone has a definite programme;
and in the 'Muss es sein?' of the string quartet,
op. 135, the natural inflections of the speaking
voice, in question and reply, have obviously given
purely musical suggestions which are carried out
on purely musical lines."

To all this there are a good many objections
to be raised. (1) In Bach's time programme
music, as we understand it, simply could *not* be
written. There was not the modern orchestra
with the modern orchestral technique; you could
no more delineate *Francesca da Rimini* with
the instruments of Bach's time than you could
adequately suggest a rainbow with a piece of
paper and a lead pencil. Further, for the expression of a number of things that we now
express in music, there were needed (*a*) the
modern enlargement of the musical vocabulary,
and (*b*) the "fertilisation of music by poetry," on
which Wagner rightly laid such stress. But in any
case Bach's neglect of programme music is no
argument against the form. We might as well
say that the fact that he wrote no operas is a
proof of the natural and perpetual inferiority of
opera. (2) Mr. Maitland passes over the fact

that, imperfect as their means of utterance were, many old composers *were* frequently obsessed by the desire to write something else than absolute music. He says nothing of the attempts of Muffat, of the composers represented in the Fitzwilliam Virginal Book, of Jannequin, of Buxtehude, of Frescobaldi, of Hermann, of Gombert, of Carlo Farino, of Frohberger, of Kuhnau, of Couperin, of Rameau, of Dittersdorf, and others, of some of whom I shall speak shortly.[1] There has always been a strong desire to write "illustrative" music, but for a long time it was checked by the imperfection of the media through which it had to work. (3) He ignores Haydn's excursions into "illustrative" music in the *Creation* and the *Seasons*—the representation of chaos, of the passage from winter to spring, of the dawn, of the peasants' joyful feelings at the rich harvest, of the thick clouds at the commencement of winter; he says nothing of the "illustrative" symphonies or parts of symphonies and other works of Haydn—"the morning," "midday," "the evening," "the tempest," "the hunt," "the philosopher," "the hen," "the bear," and so on. (4) He says nothing of the manner in which the overture, both operatic and non-operatic, became more and more "illustrative" at the end of the eighteenth and beginning of the nineteenth century; he does not refer to the works of Beethoven in which the "illustrative" function is very apparent, such as the *Battle of*

[1] See an interesting article by Max Vancsa—*Zur Geschichte der Programm-Musik*—in Nos. 23 and 24 of *Die Musik* (1903).

Vittoria, the *Leonora* overtures, the *Egmont*, the *Coriolan*, the *Ruins of Athens*, the *King Stephen*, and so on. (5) He blindly accepts Beethoven's nonsensical remark about the Pastoral Symphony being "more the expression of feeling than painting." The imitations of the nightingale, the cuckoo, and the quail may or may not be a Beethoven joke ; but if they are not specimens of "painting" in music it is difficult to say what deserves that epithet. If the peasants' merry-making, again, the brawl, the falling of the rain-drops, the rushing of the wind, the storm, the flow of the brook—if these are not "painting" but merely the "expression of feeling," well, so is the hanging of Till Eulenspiegel, the death-shudder of Don Juan, and the battle in *Ein Heldenleben*. (6) Even supposing that Beethoven's words could be taken literally, even supposing that in his music he had not given them contradiction after contradiction, still this would not settle the matter. Music did not end with Beethoven, and he might have detested "illustrative" music to his heart's content without that fact being an argument against the writing of it by other people. It is curious that the men who always tell admiringly the stories of Beethoven breaking through the fetters in which his contemporaries would have bound him, should try to use the same Beethoven as a barrier against all future innovations. *He* was great because he refused to write in any way but his own ; *we* are to be great by submitting our convictions to those of a hundred years ago. With all respect, and without any irreverent desire to pluck the beards of our fathers, we are unable to regard the question as finally settled by what Beethoven said. He himself would surely have been the last man to play the ineffective Canute, and dictate to the art the exact spot on the beach to which its flood might rise. There is no evidence that he meant his words to be a judicial condemnation of anybody or anything; there is no evidence that he had ever given much critical thought to the question; and it is quite certain that no matter how much he had thought about it he could not have seen in it all that we, with our later experience, can see.

III

One fact alone should make opponents of programme music think seriously of their position. The most significant feature of the problem is the way in which the practical musicians have dealt with it. Whereas most of the older orchestral music of any value was absolute music, most of the later orchestral music of any value is programme music; and the momentum of the latter species seems to be increasing every year. It will not do to pooh-pooh a phenomenon of this kind, nor to seek to fasten upon it the explanation that some of the new men write music depending upon literary or pictorial subjects because they cannot write music of the other kind. This is like saying that Shakespeare pusillanimously wrote dramas because he could not write epics—

which is probably a true saying, but quite irrelevant. The point is, why should Shakespeare, with a gift for good drama, force himself to write bad epics? And if a man's musical ideas spring from quite another way of apprehending life than that of the absolute musician, why should he abjure his own native form of speech in order to mouth and maul unintelligently the phrases and the forms of another musician whose mental world is wholly foreign to his? In any case, while some of the critics have been paternally warning young composers against falling into the toils of programme music, and recommending them to keep to the lines of structure as they were laid down by Haydn, Mozart, and Beethoven, the musicians themselves have been flinging programme music right and left to the world. One has only to take up a catalogue of the Russian, French, German, Belgian, American, or even English music published during the last twenty years to see how enormously this form of art has grown, and how the really big men all display a marked liking for it. You may regret, if you like, that so many modern musicians should prefer programme music to absolute music; but you cannot settle the big æsthetic problem involved by shrugging your shoulders and invoking Haydn, Mozart, and Beethoven, nor by airily flinging out a formula or two of moribund æsthetic. And as bad æsthetic, bad argumentation, are accountable for most of the confusion upon the subject, let us try to analyse it more closely down to its foundations.

Programme music—by which we mean purely instrumental (*i.e.* non-vocal) music that has its *raison d'être* in a definite literary or pictorial scheme—is not an ideal term for this kind of art; but since all names which we can give it are open to objections of some kind, we may as well use this as any other. It must be remembered, too, that though programme or representative music is indeed differentiable from abstract or self-contained music, it is not absolutely differentiable. All programme music must indeed be representative, but it must also be, in part, self-contained; that is, a given phrase must not only be appropriate to the character of Hamlet or Dante, or suggestive of a certain external phenomenon such as the wind, or the fire, or the water, but it must also be interesting *as music*.[1] On the other hand, in thousands of works that have been written without a formal programme, the expression—it may be throughout the work, or only in parts of it—is so vivid, so strenuous, so suggestive of something more than an abstract delight in making a beautiful tone-pattern, that it spontaneously evokes in us images of definite scenes or characters or actions. Surely no one can listen to the C minor symphony, for example, and feel that Beethoven's only concern was with the invention and interweaving of abstract musical themes; here at

---

[1] The reader will of course not take this to mean that a piece of programme music should sound just as well when played as absolute music, *i.e.* should be as interesting to the man who does not know the programme as to the man who does. Against that current fallacy I argue further on.

any rate we feel that there is much truth in Wagner's contention, that behind the mere tones a kind of informal drama is going on. The expression comes, at times, as close to the suggestion of definite thought and definite action as any symphonic poem could do. Thus some of the qualities of programme music are found in absolute music, and *vice versâ;* there is no hard-and-fast line of division between the two. Even in the most mathematical music that ever pedant misconceived, a human accent will sometimes make itself heard; and even the most human music—the music that has its fount and origin and its final justification in the veracious expression of definite human feeling—must be bound together by some mathematical principle of form. But we all understand what we mean by the broad distinction of absolute and poetic music.[1] In the latter we have a definite literary or pictorial scheme controlling (*a*) the shape and colour of the phrases, (*b*) the order in which they appear, (*c*) the way in which they are played off against each other, (*d*) their relative positions at the end. This it is, roughly speaking, that distinguishes it from absolute music, where the manner in which the themes are handled depends upon no conception, external to the themes themselves, that could be phrased in words.

---

[1] The term "poetic" is used as a kind of verbal shorthand. A piece of music may be suggested by a drama, a novel, a historical event, a poem, a philosophical treatise (like *Also sprach Zarathustra*), or anything else. The one phrase "poetic music" will conveniently cover the æsthetic facts involved in all these modes of suggestion.

H

Now we are often told that when music takes upon itself to represent or narrate, as in programme music, it is "stepping beyond its legitimate boundaries." We are told that it is "passing out of its own sphere"; that it is abdicating the purely musical function, and trying to do what it is the function of literature or of painting to do; that a piece of music ought to be comprehensible from its music alone; that its whole message should be written plainly on the music, without the necessity of calling in the aid of a programme. If there is anything in this thesis it will dispose of programme music at once. But I shall try to show that there is nothing whatever in it—that it is not argument, but pure assertion. I shall try to show in the first place that so far from being a passing disease of the present generation, the desire to write programme music is rooted in humanity from the very beginning; and in the second place that the argument just outlined could be made to dispose not only of programme music, but also of the song and the opera.

IV

The late Sidney Lanier, a critic of unusual sanity and freshness of vision, contended that so far from being a late and excrescent growth, programme music is "the very earliest, most familiar, and most spontaneous form of musical composition." We need not go quite so far as this, for it seems to me that it is impossible to date either kind of music first in order of time. Just as one early man placed straight and curved lines in such relations that they pleased the eye by their mere formal harmony, while another placed them in such relations that they pleased by suggesting some aspect of man or nature, so did early music spring with one musician from the mere pleasure in the successions and combinations of tones, with another from the desire to convey in sound a suggestion of the thoughts aroused in him by his intercourse and his struggles with his fellow-men and with the world. Lanier's statement is evidently a slight exaggeration; but I think he has invincible reason with him when he goes on to ask, " What is any song but programme music developed to its furthest extent? A song is . . . a double performance; a certain instrument — the human voice — produces a number of tones, none of which have any intellectual value in themselves; but, simultaneously with the production of the tones, words are uttered, each in a physical association with a tone, so as to produce upon the hearer at once the effect of conventional and of unconventional sounds.[1] . . . Certainly, if programme music is absurd, all songs are nonsense." This, I think, is the key to the problem. Let us look at it a little more closely.

Let us imagine two primitive men, each with the capacity for expressing feeling in musical

[1] That is, sound *quâ* sound (music), *plus* sound congealed into definite symbols (words).

sound. One of them manages to find a phrase of a few notes that gives him pleasure. Because it gives him pleasure he repeats it. Having repeated it a number of times he finds the mere repetition of it becoming monotonous; so next time he repeats it in a slightly different way. He now experiences, without understanding why, a subtler form of pleasure. If you told him he was making a very practical demonstration of the law that a great deal of æsthetic delight consists in realising unity in variety, he would not grasp your meaning; but all the same that is what he is doing. He still has his old pleasure in the agreeable succession of tones; but this pleasure is intensified, subtilised, by another— the |pleasure of detecting the theme in the disguises it assumes. This primitive man has made the first step towards sonata form; he is assisting at the birth of absolute music. From this root there grows up all our pure delight in agreeable tunes for their own sake, in the embroidery of them, in the juggling with them; in a word, all our delight in absolute music.[1] Now take the other man. He starts along another line. When he begins to trace his rude melodic curve, it is not primarily because he finds an all-absorbing delight in the curve itself. He

[1] I am not, of course, putting this forward as the way in which music actually and historically developed. I am simply disengaging from the historical facts, in order to throw it into stronger relief, the psychological element underlying them; just as in economics we try to understand what has actually been the course of events by isolating from the other factors of human nature the factors that concern the desire of gain, and arguing deductively from these.

begins because some definite experience has moved him emotionally, and the emotional disturbance must find an outlet in tone; his melodic curve must suggest the experience. Let us say it is the death of a friend. Here is a much more definite impulse than was acting upon the other man; and it accordingly leads to a more definite expression. The curve the melody takes is now determined not merely by the musical pleasure it gives by going this way or that, but primarily by the need to make the melody representative of a definite feeling, or suggestive of the being or the event that aroused the feeling. *This* man is at the turn of the road that leads to poetical music—to the song, the opera, and the symphonic poem. (I do not allege, let me say again, that there is an absolute line of demarcation between absolute music and poetic music, or between the states of mind from which they flow; the two are always crossing and re-crossing into each other's territory. I am simply throwing into high relief the element in each that gives it its peculiar significance.) In absolute music, as Wagner pointed out, the essential thing is "the arousing of pleasure in beautiful forms." In poetic music the essential thing is the veracious rendering in tone of an emotion that is as definite as the other is indefinite. Take two concrete examples. The opening phrase of Beethoven's 8th Symphony refers to nothing at all external to itself; it is what Herbert Spencer has called the music of pure exhilaration; to appreciate it you have to think of nothing but itself; the pleasure lies primarily in the way the notes are put together.[1] But the sinister motive that announces the coming of Hunding, in the first act of the *Valkyrie*, appeals to you in a different way. Here your pleasure is only partially due to the particular way the notes go ; the other part of it is due to the *veracity* of the theme, its congruence with the character it is meant to represent. And, to go back to our two primitive men, the first of them was in 'the mood that would ultimately give birth to the opening of the 8th Symphony, while the second of them was in the mood that would ultimately give birth to the Hunding motive.

Any one who takes the trouble to analyse the phrases of an ordinary symphony and those of a modern song will perceive a broad difference between the kinds of ideas evoked by them. In the old symphony or sonata a succession of notes, pleasing in itself but not having specific reference to actual life — not attempting, that is, to get at very close quarters with strong emotional or dramatic expression, but influencing and affecting us mainly by reason of its purely formal relations and by the purely physical pleasure inherent in it as sound—was stated, varied, worked out and combined with other themes of the same order. Take a thousand of these themes—from Haydn, Mozart, and the early

[1] There is emotion, of course, at the back of the notes ; the reader will not take me to mean that the pleasure is merely physical, like a taste or an odour. But the emotive wave is relatively small and very vague ; it neither comes directly from nor suggests any external existence.

Beethoven, for example—and while they affect you musically you will yet be unable to say that they have taken their rise from any *particular* emotion, or that they embody any special reflection upon life. It is the peculiarity of music that while on the one hand it may speak almost as definitely as poetry, and refer to things that are cognised intellectually, as in poetry, on the other hand it may make an impression on us, purely as sound, to which the words of poetry, purely as words, can offer no parallel effect. A verse of Tennyson with the words so transposed as to have no intellectual meaning would make no impression when read aloud ; no pleasure, that is, would be obtainable merely from the sound of the words themselves. But play the diatonic scale on the piano, or strike a random chord here and there, and though the thing means nothing, the ear is bound to take some pleasure in it. Musical sound gives us pleasure in and by and for itself, independently of our finding even the remotest mental connection between its parts. This connection may be great, or small, or practically non-existent ; and the greater it is, of course, the more complicated becomes our pleasure ; but it is not essential to our taking physiological delight in music considered purely as sound. Now it is quite possible to construct a lengthy piece of music that shall have absolutely no emotional expression, in the sense of suggesting a reference to human experience—that shall be purely and simply a succession and combination of pleasurable sounds. In the nature of the case, it is clear that not much of the actual music that is written could be of this order throughout. Emotion of some quality and degree is sure to intrude itself here and there into even the most "mathematical" music; but it is quite unquestionable that while some music is alive with suggestions of human interest, of actual man and life, there is an enormous quantity of very pleasant music from which the interest of actuality is wholly absent, that reaches us through physiological rather than through psychological channels, or at any rate, if this is putting it unscientifically, through quite other psychological channels.

Compare with music of this kind the phrases of a highly expressive modern song, or of such a piece as Wagner's *Faust Overture*, or of one of Liszt's or César Franck's symphonic poems. Here the inspiration comes direct from some aspect of external nature or from some actual human experience; and the musical phrase becomes correspondingly modified. While there still remain (1) the physiological pleasure in the theme as sound, and (2) the formal pleasure in the structure, balance, and development of the theme, there is now superadded a third element of interest—the recognition of the veracity of the theme, its appropriateness as an expression of some positive, definite emotion, something seen, some actual experience of men. And music with a content of this kind, it is important to note, can depart widely from the manner of expression and of development of absolute music, and still be interesting. The proof of this is to be had in

recitative. Here there is a very wide departure
from the more formal music in every quality—
melodic, rhythmic, and harmonic. Attempt to
play an ordinary piece of recitative as pure music,
without the voice and without a knowledge of the
words, and its divergence from music of the self-
sufficing order generally becomes obvious. The
justification of recitative is to be sought not |in its
compliance with the laws that govern pure non-
dramatic instrumental music, but in its congruence
with a definite literary idea that is seeking expression through the medium of tone ; and our
tolerance of it and appreciation of it are due
to this supplementing of the somewhat inferior
physical pleasure by the superior mental pleasure
given by the sense of dramatic truth and fitness.
So again in the song. Let any one try to imagine
how little the ending of Schubert's *Erl-King*
would suggest to him if he were totally ignorant
of the words or the subject of the song, and he will
realise how the literary element at once modifies and
supports music of this kind. As a piece of absolute
music, the final phrase of the *Erl-King* means
nothing at all ; it only acquires significance when
taken in conjunction with the words ; and the
justification of its relinquishment of the mode of
expression of pure self-sufficing music is precisely
its congruence with the literary idea. To go a
step further, the phrases typical of Mazeppa in
Liszt's symphonic poem, both in themselves and
in their development, would probably puzzle us
if we met with them in a symphony pure and
simple ; they only become such marvels of poig-

nant and veracious expression when associated in the mind with Mazeppa. And, to go still further, and to show not from the structure of a theme but from the treatment of it the change that may be induced by a "programme," I may instance the repetitions in the last movement of Tchaikovski's "Pathetic" Symphony, which, though unwarrantable in a symphony of the older pattern, seem to many of us surcharged with the most direct psychological significance. Right through, from recitative to the symphonic poem or the programme symphony, we see that the fusion of the literary or pictorial with the musical interest necessarily leads to a modification of the tissue of the musical theme and of the musical development. You could not, if you would, express the story of Mazeppa in such phrases as those of the "Jupiter." So that, while we thus have an *a priori* justification of the programme phrase, we begin to understand the difficulties that attend programme development, and some reasons for its many failures in the past. Much of the work that had been done by the older men in consolidating and elaborating the form of the symphony was found to be of little help to the new school. A new type of phrase had to be evolved, and with it a new method of development.

No one, I think, will dispute the broad truth of the principles here laid down. That absolute music *per se* and vocal or programme music *per se* have marked psychological differences between them, and that, while the older bent was towards

the one, the modern men show a marked preference for the other—these are fairly obvious
facts. Hence the necessity of urging it upon the
classicists that it will not do to apply the formal
rules of the old music to the new *en bloc*, as if
they were equally valid in both *genres*. If the
modern men reject the classical forms, and try to
produce new ones of their own, it can only be
because their ideas are not the classical ideas, and
must find the investiture most natural and most
propitious to them. When Wagner rejected the
current opera-form, and strove to attain congruence of the poetical and the musical schemes
at all points of his work, the pedants told him
that he avoided the long-sanctioned forms because
he could not write in them. They did not see
that it would have been much less trouble for him,
as a mere musician, to shelter himself behind the
old forms than to evolve a consistent new one,
and that he aimed at a new structure simply
because he had something quite new to say.
Similarly, when the pedants lay it down that the
programmists choose the programme form because it is an easier one to work in than the
absolute form, they fail to see how much originality of mind is needed to get veracity of
expression in the song or the symphonic poem,
where the work, besides having to satisfy our
musical sense, will be tested by the standard of
the literary utterance or the literary idea with
which it deals.

V

Without making too wide a digression into the æsthetics of music, we can see that the tendency to write the one kind of music is as deeply rooted in us as the tendency to write the other kind. Some musicians, by constitutional bias, take the one route, some the other; but neither party has the right to assume that the kind of music it prefers is the only kind. Hence it is an error to say that music is stepping out of her own province when she becomes programme music. Her real province includes both absolute and programme music; the one is as inherent in us as the other.

But for reasons that will become apparent later, the absolute branch of the art developed more rapidly than the poetical branch. Even by the time absolute music had come to its magnificent climax in Beethoven, programme music had really done nothing at all of any permanent value. Many composers seemed to have a vague idea that purely instrumental music *could* be made to convey suggestions of real life just as poetry does, and just as the song does; but they had not yet learned where to begin and where to end, what was worth doing in this line and what was not worth doing. Their attempts at programme music were mostly crude imitations of external things, in a language not yet rich enough to express what they wanted to say; they contain, for our ears, rather too much programme and rather too little music. In the sixteenth and seventeenth centuries the minds of the men who tried to write poetic music for instruments alone, ran in two main directions. They either wrote pieces musically interesting in themselves, and gave them fanciful titles, such as "Diana in the wood," "The virtuous coquette," "Juno, or the jealous woman," and so on, or they frankly began with the intention of representing appearances and events in music. Thus in the Fitzwilliam Virginal Book we have pieces with the titles, "Faire wether," "Calm wether," "Lightening," "Thunder," and "A clear day." These things were not confined to one country; they are met with all over Europe. Occasionally the programme writers worked through vocal as well as instrumental forms. Muffat wrote pieces of the "Diana in the wood" order. Jannequin described the battle of Malegnano in music, Hermann the battle of Pavia. In the seventeenth century Carlo Farina wrote orchestral pieces in which the voices of animals were imitated. Buxtehude wrote seven klaviersuites, describing in music the nature and quality of the seven planets. Frescobaldi did a battle capriccio. Frohberger wrote a suite showing the Emperor Ferdinand IV. making his way up into heaven along Jacob's ladder. Frohberger, indeed, was realistic beyond the average. He' not only painted nature, for example, but indicated the locality as accurately as a geography or a guide-book could do; and it was not merely humanity in general that moved about among his scenes, but the Count this or the Prince that. In some suites, that are unfortunately lost to an admiring world, he painted a storm on the Dover-Calais route, and gave a series of pictures of what befell the Count von Thurn in a perilous journey down the Rhine.[1]

All this seems very crude now, but the very prevalence of the practice points to a widespread feeling in those times that music *could* be made to serve as an art of representation. Indeed, a much earlier example of this tendency can be quoted, showing that even the ancient Greeks had their programme-music writers. There is a passage in the Geography of Strabo, in which he describes what he heard at Delphi. Here, he says, they had a musical contest " of players on the cithara, who executed a pæan in honour of Apollo. The players on the cithara were accompanied by players on the flute, and by citharists, who performed without singing. They performed a melos (strain) called the Pythian mood. It consisted of five parts—the anacrusis, the ampeira, cataceleusmus, iambics and dactyls, and pipes. Timosthenes, the commander of the fleet of the second Ptolemy, and who was the author of a work in ten books on Harbours, composed a melos. His object was to celebrate in this melos the contest of Apollo with the serpent Python. The anacrusis was intended to express the prelude ; the ampeira, the first onset of the contest ; the cataceleusmus, the contest

---

[1] I take some of these historical facts from the article of Max Vancsa, already cited.

itself; the iambics and dactyls denoted the tri-
umphal strain on obtaining the victory, together
with musical measures of which the dactyl is
peculiarly appropriated to praise and the iambics
to insult and reproach; the syrinxes and pipes
described the death, the players imitating the
hissings of the expiring monster."[1] The unsympathetic may say it is to be hoped that the gentleman was a better admiral than he seems to have
been a musician.

But to get back to modern Europe again.
These crude imitations of birds and beasts and
the rolling of the waves are not programme
music; they are the rawest part of the raw
material out of which programme music is
made. The difficulty is to make the piece
interesting both as music, and as a representation of what it purports to describe. A composer
may fling a phrase before us and tell us this
represents Hamlet, or Othello, or a death-rattle,
or the Israelites crossing the Red Sea, or anything else he likes; but unless the phrase has an
interest of its own, and unless he can satisfy our
musical as well as our literary sense by the way
he handles and combines and transforms it in the
sequel, he will not arrest our attention. The
great problem, indeed, of both the modern
symphonic poem and the modern opera is to
tell a story adequately and at the same time to
satisfy our desire for interesting musical development. If the composer fixes his attention too
exclusively on the literary part of his subject, his

---

[1] See Strabo's *Geography*, Bohn edition, vol. ii. p. 120.

work will lack organic *musical* unity ; if he is too intent on achieving this, he will probably fail in dramatic definiteness. This, I shall soon try to show, is really the crux both of opera and of programme music ; and if *we* rarely succeed in solving so knotty a problem, it is not to be wondered at that the solution did not come to the men of the sixteenth or seventeenth or eighteenth century.

As a matter of fact, however, one old composer *did* try to effect a union of the programme purpose with some real sense of musical form. This was Johann Kuhnau (1660 ?–1722), who, in his six Bible Sonatas, describes " the fight between David and Goliath," " the melancholy of Saul being dissipated by music," " the marriage of Jacob," and so on. Kuhnau was a really remarkable man. He was a good musician who could write interesting clavier-pieces apart from any programme scheme. He was moreover a keen-witted man who tried to think out seriously the problem of the union of musical expression and poetical purpose, so far as any man in those days could do so. In the preface to the Bible Sonatas he points out that the musican, like the poet, prose-writer, and painter, often wants to turn his hearer's thoughts in a particular direction. If he wants to express in his music not merely sadness but the sadness of this or that individual—to distinguish, as he says, a sad Hezekiah from a weeping Peter or a lamenting Jeremiah—he must employ words in order to make the emotion definite. But not necessarily, be it observed, by writing the music *to* the words, as in a song. His own plan is to illustrate his subject in music, and make his poetic purpose clear to us by giving a detailed verbal account of it. Thus he prefaces each of his Bible Sonatas with an elaborate account of the event it deals with, and then summarises the main motives. This, for example, is the summary of the first Sonata, after a long general introduction. The Sonata expresses, he says—

1. The stamping and bravado of Goliath.
2. The trembling of the Israelites, and their prayer to God at sight of their awful enemy.
3. The courage of David, his desire to break the proud spirit of the giant, and his childlike trust in God's help.
4. The contest of words between David and Goliath, and the contest itself, in which Goliath is wounded in the forehead by the stone, falls down, and is slain.
5. The flight of the Philistines, and how they are pursued by the Israelites, and slaughtered with the sword.
6. The jubilation of the Israelites over the victory.
7. The chorus of the women in praise of David.
8. And, finally, the general joy, finding vent in vigorous dancing and leaping.

It will be seen at once that the programme here is of a different kind from those of some of

I

Kuhnau's predecessors and contemporaries. It does indeed aim at representing some external things—such as the stamping of Goliath, the impact of the stone against his head, and so on— but they are not inherently absurd or impossible ; while he gives a great deal of his space to the really emotional moments of the story. Throughout the sonatas, however, it is the poetic purpose that directs the music, determining both expression, sequence, and form. Every episode that occurs in the story has to be represented in the music ; and Kuhnau is careful to print, in his score, the verbal indication at the precise point where the music follows it. He tells us the exact bar at which the stone is aimed at Goliath, and the bar in which the giant falls down ; where Laban begins to practise his deceit on Jacob, where Jacob is "amorous and contented," and where "his heart warns him that something is wrong" ; and so on—thereby setting an example to composers like Strauss, who foolishly give the purchaser of such a score as *Till Eulenspiegel* no guide to the various adventures of the hero. Some of Kuhnau's devices provoke a smile, as in the Fifth Sonata—"Gideon, the Saviour of the People of Israel." The sign to Gideon was that the fleece was to be wet with dew, but the ground dry ; the next night the ground was to be wet and the fleece dry. Kuhnau naïvely expresses the second sign by giving the theme of the first sign in contrary motion. But all *naïvetés* apart, a great deal of the music of the Sonatas is very fine ; and it is noteworthy that Kuhnau points out, in his general preface, that the writer of programme music must be allowed more liberty than the absolutist to break a traditional "law" when the expression demands it.[1] Kuhnau, indeed, was on the right path. He was a man born before his due time ; had he lived in our days, and had at his command all the resources of modern expression and our enormous orchestras, he might have taken up very much the same position towards music as the modern programmists.

John Sebastian Bach, who succeeded Kuhnau at the Thomas Church in Leipzig, made one, and only one, experiment in the same line. This was the "Capriccio on the departure of my dearly beloved brother." The first movement, he says, depicts "The cajoleries of friends, trying to induce him to give up the idea of the journey"; the second is "a representation of the various things that may happen to him in foreign lands"; the third gives utterance to a "general lament of his friends as they say good-bye to him"; and the finale is a fugue on the postillion's signal.

Bach, however, made no further attempt to develop along these lines. The work *he* had been sent into the world to do was of another order.

About the same time Couperin, in France, was

---

[1] The Bible Sonatas, together with Kuhnau's other piano works and his prose writings, may be had in vol. iv. of the *Denkmäler Deutscher Tonkunst*, carefully edited by Karl Päsler. Mr. Shedlock, in his book on *The Pianoforte Sonata*, gives a pretty full account of Kuhnau ; but it is a pity he could not have found space for a complete translation of the preface to the Bible Sonatas.

cultivating the programme *genre* with some success. He not only wrote harmless little things with titles like "La Galante," but also connected pieces of musical delineation, such as "The Pilgrims." Like Kuhnau, he justified his principles in a preface. "In the composition of my pieces," he says, "I have always a definite object or matter before my eyes. The titles of my pieces correspond to these occasions. Each piece is a kind of portrait."

In Rameau again, we get such things as "Sighs," "Tender Plaints," "The Joyous Girl," "The Cyclops," etc.; and at a slightly later date Dittersdorf (1739–1799) wrote twelve programme symphonies, illustrating Ovid's "Metamorphoses" and "The War of Human Passions."

Mozart's father wrote a musical description of a sledge-journey, in which the ladies are represented shivering with the cold; but Mozart himself avoided the programme form as positively as Bach. Haydn, however, dabbled in it more extensively, as I have already pointed out.

Beethoven's position in the history of programme music is somewhat peculiar. Just about that time, when the Napoleonic wars had familiarised every one with the pomp of armies, there was a perfect deluge of battle pieces. There was probably not a battle of any importance in those days that had not a fantasia written upon it, each differing from the others in little else but its title. In a weak moment Beethoven succumbed to the general temptation and wrote his "Battle of Vittoria," which is not only one of the least

significant of his works, but one of the least
significant works in the history of programme
music. Beethoven's real contributions to this
form of art were indirect rather than direct. He
told one of his friends that he had always a
picture in his mind when composing; and if this
could be taken quite literally, it would seem as if
we were on the trail of programme music pure
and simple. But we shall probably never know
the extent to which Beethoven relied on poetic
suggestions for his musical inspiration; and if
we look at the internal evidence of his music, we
shall see that although it often deals with poetic
subjects, it treats them from the standpoint of
the old forms rather than from that of the new.
So far as their intellectual origin is concerned, the
superb *Leonora, Egmont,* and *Coriolan* overtures
are poetic music; that is, they aim, in a musical
texture, at sketching a character or telling a story.
But so far as the form is concerned in which the
composer has chosen to work, the procedure is
determined almost entirely by the laws of absolute
music. Wagner has drawn attention to this in
a well-known passage in his essay on " Liszt's
Symphonic Poems." He shows what the formal
laws of the old symphony were, and how necessary they were to give logical coherence to abstract
music. But, he says, when these laws were
applied uncompromisingly to a different kind of
art-work—the overture—a disturbance occurred
at once between the aims of the overture and the
demands of the symphonic form. All that the
latter was concerned with was *change*—the con-

stant re-presentation of themes in new lights. The overture had, in addition to this, to concern itself with dramatic development. "Now it will be obvious," he says, "that, in the conflict of a dramatic idea with this form, the necessity must at once arise either to sacrifice the development (the idea) to the alternation (the form), or the latter to the former." He goes on to praise Gluck's *Iphigenia in Aulis* overture for the skilful way it keeps the dramatic development from being spoiled by compliance with extraneous laws of form. Then, he says, Beethoven, working on a bigger scale and with a more stupendous imagination than Gluck, nevertheless came to grief on the rock Gluck managed to escape. "He who has eyes," says Wagner, "may see precisely by this overture (*i.e.* the great *Leonora No. 3*), how detrimental to the master the maintenance of the traditional form was bound to be. For who, at all capable of understanding such a work, will not agree with me when I assert that the repetition of the first part, after the middle section, is a weakness which distorts the idea of the work almost past all understanding; and that the more, as everywhere else, and particularly in the coda, the master is obviously governed by nothing but the dramatic development. But whoso has brains and lack of prejudice enough to see this, will have to admit that the evil could only have been avoided by entirely giving up that repetition; an abandonment, however, which would have done away with the overture-form—*i.e.* the original, merely suggestive, symphonic dance-form—and have constituted the departure-point for creating a new form."

Wagner is undoubtedly right. Beethoven hovered uncertainly at times between the demands of poetic expression and the demands of absolute form. To write poetic music pure and simple, of course, was not his mission in the world. That was reserved for other men. One side of his powerful genius was to be taken up by Wagner and pushed to its logical conclusion in the music-drama. Another side, cultivated by Berlioz, Liszt, and Richard Strauss, comes to its logical end in the symphonic poem ; and just as Wagner criticised the Beethoven overture from the standpoint of music-drama, I propose, shortly, to criticise Wagner from the standpoint of the symphonic poem. I shall try to show that so far from the Wagnerian opera representing, as Wagner thought, the ideal after which the music of Beethoven was striving, it is really only a transitional form ; and that the symphonic poem is the completely satisfactory, completely logical form, to which the Wagnerian opera stands in the same relation as the *Leonora* overture does to *Tristan and Isolde*.

VI

Before embarking on this æsthetic argument, however, let us briefly conclude our historical view of the development of programme music. It was with the Romantic movement that the infusion of poetry into music became complete, and at the same time the vocabulary and the colour-range of music became adequate to express all kinds of literary and pictorial ideas. The older musicians could not, if they had tried, have written the modern symphonic poem or the modern song. And this for several reasons. In the first place, they were pretty fully occupied with making music the language it now is; they had to form a vocabulary and think out principles of architecture; and the last thing they could have done was to leave the safe and formal lines of their own art—safe because they were precise and formal—and plunge into a mode of expression that would have seemed to them to offer no coherence, no guiding principle. In the second place, they lacked one of the main stimuli to the development of modern programme music, the suggestion of a vivid, living, modern, highly emotional and picturesque poetry. A Schumann, a Brahms, a Franz could not have written such songs as they have done in any century but this; for the mainspring of their songs has been the emotional possibilities contained in the words. It was only when composers really felt the deepest artistic interest in the words they were setting, instead of regarding them as merely a frame for musical embroidery, that they attained the modern veracity and directness of phrase. You cannot do much more with words like those of the older song or opera than set them with a view to their purely musical rather than their musico-poetical possibilities; and if you persist, out of deference to a foolish tradition, in setting to music the words of a foreign and relatively unfamiliar language, you will perforce become more and more conventional in your phrases and in your general structure. It was the peculiar advantage of the modern German song-writers that they could set lyrics of their own language, alive with every suggestion that could lend itself to musical treatment. The emotion was intense, the form concentrated and direct, the idea definite and concise; and the musicians, having by this time a fully developed language for their use, set themselves to reproduce these qualities of the poem in their music. Hence the new spirit that came into music with the Romantic movement, and that reacted on opera, on piano music, and on the symphonic poem.

Another great difference between the pre-Romantic and the post-Romantic composers was that the latter were, on the whole, much more cultured men than the former. This was due, of course, not to any particular merit of their own, but to the changed social circumstances of the musician. The system of patronage in the eighteenth century, while it undoubtedly helped the musician to develop *as* a musician, must have retarded his development in other ways. Under that system, where he was often little better than the servant of some aristocrat, he must often have been debarred from studying the world at first-hand, meeting it face to face, looking at it through his own eyes. Neither Haydn[1] nor

[1] "He was and remained," says Wagner, "a prince's musical officer, with the duty of catering for the entertainment of his pomp-

Mozart, for example, stood on the level of the best culture of the time. The great German historian of music, Ambros, has pointed out how, in Mozart's letters from Italy, the talk is all of the singers and dancers ; "he scarcely seems to have noticed the Coliseum and the Vatican, with all that these contain." And Ambros goes on to say that the modern musician reads his Shakespeare and his Sophocles in the original, and knows them almost by heart. He reads Humboldt's Cosmos and the histories of Niebuhr and Ranke ; he studies the dialectic of Hegel as well as, or perhaps more than, the art of fugue ; and if he goes to Italy he does not trouble himself about the opera, but occupies himself with nature and the remains of classic art. He is, in fact, says Ambros, " Herr Microcosmos."[1]

For a fair picture of the ordinary life of a musician in the house of his patron in the eighteenth century we have only to turn to the Autobiography of Dittersdorf. Among them all, indeed, Gluck and Handel seem to be the only musicians who possessed much culture,[2] and who strike us as

struck master. . . . Docile and devout, the peace of his kind and cheerful temper stayed unruffled till advanced old age ; only the eye, that looks upon us from his portrait, is suffused with a gentle melancholy."

[1] See Ambros : *Die Grenzen der Musik und Poesie* (1885), iv. v.

[2] It is significant that even the sturdy, independent Gluck too fell a victim to princely patronage in the very middle of his career. After striking out for himself in *Telemacco* (1749) and *La Clemenza di Tito* (1750), and apparently being well on the way to the reform of the opera, he became, in 1754, Kapellmeister at Vienna. From that date to 1762, when *Orfeo* was produced, he wrote, not like Gluck, but like a court servant. See a pithy paragraph on the subject in Mr. Hadow's book, *The Viennese Period* (vol. v. of the Oxford History of Music), p. 90.

being, apart from music, the intellectual equal of
the great men of the time—of Voltaire, Rousseau,
Condorcet, Diderot, Lessing, and the rest. There
is no evidence that Beethoven was either a man
of wide culture, or a respectable thinker outside
his own art. It is, indeed, probable that the
enormous musical power of many of these men,
and the centuries of progress through which they
rushed music in comparatively a few years, was
due to their being nothing else but musicians, to
the concentration of all their faculties, all their
experiences, upon the problem of making sound
a complete, living, flexible medium of expression.
But the later musicians were of another order.
The Romantic movement bred a new type of
musician. He no longer sat in the music-room
of an aristocrat, clothed in the aristocrat's livery,
and spun music out of his own inner consciousness. He moved about in the world and saw and
learned a good deal. He associated with poets;
he frequented the studios of painters. We get
men like Hoffmann, at once novelist, painter,
musician, and critic; like Liszt, pianist, composer,
author; like Schumann, musician and musical
critic; like Wagner, ranging greedily over the
whole field of human knowledge, and mixing
himself up—in more senses than one—with every
possible and impossible subject under the sun.
I am not using the term in any offensive or disparaging sense when I say that the average
modern musician, in matters outside music, is a
much better educated and more all-round man
than his predecessor; he knows more, sees

more, reads more, thinks more. Men like Wagner, Brahms, Richard Strauss, Hugo Wolf, and Bruneau, stand much closer to the general intellectual life of their day than any of the older musicians did to the intellectual life of *his* day. I am not for a moment contending that they are any greater *musicians* merely on this account; I simply state it as a psychological factor in their work, as something that determines, to a great extent, the quality of that work, and certainly determines their choice of subjects.

The way it does this is by making them anxious to express in their music all the impressions they have gathered from the world and from their culture. But in order that they might do this, two things were necessary, as we have already seen. The vocabulary of music — its range of melody and harmony—had to be increased, and the capacity of the orchestra had to be enormously developed. It is folly to laugh at the men of the seventeenth and eighteenth centuries for not getting on further with poetical music. They had not the means at their disposal to do so. Sonata-form grew up to a great extent on the piano and the violin; and the nature of these instruments largely determined what could and should be uttered upon them. It was not till harmony got richer and deeper and fuller, and men had learned to extract all kinds of expression from the orchestra, that programme music in the true sense of the word became possible.

The broad historical facts, then, are that the

stimulus to poetic music in the nineteenth century came from the wider education of the musician, the great development of the means of musical expression, and the incessant stimulation of the musician by poetry and literature in general.[1] As we know, the new spirit broke out in three forms—in the highly emotional song of Schubert, Schumann, Brahms, Franz, and the others ; in the poetical music-drama of Wagner ; and in the symphonic poems or programme symphonies of Berlioz, Liszt, Tchaikovski, Raff, and a dozen others, leading up to Richard Strauss. Even the men who did not actually dabble much in the last-named form helped the cause of instrumental poetic music in other ways. Schumann, for example, with his poetic little piano pieces, his delicate sketches of character in the *Carneval* and *Papillons* and elsewhere, was really following up the same trail as led to Liszt's *Mazeppa*, Berlioz's *Harold en Italie*, and Strauss's *Till Eulenspiegel*.

VII

On two lines of inquiry, then, we have found the case for programme music somewhat stronger than its hasty opponents have imagined. On the one hand, we have seen that when the nature and origin of music are psychologically analysed,

---

[1] The development of the opera, too, was an important factor. It was not till men had mastered dramatic musical expression in association with words that they could properly aim at the same kind of expression without words.

there are two mental attitudes, two orders of expression, and two types of phrase, from one of which has arisen absolute, from the other, programme music. On the other hand, we have seen that, from a variety of reasons, programme music could not have been cultivated by the great masters of the eighteenth century who beat out the form of the classical symphony; while its fascination for the modern men is due to its being the only medium of expression for a certain order of modern ideas. It is quite time, then, that not only critics but composers realised that when the brains are out the form will die; that you cannot write a symphony in the form of Mozart or Beethoven unless your mental world is something like theirs, and that if the literary, or pictorial, or dramatic suggestion is all-potent with a composer, it is folly for him to throw it aside, and try, by using a form that is uncongenial to him, to get back into an emotional atmosphere it would be impossible for him to breathe.

The change that came over music about the beginning of the nineteenth century, and that first came to full fruition in Wagner's operas, is best described in the oft-quoted words of Wagner himself, as "the fertilisation of music by poetry." He felt that there was considerable evidence of the action of poetry upon music in Beethoven, though, as can be seen from the passages on the *Leonora* overture already quoted, in Beethoven the reins are still too tightly clutched by absolute music. He always, no matter what the origin of his conceptions may have been, worked them out within the limits of symphonic form. Berlioz, roughly speaking, went the other way, always keeping his eye fixed intently on the lines of his poetic scheme. Wagner's criticism upon this practice of Berlioz is interesting, even if not final. In listening to music of this kind, he says, "it always happened that I so completely lost the musical thread that by no manner of exertion could I re-find and knit it up again." His point was this, to put it in words of our own: if he was listening to a Berlioz work, he could not get complete pleasure out of the music, *as* mere music, because it was not developed along purely musical lines; the chief theme, let us say, gave him pleasure on its first announcement, but he could not see the *rationale* of its future treatment, as one can always see the *rationale* of the return of the themes in a symphony. This was because the course of the music was determined not by abstract musical intentions, but by poetic intentions which were not made clear to him; and the result was, as it were, that he fell between two stools. "I discovered," he says, "that while I had lost the musical thread (*i.e.* the logical and lucid play of definite motives), I now had to hold on to scenic motives not present before my eye, nor even so much as indicated in the programme. Indisputably these motives existed in Shakespeare's famous balcony scene" (Wagner is speaking of Berlioz's *Romeo and Juliet*); "but in that they had all been faithfully retained, and in the exact order given them by the dramatist, lay the great mistake of the composer." And Wagner's contention was this, that when a composer wants to reproduce in music a certain scene from a drama, he must not take the thing as it stands and move on from point to point in exactly the same way as the poet did. What was right for the poet would be wrong for the musician. *He* must tell his story or paint his scene according to the laws and capacities of music, not those of poetry ; and Wagner goes on to praise Liszt for having, by superior artistic instinct, avoided the pitfall that nearly proved fatal to Berlioz. Liszt, instead of trying to tell us in music precisely what the poet had already told us in verse, rethinks in music what the poet has said, and gives it out to us as something born of musical feeling itself.

Now we need not go into the question of how far Wagner is right in what he says of Berlioz. This, at all events, is certain, from his own words in praise of Liszt, that Wagner had no *à priori* objection to the symphonic poem, but only to the symphonic poem when it went on what he took to be the wrong lines. All that is needed is for the proper compromise to be agreed upon between the poetic purpose and the musical form. This, I think, Richard Strauss has effected, and it would be interesting to have had Wagner's criticism of Strauss. But since we cannot get that, *we* may criticise Wagner from the standpoint of the symphonic poem.

VIII

Before doing this, however, let us briefly touch upon one or two other main issues.

The first point I lay stress on is this, that "form" in programme music cannot mean the same thing as form in absolute music; and for this reason. So long as you work in one medium alone, the form is controlled simply by the necessities and potentialities of that medium. In a symphony or a fugue you have to consider nothing but the nature of absolute music; in the drama, you have to worry about no problems except those that lie in the nature of drama. But as soon as you begin to work in a form that is a blend of the two, each of them wants to pull the other along its own road, and a compromise has to be arrived at. This is why it is easier to satisfy our sense of form in a drama or a symphony than in an opera or a symphonic poem. We see the same thing in prose literature. If you are going to write a pure romance, concerned with nothing but romance, your course is fairly easy. If you are going to write a treatise on society, again, you are bound by no laws but those pertaining to this kind of work. But if you want to combine the two—if you want to write a novel that shall not only depict character but also enforce a sociological lesson, as in Zola's novels or some of the stories of the American Frank Norris, then there is a wrench between the two tendencies. The sociology is apt to spoil the

K

fiction, and the fiction the sociology. So it is in poetic music; the poetry wants the music to go *its* way, the music insists on the poetry going *its* way. In the case of the sociological novel, what really happens is this. We admit that Zola's *Débâcle* is not so artistic a piece of work as, say, R. L. Stevenson's *Prince Otto;* but we make allowances; we give up a little purely æsthetic pleasure in consideration of getting a great deal of another kind of pleasure—that of seeing a bigger picture of a more real life put on the canvas. If we can only get the larger human quality in fiction by giving up a little of the æsthetic gratification that comes from perfect form—well, being reasonable creatures, there are times when we will cheerfully accept the situation and make the compromise.

And so it is in poetic music. Wagner's *Tannhäuser* overture and the *Tristan* prelude are not so satisfactory, from the point of view of pure form, as a movement from a Beethoven symphony. We get the repetitions of the themes determined by poetic rather than musical necessities. Push the principle a little further, and you will get almost no musical continuity at all, but a continuity of picture only. If we examine the prelude to the *Dream of Gerontius*, we see that the order of the themes follows a poetic or scenic purpose rather than a musical purpose. This is legitimate so long as it does not go too far, so long as we are not made to feel that the musical continuity is absolutely thrown overboard to secure didactic or literary continuity. But the

broad principle is, that a piece of musical development, like the *Tristan* or *Gerontius* prelude, that
would not be altogether satisfactory in absolute
music, is quite satisfactory in poetic music. It
tells the literary story well enough, and yet does
not starve our musical sense.

IX

This brings us to a second point. We are
often told that programme music is all right if it
is so conceived and so handled that it suffices *as
pure music*, whether we know the programme or
not. And as this seems to many people like a
fair compromise, and as programme-musicians
have been ill-treated so long that some of them
are positively thrilled with gratitude now for *not*
being kicked, there is a tendency to accept this
quasi-solution of the problem as something like
the final one. The programmist is willing to
admit that a number of themes, no matter how
agreeable, do not constitute symphonic music
unless they have some emotional connection and
some logical musical development; while the
absolutist graciously allows that a concrete subject may be the basis of a symphony, if only the
music is of such a kind that it will appeal to the
hearer just as much, although he may not know
what the subject is.

It is precisely against this compromise that I
think we ought to protest, for it seems to me to
be based on a complete misunderstanding of the

natures of absolute and of programme music. Not only does it ignore the difference in intellectual origin between a phrase such as that which opens the finale of the *Jupiter* symphony, and such a one as that which symbolises *Till Eulenspiegel*, but it overlooks the fact that along with this difference in the thing expressed there must necessarily go a difference in the manner of expressing it. It is impossible to subscribe to the insidious compromise that programme music ought to "speak for itself," without a knowledge of the programme being necessary.[1] We not only need the programme— the statement of the literary or pictorial subject of the composition—but this is at once answerable for half our pleasure and a justification of certain peculiarities of form which the music may now safely assume. If the shape and colour of the themes of a piece of music, the order of their occurrence, and the variations they undergo, are all determined by the composer having a certain picture in his mind, it is surely necessary for us to be told what that picture is. If it was necessary for him when he was composing, it is necessary for us if we are to listen to the music as he meant us to listen to it. To put a symphonic poem before us without telling us all the composer's intentions in it, is as foolish as to make us listen to the music of a song or an opera

[1] Even Berlioz, in a weak moment, said he hoped that the music of the *Symphonie fantastique* would itself "have a musical interest, independent of the dramatic intention," though he insisted on the title, at any rate, of each movement being given to the audience. See his Preface to the Symphony.

without hearing the words. In the opera and the song, things go this way or that because the poetic purpose requires it, and the justification of them is precisely their appropriateness to the poetic purpose. Similarly, things go this way or that in the symphonic poem because the poetic purpose requires it; and here also we require to know what that poetic purpose was before we can justify or condemn what the musician has done. Let us examine a simple case, say the *Romeo and Juliet* overture of Tchaikovski, and see whether this particular work could be equally understood and appreciated, as pure music, by the man who knows and the man who does not know the programme.

There is not the slightest doubt that the *Romeo and Juliet* would give intense pleasure to any one who simply walked unpremeditatedly into a concert room and heard the overture without knowing that it had a poetical basis—who listened to it, that is, as a piece of music pure and simple in sonata form. But I emphatically deny that this hearer would receive as much pleasure from the work as I do, for example, knowing the poetic story to which it is written. He might think the passage for muted strings, for example, extremely beautiful, but he would not get from it such delight as I, who not only feel all the *musical* loveliness of the melody and the harmonies and the tone colour, but see the lovers on the balcony and breathe the very atmosphere of Shakespeare's scene. I am richer than my fellow by two or three emotions in a case of this kind.

My nature is stirred on two or three sides instead of only one. I would go further, and say that not only does the auditor I have supposed get less pleasure from the work than I, but he really does not hear Tchaikovski's work at all. If the musician writes music to a play and invents phrases to symbolise the characters and to picture the events of the play, we are simply not listening to *his* work at all if we listen to it in ignorance of his poetical scheme. We may hear the music, but it is not the music he meant us to hear, or at all events not heard as he intended us to hear it. If melody, harmony, colour and development are all shaped and directed by certain pictures in the musician's mind, we get no further than the mere outside of the music, unless we also are familiar with those pictures. Let us take another example. The reader will remember that the overture opens with a *religioso* theme, in the clarinets and bassoons, that is intended to suggest Friar Lawrence. In the ensuing scenes of conflict between the two opposing factions, this theme appears every now and then in the brass, sometimes in a particularly forceful and assertive manner. The casual hearer whom I have supposed would probably look upon this simply as a matter of counterpoint; Tchaikovski has invented two themes, he would say, and is now simply combining them. But here again he would be wrong. These passages certainly give us musical pleasure, and are as certainly meant to do so, but they are intended also to do something more. The reappearance of the

"Friar Lawrence" theme has a dramatic as well as a musical significance. Taken as it is from the placid wood-wind and given to the commanding brass, and made to stand out like a warning voice through the mad riot that is going on all round it, it tells its own tale at once to any one with a knowledge of the subject of the overture. So again with the mournful transformation of the love motive at the end of the overture. Tchaikovski does not alter the melody and the harmony in this way for merely musical reasons. He has something more in his mind than an appeal to the abstract musical faculty; and I repeat that the hearer who is ignorant of this something more not only gets less than the full amount of pleasure from the work, but really does not hear the work as Tchaikovski conceived and wrote it, and intended it to be heard. The same argument holds good of the song. Imagine one of the most highly and subtly expressive of modern songs—say the "O wüsst' ich doch" or the *Feldeinsamkeit* of Brahms—sung to you at a concert without your having the slightest knowledge of the words. Some pleasure, of course, you could not help feeling in the music; but it would be nothing compared with the sensations you would have if you knew the words or could follow them in a programme. Then you would find not only that certain passages that seemed to you the least interesting before, as mere music, are poignantly expressive, but these apparent peculiarities are justified, and indeed necessitated, by the poetry. Now imagine that you hear the same song three months later. You have forgotten the actual words point by point; but you still retain the recollection of the emotional moods they suggested; and so you are still responsive to each *nuance* of expression in the music. Listening to a song under these conditions is precisely the same as listening to a symphonic poem. In *Die Ideale*, for example, Liszt divides Schiller's poem into sections of different intensity or different *timbre* of feeling, and places each of these in the score before the section of the music that illustrates it. *Die Ideale* is, in fact, an extension of the song-form, in which the words are not sung but are either suggested to us or supposed to be known to us. But it is folly to suppose that either in the Brahms song or *Die Ideale* the man who does not know the literary basis can get the same pleasure as the man who does.

We have only to treat all other symphonic poems in the same way as we have just treated Tchaikovski's *Romeo and Juliet*—to ask ourselves what the composer meant us to hear, and how much of it we really *do* hear if we do not know his poetical scheme—to see the folly of holding up absolute music as the standard to which programme music ought to conform. Occasionally, however, the objection is put in the inverse way, and we are told that programme music is absurd because it does not speak intelligibly to us, does not carry its story written upon it so plainly that no one can mistake it. The charge of absurdity must be really laid at the door of the composer. The plain truth is that a composer has no right to put before us a symphonic poem without giving us the fullest guide to his literary plans. It would be ridiculous of Wagner or Schubert to think their business was ended when they had simply given their music the title of, say, *The Ring of the Nibelung* or *The Erl-king* ; it is equally ridiculous of Strauss to call a work *Till Eulenspiegel* or *Don Juan*, and leave us to discover the rest for ourselves. If Strauss, for example, put together the Don Juan theme (the one on the four horns) in that particular order not merely because he liked the sequence of sounds, but because they accurately limned the picture of Don Juan which he had in his eye at that moment, it is folly of him to throw it before *us* as a mere self-existent sequence of sounds, and not to tell us what aspect of Don Juan it is meant to represent.

As for " the inherent stupidity of programme music "—to which opinion one critic was led by having, in the innocence of his heart, thought the motive just mentioned signified one thing, while, he afterwards discovered, it signified quite another—I would put it to him that he is never likely to go wrong again over this phrase, and that each time he hears *Don Juan* he will, to this extent, be nearer seeing what the composer meant him to see than he ever was before. And if he had an equal certainty of the meaning of all the other subjects in *Don Juan*, would he not then be able to recreate the whole thing in accordance with Strauss' own ideas? And would not all difficulty then vanish, and the " inherent stupidity " seem to be in those who cursed the form because they had not the key to the idea? Let any one listen to *Till Eulenspiegel* with no more knowledge of the composer's intentions than is given in the title, and I can understand him failing to make head or tail of it. But let him learn by heart the admirable German or English analyses that can now be had in almost any programme-book, and if all does not then become as clear to him as crystal, if then he cannot follow all the gradations of that magical piece of story-telling—well, one can only say that nature has deprived him of the symphonic-poem faculty, just as she makes some people insensitive to Botticelli or Maeterlinck. He does but throw an interesting light on his own psychology; the value of the musical form remains unassailed.

Now why does not Strauss, or any other composer of programme music, spare himself and us all this trouble by showing us, once for all, the main psychological lines upon which he has built his work? The composer himself, in fact, is the cause of all the misunderstanding and all the æsthetic confusion. Nothing could be clearer than the symbolism of the music in Strauss' *Don Quixote*, when you know the precise intention of each variation; but the fact that Strauss should give the clue to these in the piano duet and omit it all from the full score shows how absurdly lax and inconsistent the practice of these gentlemen is. *Also sprach Zarathustra*, again, is quite clear, because indications are given here and there of the precise part of Nietzsche's book with which the musician is dealing ; while *Ein Helden-leben*, in the absence of an official "Guide," simply worries us by prompting futile conjectures as to the meaning of this or that phrase. Wagner would not have dreamt of throwing a long work before us, and simply telling us that the subject of it was *Parsifal*. Why, then, should the writer of symphonic poems expect us to fathom all his intentions when he has merely printed the title of his work? If the words of the opera are necessary for me to understand what was in Wagner's mind when he wrote this or that motive, surely words—not accompanying the music, but prefixed to it—are needful to tell me what was in Strauss' mind when he shaped the violin solo in *Ein Heldenleben*. If it is absurd to play to me a song without giving me a copy of the words, expecting me to understand the music that has been born of a poetical idea as if it had been written independently of any verbal suggestion, it is equally absurd to put before me, as pure music, an orchestral piece that was never conceived as pure music. If the poem or the picture was necessary to the composer's imagination, it is necessary to mine ; if it is not necessary to either of us, he has no right to affix the title of it to his work.

It is curious, again, that people who can defend Wagner as against the absolutists cannot also see that they are implicitly justifying Strauss and his fellows. Thus another critic writes that " Wagner saw that the intellectual idea could not be conveyed by music alone; that together with the colour—the music—must go the spoken word to make clear what was meant." So far, good. But then he quarrels with Strauss for trying to make *his* themes expressive of something more than music pure and simple, and giving us a programme to help us. Why, where in the name of lucidity is the difference between singing to a phrase of music the words that prompted it, and printing these words alongside the phrase or at the beginning of the score? Does it matter whether the composer writes a love-scene and has the actual words *sung* by a tenor and a soprano, or merely puts the whole thing on an orchestra, and *tells* us that this is a scene between two lovers, and that their love is of such and such a quality? For the life of me I cannot see why the one proceeding is right and the other wrong. And once more, if it is essential that we should not be left in the slightest doubt in the case of the opera as to who the protagonists are and what is the nature of their sentiments, it is equally essential, in the case of the symphonic poem, that we should not be left in ignorance of any of the points that have gone to make the structure of the music what it is. No symphonic poem ought to be published or performed without the fullest analysis of it by the composer himself, just as he would never think of publishing the music of his song or his opera without the words. There is no compromise possible. If the song and the opera are legitimate blends of literary ideas and musical expression, so is the symphonic poem, and if the literary basis has to be given us in full in the case of the opera, we equally need it in the other case as completely as it can be set before us. The great trouble is that composers like Strauss so often do neither the one thing nor the other ; they neither put their work before us as music pure and simple, nor give us sufficient clue to what the representative music is intended to represent.

And now let me try to show briefly that Wagner misunderstood the meaning of his own reforms, and that the ideal poetic art-form after which he was striving was not the opera but the symphonic poem.

X

To make the following argument clearer I will state its conclusion at once ; I am going to try to show that Wagner's own analysis of the natures of poetry, music and drama conclusively proves that if there can be said to be such a thing as the ideal form of art, it is not the opera but the symphonic poem. I am not going to criticise Wagner's theory, except for a moment here and there. I am going to accept it broadly just as it stands, assume it to be perfectly founded on facts and perfectly logical in the bulk of its exposition, and prove from it that he stopped short at the final conclusion—that had he been quite con-sistent to the end he would have seen, all through his own argument, the finger of demonstration beckoning him on to a point further than that of opera, to a point still higher up the road, where the symphonic poem was awaiting him. And to draw this conclusion I think we do not need to call in the aid of anything but his own words.

In *A Study of Wagner* (1899) I contended that, owing to the structure of his mind, Wagner was to a large degree insensitive to the charms of poetry purely as poetry and of music purely as music. He did not, that is, and could not, get from poetry or from abstract music the precise sensations, completely satisfactory in themselves, that a lover of poetry or a lover of abstract music would get. Poetry to him had something unsatisfactory, imperfect, incomplete in it, unless it reached out a hand to music ; music was similarly defective unless it was born of a poetic stimulus. To dispute this is to be blind to the plain evidence of Wagner's prose works ; the mere assertion to the contrary of his more uncritical admirers counts for simply nothing against the numerous passages that can be brought up in proof. Remarks such as this, " What is not worth the being sung, neither is it worth the poet's pain of telling," or this, " that work of the poet's must rank as the most excellent, which in its final consummation should become entirely music," or this, " A need in music which poetry alone can still," or this, " If the work of the sheer word-poet appears as a non-realised poetic aim, on the other hand, the work of the absolute musician is only to be described as altogether bare of such an aim ; for the Feeling may well have been entirely aroused by the purely-musical expression, but it could not be *directed*,"[1]—remarks such as these are not to be explained away. Nay, Wagner's very notion of an art-work that should embrace all the arts was a sure proof of there being a specific something in each art to which he was impervious.

This, then, is the prime fact in Wagner's artistic psychology. When a poetical idea occurred to him, it was one that cried out for the emotional colour of music to complete it; when a musical idea occurred to him, it was one controlled and directed from the start by a poetic concept. Hence not only his dramatic work but his theoretical work is simply the expression of this psychological bias. His opponents did him an injustice when they said he worked out certain theories and then wrote operas to illustrate and justify them. The fact was that the theories and the operas were only two branches from the same trunk—not cause and effect, but two effects of the same cause. In the operas and the prose works alike he was simply seeking self-expression. But muddled thinker as I hold Wagner to have been upon most of the subjects his busy brain took up, he was perfectly clear as to what he wanted to do in opera, and what he wanted to say in explanation of it. Even the distressing opacity of his style, that makes the reading of him so severe a trial to one's literary sense, cannot prevent the big outlines of his system standing out in perfect clearness. In that system

[1] Here, and elsewhere in this article, I venture to make my quotations from Mr. W. Ashton Ellis's translation of Wagner's prose works.

he thought he had demonstrated three things—
(1) that at a certain stage of its evolution poetry
has to call in the aid of music in order fully to
realise its desires, (2) that music for the same
reason has at a certain stage to call in the aid of
poetry, and (3) that in the musical drama we get
the best powers of music and of poetry exerted to
the fullest, and combined in a harmonious whole.
(He also held that the scene-painting, the stage-
setting, and the gestures of the actors gratified
adequately our other æsthetic senses; but we
need not concern ourselves with this aspect of his
theory here.)

Let me first make it quite clear that Wagner
wished to get an ideal musical-poetic art-form by
shearing off from music all that did not tend
towards poetry, and from poetry all that did not
tend towards music. "Unity of artistic Form,"
he says in *Opera and Drama*, "is only thinkable
as the emanation of a united Content: a united
Content, however, we can only recognise by its
being couched in an artistic expression through
which it can announce itself *entirely* to the Feeling. A Content which should prescribe a twofold
expression, *i.e.* an expression which obliged the
messenger to address himself alternately to the
Understanding and the Feeling—such a Content
could only be itself a dual, a discordant one.
Every artistic aim makes primarily for a united
Shape. . . . Since it is the instinctive Will of
every artistic Aim to impart itself to the Feeling,
it follows that the cloven Expression is incompetent to entirely arouse the Feeling. . . ." "This,"

he goes on to say, "This entire arousing of the Feeling was impossible to the sheer Word-poet, through *his* expressional organ ; therefore what he could not impart through that to Feeling, he was obliged to announce to Understanding, so as to compass the full utterance of the content of his Aim : he must hand over to Understanding, to be thought out, what he could not give to be perceived by Feeling." Thus poetry falls to the ground, as it were, between two stools ; the poet wants to make a direct appeal to Feeling, but he is partly defeated by having to make this appeal through the medium of words, which are more the organ of Understanding than of Feeling. The one thing to be done, then, is to supply this deficiency of Feeling by a resort to music, whose appeal *par excellence* is to the Feeling.

But *per contra*, music itself, as abstract music, is incomplete ; because, although it does indeed move us, it leaves us in doubt as to the cause and purpose of the emotion. "If the work of the sheer Word-poet," says Wagner, "appears as a non-realised poetic Aim, on the other hand the work of the absolute Musician is only to be described as altogether bare of such an Aim ; for the Feeling may well have been entirely aroused by the purely-musical expression, but it could not be *directed*." Or, as he phrases it in another place, instrumental music had worked away at its regular sound-patterns until it "had won itself an idiomatic speech—a speech which in any higher artistic sense, however, was arbitrary and incapable of expressing the purely-human, so long as

L

the longing for a clear and intelligible portrayal of definite, individual human feelings did not become its only necessary measure for the shaping of those melodic particles."

So much, then, is clear ; according to the Wagnerian theory, mere poetry needs music to help it to make its direct appeal to Feeling ; mere music needs the concrete suggestions of poetry to give it order and direction. Even in the later works of Beethoven the pendulum shifts from absolute, abstract musical tone-weaving to the effort to say more definite things; there awoke in him, says Wagner, "a longing for distinct expression of specific, characteristically individual emotions," and he "began to care less and less about merely making music." The climax of this impulse to blend musical feeling and poetic purpose in the one art-work was, of course, to be the Wagnerian opera or music-drama.

This line of argumentation leads to two other propositions :—

(1) In the first place, given that music and poetry are to co-operate to make one product, and given that the most perfect art-form is that which makes a single, undivided, undistracting appeal to us, it follows that the more intimately the two factors are blended the better the result will be. There must be no little bit of music that hangs out, as it were, and declines to meet the poetry on equal terms ; there must be no little bit of poetry that refuses to be amenable to musical expression. The compromise must be

perfect; there must be just so much poetic purpose as is necessary to keep the musical utterance
definite and unmistakable, and just so much
musical outpouring as is necessary to lift *all* the
poetry into the ideal realm of Feeling; just so
much in each case and no more. There must be
a complete "emotionalisation of the intellect";
or, to use yet another of Wagner's phrases, we
must have "a truly unitarian" form. And in
answer to the question, "Has the poet to *restrict*
himself in presence of the musician, and the
musician in presence of the poet?" he says that
they must not restrict each other, "but rouse
each other's powers into highest might, by
love . . ." ". . . If the *poet's aim*—as such—
is still at hand and visible, then it has not as yet
gone under into the Musical Expression; but if
the *Musician's Expression*—as such—is still apparent, then it, in turn, has not yet been inspired
by the Poetic Aim." In the *Zukunftsmusik* he
puts the same idea in other words: the ideal
text can be achieved only by "that poet who is
fully alive to Music's tendence and exhaustless
faculty of expression, and therefore drafts his
poem in such a fashion that it may penetrate the
finest fibres of the musical tissue, and the spoken
thought entirely dissolve into the *Feeling*."

(2) In the second place, the new circumstances
must sanction a new form. What was quite right
in the symphony, having regard to its peculiar
purpose, will be quite wrong in the music-drama,
where the purpose is altogether different. Nowhere, perhaps, is Wagner on safer ground, or

more illuminative in his reasoning, than he is here. He shows how the symphony—like all purely abstract musical utterances—must adopt certain definite formal methods of procedure if it is to hang together at all. The growth of sonata-form in the eighteenth century was determined not by the arbitrary desires of individuals here and there, but by a deep underlying logic—a logic of the emotions—that ran unconsciously through them and through their hearers. It was this obscure, intuitive logic that made the need felt for a second subject in contrast with the first, for an exposition of these two subjects, for their working out, and for their final recapitulation ; it was this logic that determined the contrast of character between the different movements. The kaleidoscope had to be perpetually bringing the picture before us in new aspects ; the essence of dramatic working is *development;* the essence of "all forms arisen from the March or Dance" is *change.* Thus the new form for dramatic music must be sought in the nature of that *genre,* not in the nature of a quite alien *genre.* In the essay *On Franz Liszt's Symphonic Poems,* Wagner points out, as we have seen, how the laws of drama and the laws of symphony are at variance. Let me quote the gist of his remarks again. "It will be obvious that, in the conflict of a dramatic idea with this (symphonic) form, the necessity must at once arise to either sacrifice the development (the idea) to the alternation (the form), or the latter to the former" ; whereupon follows the criticism of the *Leonora* overture which I have already quoted. When he reaches the point that a new form would have been necessary to allow free and consistent play to Beethoven's ideas in the *Leonora*, he asks, "What, now, would that form be?" and replies, "Of necessity a form dictated by the subject of portrayal and its logical development."

Having briefly sketched out the two leading principles of Wagner's theory, let us now leave the second, which is perfectly clear in itself and in all its implications, and return to the first, the implications of which are perhaps not quite so clear. Wagner himself held that as he grew in artistic wisdom, his opera-poems came closer and closer to the ideal form, in which there should be just as much music as the poetry required, and just as much poetry as the music required. He admitted that the poems of *Rienzi*, *The Flying Dutchman*, *Tannhäuser*, and *Lohengrin* were not quite all they should be ; they were simply stages in his evolution. But he was willing to submit the poem of *Tristan* to the severest possible test of conformity with his ideal. "Upon that work," he says, "I consent to your making the severest claims deducible from my theoretic premisses : not because I formed it on any system, for every theory was clean forgotten by me ; but since here I moved with fullest freedom and the most utter disregard of every theoretic scruple. . . ."

What now is the great advantage, according to Wagner's theory, that the musical dramatist has over the poet or the novelist? Simply this, that he can discard all the more or less uninspired matter that they require in order to make their purpose clear, and plunge at once into the heart of his subject. Take, as an example, this very poem of *Tristan and Isolde*. The poet or the novelist, before he can begin to move you, must descend to a relatively unemotional plane in order to acquaint your understanding with certain positive facts it is essential it should know. He must tell you who Tristan and Isolde were, when and where they lived, what was their relation to the other people of the drama, and a score of other things that can hardly be made emotional in themselves. A long poem or drama is bound, by the nature of the case, to have a certain amount of dross scattered about among its gold ; the beautiful appeals to Feeling are only made into a coherent story or picture by the use of this less emotional tissue. From this difficulty the musical dramatist escapes ; in music he has a powerful engine that enables him to dispense with all these mere wrappings of his Feeling, and reach directly and immediately to the Feeling itself. He avoids the arbitrary, and takes up his stand at once in the centre of the " purely human." Thus Wagner needs no preliminary fumbling about for *his* tragedy ; the first bar of the overture transports you at once into the world and the mood to which the poet must drag you through twenty explanatory pages. " All that detailed description and exhibition of the historico–conventional which is requisite for making us clearly understand the events of a given, remote historical epoch, and

which the historical novelist or dramatist of our
times has therefore to set forth at such exhaustive
length—all this I could pass over." He concerns
himself not with historical subjects but with the
simple myth or legend, for "the legend, in whatever age or nation it occurs, has the merit of
seeing nothing but the purely human content of
that age and nation, and of giving forth that
Content in a form peculiar to itself, of sharpest
outline, and therefore swiftly understandable."
The musician, in fact, must discard everything but
the purely human ; he must take a poetical subject of which this is the core, and then kindle it
into incandescence by means of music. In *Tristan*,
says Wagner, " I plunged into the inner depth of
soul-events, and from out this inmost centre of
the world I fearlessly built up its outward form.
A glance at the volumen of this poem will show
you at once that the exhaustive detail-work which
an historical poet is obliged to devote to clearing
up the outward bearings of his plot, to the detriment of a lucid exposition of its inner motives, I
now trusted myself to apply to these latter alone.
Life and death, the whole import and existence
of the outer world, here hang on nothing but the
inner movements of the soul." The object, of
course, was—to recur to a previous order of
imagery—to reduce the amount of dross in the
work and to increase the amount of pure gold ;
all the available space ought to be devoted not
to demonstrations or recitals of fact but to the
evocation of feelings, to "exhibiting the inner
springs of action, those inner soul-motives which

are finally and alone to stamp the Action as a *necessary* one."

So much, then, is clear. Without questioning one of Wagner's contentions—accepting his theory as true, without disagreeing with his data or his reasoning—we come to these positions :—

(*a*) Poetry without music is lacking in expression, in appeal to Feeling : music without poetry is lacking in the power to give a definite direction to Feeling.

(*b*) An art-form therefore must be sought that will be an amalgam of the two, with the advantages of each and the defects of neither.

(*c*) In proportion as the advantages are retained and the defects eliminated will the new art-form approach ideal perfection.

(*d*) The musical defect to be guarded against is the attempt to subject dramatic music to the laws of symphonic music : this is easily overcome, and there only remains the poetic defect to be avoided, *i.e.*

(*e*) All poetic or verbal material that cannot be "musicalised," or caught up into the spirit of music, is superfluous and harmful ; therefore in proportion as the music-drama is perfected will this kind of material tend to disappear.

So far, so good. The point remaining to be considered is this : can we *ever* totally eliminate this non-musical material from opera ? Let us say, for example, in terms of the Wagnerian æsthetic, that a good opera on the subject of Romeo and Juliet will be nearer artistic perfection than Shakespeare's play, because it will dispense with all the poet's clumsy methods of reaching the Feeling through the viscous waters of the Understanding—that it will concern itself only with the "purely human," with the "inner springs of action" of the souls of the characters, and that it will raise these — to use a term borrowed from electrical science—to the highest potential, the highest incandescence. Granting all this, let us then press our question a point further still. There will, let us admit, be less non-emotional matter in the opera than in the drama, less hard, incalcitrant material that cannot be emotionalised, but that has to be there because without it the structure cannot hang together. Admitting that there will be less of it, will any one venture to say that there will be *none* of it in the opera ? I think not. *À priori* considerations apart, an appeal to practical experience will soon disillusionise us. Of all the thousands of operas that have been written since opera began, not one, outside the works of Wagner, will pass successfully through the ordeal. Of Wagner's operas, *Rienzi, The Flying Dutchman, Tannhäuser*, and *Lohengrin* are, by his own admission, as I have already shown, put out of court. *The Ring* will certainly not stand the test ; *Parsifal* certainly will not ; *The Mastersingers* certainly will not. There only remains *Tristan*, of the form and substance of which he himself was justly proud. It will pass the judges with a lighter sentence than any of the others ; but will it be dismissed without a stain on its character? By no means. Even in the pure, dazzling, magnificent metal of *Tristan* itself we find embedded, here and there, a refractory piece of alien ore, of raw material not yet put through the subtle alchemy that must divinise it. If then this last straw fails us, where shall we look for salvation? The only answer can be that *salvation on these lines is impossible.* Reduce the coarser, explanatory, unemotional matter of opera — the merely utilitarian stuff, the paste that binds the more precious things together — reduce this as you will, *some* of it you are still bound to retain in opera, for without it opera cannot have enough intellectual, dramatic consistency to ensure our getting hold of it. And if (1) granting the premisses, the reasoning by which the Wagnerian theorem is supported has been flawless, and (2) the brain that strove to embody that theorem in practical art was an organ mightier than anything the sons of men are likely to see for a very long time to come —then, I take it, there is only one conclusion possible, that the failure occurs through attempting to realise the theory in the wrong medium. To phrase it differently, the logic of the case is not rigorously enough applied at the last stage, when it comes to be pushed to its ultimate conclusion. Always bearing in mind that, according to Wagner, the strong point of the musical drama, as compared with any other poetic art-form, is that the non-emotional matter

in it can be reduced to a minimum, let us ask
ourselves whether a form cannot be found in
which even this minimum can be dispensed with.
The answer will be that the necessary conditions
are united in the symphonic poem, which is
therefore the true heir of Wagner's theory,
and has been too long kept out of its lawful
inheritance.

Two points now fall to be considered : (1)
Can the affiliation of the symphonic poem to
the Wagnerian theory be properly established,
and the superiority of its rights of succession
over those of its half-brother opera be fully
demonstrated ; and (2) are there no defects,
suggested by Wagner himself, that unfit the
symphonic poem to hold sway over opera?

The first point need not detain us long ; least
of all can the thorough-going Wagnerian here
have much right to protest. If Wagner's
reasoning is right his conclusion must be accepted—namely, that the less waste matter you
have in your poetic music the better. Now he
himself attributed the failure to "musicalise"
the poetic subject completely to this cause, that
instead of addressing the Feeling we were too
prone to address the Understanding. He tells
us, too, that *words* are the channel through which
the Understanding operates. In all cases, then,
where words are employed, there is a strong
probability of their carrying us with them further
along the path of mere Understanding than the
ideal art requires ; and diminish this feature as
much as you can, some of it is still bound to

persist. So that your only resort is to find a form that shall make use of all the advantages of poetic music and keep clear of this one defect. This form is unquestionably the symphonic poem. It *does* eliminate the defects that attend the use of words, for it dispenses with words; it meets Wagner's demand that music shall not sing merely for its own sake, but for a poetic purpose; it can order its structure upon the same lines as opera, *i.e.* the themes are conceived at once in terms of musical beauty and in terms of poetic appropriateness, and they suggest, by the modifications they undergo, the changing aspect of the personages and scenes of the drama. A symphonic poem is the concentrated essence of opera; it is to the opera as Bovril is to the ox.

But Wagner himself, it may be said, expressly warned us against programme music as being an artistic error. That is quite true. Wagner's argumentation here, however, is exceptionally weak. It is clear that he had no properly thought-out principles to guide him at this point. To begin with, his differentiation of programme music from the symphonic poem is thoroughly fallacious. If programme music is music based upon a programme—*i.e.* upon a literary subject— then every symphonic poem, nay, every opera, necessarily belongs to that category. The truth probably is that Wagner clung to this false distinction because he thought it would help him out of an embarrassing situation. He found himself compelled to say something publicly upon Liszt's symphonic poems; and I am afraid his essay on

that subject is hardly a model of the ingenuous.
To condemn Liszt was, of course, impossible for
many reasons. At all costs he had to be com-
mended ; but if we critically examine the essay of
eighteen pages, we shall find that surprisingly
little of it really deals with Liszt's work. There
is much declamation, and much æsthetic theorising
—most of it very good ; but surprisingly little
rational criticism of Liszt's symphonic poems.
Practically all that Wagner does is (1) to admit
the *à priori* proposition that it is just as sensible
to write a symphonic poem as a symphony—he
asks "whether March or Dance . . . can supply
a worthier motive of form than, for instance, a
mental picture of the . . . characteristic features
in the deeds and sufferings of an Orpheus, a
Prometheus, and so forth," and whether it is not
nobler for music to take its Form "from an
imagined Orpheus or Prometheus motive, than
from an imagined march or dance motive"; and
(2) to contrast disparagingly the procedure of
Berlioz with that of Liszt. But the final impression the essay leaves on me is that it was a
duty which Wagner performed rather unwillingly.
He did not want to say too much for Liszt's
music ; so on the one hand he argued that at any
rate the symphonic poem was permissible, and on
the other hand that it was preferable to the programme music of Berlioz.

Here his distinctions and his reasoning will
not hold. He objected in Berlioz, as we have
seen, to the way in which the musician followed
the literary clues of his subject, without recasting

these so as to fit them in with a scheme that was *musically* logical. Now it is absurd to condemn programme music *en masse* because a particular man blunders in it; Berlioz may quite well be wrong[1] and programme music still be right. But take Wagner's criticism as it stands, and correlate it with the previous arguments of this paper, and what is the conclusion to be drawn? Just this, that if Wagner could not, as he says, "hold on to scenic motives not present" before his eye, he was not listening to the music in the proper way. It is *not* necessary, for most of us, to have a poetic scene put visibly before us; we can easily reconstruct it in imagination; and what the symphonic poem does is to give us the musical feeling the opera aims at giving us, and to tell us to *imagine* the occasion of it all, instead of putting this occasion on a stage before us. The prelude and finale of *Tristan* constitute a rudimentary symphonic poem, in the hearing of which we never ask to hear a word or see an actor. A more explicit symphonic poem does the same thing on a larger scale. We can, if we like, make a three-act opera out of *Romeo and Juliet*, but on Wagner's own principles the essence of the thing is contained in Tchaikovski's concert overture. And if I am told that this theme is to be associated with the lovers, this with Friar Lawrence, and so on, then during the playing of the overture the whole drama is acted

---

[1] I am not, of course, agreeing with Wagner's criticism of Berlioz; it seems to me quite superficial and unilluminative, but to discuss it would be foreign to our present purpose.

in my brain, and is quite as real for me as if I beheld artificial men and women acting artificially in an artificial stage-setting. So with *Ein Heldenleben.* Nothing would be easier than to make an opera out of this subject; but who wants the opera, with its eking out of the parts that really do matter with a number of parts that really do not matter, with all its stage absurdities, its posturing actors? We have the diffuse emotions of three or four hours concentrated into the rich emotions of forty minutes. We have the whole life of the hero just as we would get it in the opera; but the small basket of strawberries has fewer pieces of grit in it than the bigger basket.[1]

I hope I shall not be taken to mean that the opera is a false and useless form, and that composers should henceforth all work frenziedly at the manufacture of symphonic poems. My position is that for certain purposes we *must* have opera; by it alone can certain needs of our soul be satisfied, just as—though Wagner did not know it—for the satisfaction of other needs we must resort to pure poetry and pure music. But for certain other satisfactions we must have recourse to the symphonic poem; and this form, I contend, is the only form that can be deduced

[1] The reader will understand that I am not founding my case on the actual musical value of *Ein Heldenleben;* I am only using that work as an illustration of an æsthetic theory. In the actual *Heldenleben* there is rather more grit than I like; but there is no real need for it to have been put there. In the article on Strauss in the present volume I have tried to show how he has needlessly weakened his scheme by not keeping to the one piece of portraiture throughout.

logically from Wagner's own æsthetic theory. As I have tried to show, in the symphonic poem alone can you get music fertilised by a poetic purpose, and yet, by eliminating the actual words, avoid the intrusion even of the minimum of non-emotional substance. In *The Ring and the Book*, Browning describes how the artificer has to fashion a gold ring. In order to make his material workable, he has to blend an alloy with the gold ; but when the circle is complete he drives out the alloy with a spirt of acid, leaving the pure metal only. That is the symphonic poem ; the opera is the ring with the alloy left in it. If perfection of form is what we want—the consummate, intimate transfusion of matter and form, the "truly unitarian" form to which Wagner aspired — then it is in the symphonic poem that we must look for it, not in the opera.

Only one objection that Wagner might urge against this has, I believe, not yet been considered. He expressly laid it down, it may be pointed out, that it is *not* sufficient for us to carry the external, moving, concrete features of the drama in our heads ; they must be set before us, in the fulness of real life, on the stage. " Not a Programme," he says in *Zukunftsmusik*, " which rather prompts the troublous question 'Why'? [1] than stills it—not a Programme, then, can speak the meaning of the symphony ; no, nothing but a stage performance of the Dramatic Action itself."

[1] *i.e.* the troublous question as to what the music "means" poetically.

This was an opinion he always maintained; but after all is it anything more than a mere *obiter dictum?* Wagner had a passion for seeing anything and everything upon the stage—a passion that at times becomes rather childish, for he was quite unconscious of a number of the absurdities of his characters and his situations that are painfully evident to the audience. Truth to tell, his notions of the stage were just a little crude at times; in any case he did not see that even the best acting in opera is *per se* bound to be inferior to the best acting in drama—people cannot sing and at the same time be wholly natural in demeanour. I take it, then, that his predilection for stage-settings was a purely personal one; it has no logical relation to his general æsthetic theory; and we can refuse to be bound by it. We all like opera, and we tolerate its absurdities and its intellectual deficiencies because we know these are inseparable from it; but once more it has to be said that from these stage absurdities the symphonic poem is free. Mr. Arthur Symons has recently pointed out the strain that is put on our sense of the ridiculous when what should be merely a symbol is thrust visibly before our eyes. The Stranger in Ibsen's *Lady from the Sea* is very impressive as a symbol of the call of the sea to the blood of Ellida Wangel; but when an ordinary human being in a tourist suit comes on the stage and purports to be the symbol incarnate, our sense of the poetry of the thing is severely tried. So with the scene where Wotan attempts to bar Siegfried's progress with his spear, and

M

Siegfried shatters it with his sword. This is all very fine as a symbol of "the last ineffectual stand of constituted authority against the young, untrammelled individuality of the future"; but what the candid eye sees on the stage is a young man chopping in two a piece of stick held by an old man, who picks up the pieces, walks off with them, and says, "Advance! I cannot stop thee!" What is very impressive, merely conceived imaginatively as a symbol, becomes unimpressive when narrowed down to ordinary men with legs and arms, holding "property" swords and spears.

Opera, indeed, has no lack of absurdities, and this will always prevent it taking rank as the highest form of dramatic art; and Wagner, as I have said, must be held to have taken some of his own stage absurdities and puerilities with quite abnormal seriousness. It stands to reason, too, that the symphonic poem suffers from no such disabilities. If Wagner's theory be correct, then a symphonic poem on a given subject can follow, as regards its musical form, the lines laid down for it by the poetic impulse, just as efficiently as an opera on the subject could do; while it avoids the "padding" that is inseparable from opera by simply giving us, in our programme, an outline of the poetic subject, instead of daubing the subject over, from head to foot, with pseudo-poetry that rarely rises above the level of rhymed or rhythmic prose. As for the inability to follow the poetic motives of the subject from the programme—well, I fancy we are not all so imperfectly endowed with imagination as Wagner seems to have been here. I quite admit that there are minds like his in this respect, to which poetic music conveys little or nothing without speech and action—that are unable, while they listen, say to *Ein Heldenleben*, to keep all the details of the story moving at equal pace with the music; but the sufficient answer to such people is that other people *can* do this. To sum it all up, the symphonic poem is theoretically deducible from Wagner's own æsthetic; while in practice, if we miss in it some of the elements that make opera interesting, we are compensated by the absence of other elements that make opera tedious and absurd.

XI

One point still remains to be discussed, though we need only touch on it very briefly. How far can music represent external things—ought it, indeed, to try to represent external things at all? It was Schopenhauer, I think, who said that music was not a representative but a presentative art. But that was very superficial psychologising even in his day, and it is still more superficial in ours. The whole problem is exceedingly simple if people, in their anxiety to prove that music cannot "imitate," would not confuse it unnecessarily. Heaven only knows how much bastard æsthetic has been born of that unfortunate remark of Beethoven's about the Pastoral Symphony, which we have already had occasion to examine. As a specimen, look at this quotation

from Victor Cousin, intended to demonstrate, in
its own way, that music must not be "painting,"
but only an "expression of emotion." "Give
the wisest symphonist a tempest to render.
Nothing is easier than to imitate the whistling
of the winds and the noise of the thunder.
But by what combination of ordered sounds
could he present to our sight the lightning
flashes which suddenly rend the veil of night,
and that which is the most terrific aspect of
the tempest, the alternate movement of the
waves, now rising mountain high, now sinking
and seeming to fall headlong into bottomless
abysses? If the hearer has not been told
beforehand what the subject is, he will never
divine it, and I defy him to distinguish a
tempest from a battle. In spite of scientific
skill and genius, sounds cannot represent forms.
Music, rightly advised, will refuse to enter upon
a hopeless contest; it will not undertake to
express the rise and fall of the waves and other
like phenomena; it will do better; with sounds
it will produce in our soul the feelings which
successively arise in us during the various scenes
of the tempest. It is thus that Haydn will
become the rival, even the conqueror of the
painter, because it has been given to music to
move and sway the soul even more profoundly
than painting."[1]

The point is, be it observed, that unless you
were told beforehand, you could not say whether

[1] *Du Vrai, du Beau, et du Bien.* I make the quotation from
Mr. Basil Worsfold's little book on *Judgment in Literature.*

a given orchestral piece was meant to represent
a tempest or a battle; the composer is therefore
advised not to try to paint a tempest, but to
"produce in our soul the feelings which successively arise in us during the various scenes
of the tempest." Why, how in the name of all
æsthetic innocence does this help us? How
are we, in the absence of a verbal indication,
to distinguish "the feelings which successively
arise in us during the various scenes of the
tempest" from the feelings which would arise
in us during the various scenes of a battle?
We only hear, that is, a certain mass of sound;
how are we to know, from the mere "feeling"
this arouses in us, that it refers to a battle or
a tempest or anything else? What man, for
example, listening to solemn music, can possibly
know whether it is meant to describe the death
of Napoleon, the funeral of Mr. Gladstone, the
poetic contemplation of nature, the opening of
the St. Louis Exhibition, the life-work of John
Stuart Mill, or anything else under the sun?
The "feelings" are perfectly incompetent to
pierce through the indefinite tone to the definite
scene that inspired it. What the composer has
to do is to tell us what this definite scene is;
nobody, for example, would have guessed that
the fourth movement of Schumann's *Rhenish*
symphony had its origin in the installation of the
Archbishop of Geissel as Archbishop of Cologne,
if the composer himself had not told us so.
Nobody would have known that a certain part
of the Pastoral Symphony represents a peasant's

gratitude after a storm, if Beethoven had not said so himself. The "feelings" are no more reliable guides in cases of this kind than the "painting" is. And if the composer has to give us a verbal clue in order to let us know definitely what feelings he is representing, he has only to give us a verbal clue to make it quite clear to us what his painting is intended to represent; and there is no more odium in needing the verbal clue in the latter case than there is in the former.

No one in his senses has ever pretended that music alone could depict external things so accurately that we could recognise them infallibly at once, without any assistance from the sight, as in opera, or from a verbal accompaniment. As M. Alfred Ernst has put it: "It is not a question of painting an object—music could not succeed in doing that; nor is it a question of reproducing exactly the sounds of nature, such as the murmur of flowing water, the rumbling of thunder, the song of birds; but, when these phenomena are in the subject that is being treated, of recalling them to the mind by means of tone. . . . Thus conceived, music does not materialise itself in becoming descriptive; it would be more accurate to say that it spiritualises the phenomena of nature. . . ." And he shows how Mozart, for example, employs description. "In his *Don Juan* he has more than once translated the gesture, the mimic, of his personages. We may cite, for instance, the ascending scales in the orchestra in the duel between the Commandant and Don Juan.

The figures in the bass refer to the old man, those above to Juan; each time that one of the two adversaries steps towards the other and attacks, this figure comes out, strident, quick as the thrust of a sword, and at the moment when Don Juan presses the Commandant, lunges at him time after time, strikes him and kills him, the violin scales succeed each other without giving the auditor time to breathe. . . . At the beginning of the sextett, when Leporello tries to slip away, fearing to be taken for Don Juan, the orchestra reproduces his stealthy movements; we see the unhappy wretch creeping along cautiously, his back bent, feeling round for a way out."[1] Nor does one need to be reminded of the numerous pieces of "description," of "imitation," in Wagner—of the water-music, the fire-music, the swish of Klingsor's spear, the voices of the forest, and so on. Every dramatic, or, indeed, vocal writer is full of passages of this kind; it simply cannot be avoided in music that aims at something beyond abstract note-spinning.

But in every case, as we can see, the music is not left to tell its story alone; we are not compelled to guess the subject represented merely from the tones themselves. The subject is told us in some way or other—we see Don Juan thrusting at the Commandant, or the spear flying at Parsifal's head, or the fire licking the couch of Brynhilde; or else there is, in the words of the song or opera, some suggestion of the external thing that is being illustrated in the music. And

[1] *L'Œuvre dramatique de Berlioz*, pp. 30–34, etc.

in the symphonic poem, all that we require in order that everything may be perfectly clear is a statement, in the programme, of the picture upon which the music is based. I am not expected to know, merely from the tones alone, what the "giant" motive in the *Rheingold* is meant to represent; but when I am told that it relates to the giants, I can take delight in the expressiveness of its lumbering, unwieldy movements. Similarly I must be told that the opening pages of *Also sprach Zarathustra* are meant as a representation of the majesty and spaciousness of Nature. And —again to draw upon the argument of the foregoing pages—there is nothing that can be done in this line in the song or the opera that cannot be done quite as effectually in the symphonic poem, if composers would only give their hearers the same full insight into their literary intentions as the song or opera writer does, and if hearers would only take the trouble to master these intentions before they listen to the music that is based upon them. If they would do this, their pleasure in the symphonic poem would be enormously increased; everything in it would be alive to them. For myself, at any rate, to listen to *Till Eulenspiegel* or *Ein Heldenleben* or *Don Quixote* is not only to enjoy the music but to see the whole action as clearly as if I were reading it in a book or watching it on the stage. I get none of the boredom, none of the unfortunate provocations to laughter, that are inseparable from that artificial, stagey form of art, the opera. I miss, of course, some of the factors that make opera so glorious—the inexpressible thrill communicated by the human voice, the quickening of the pulse that is given by the movements of the actors and the catastrophes of the stage; but on the other hand I am spared a great many things, and I have the satisfaction of knowing that my sense of form is receiving the purest, most undiluted pleasure it is possible for it to receive in poetic music. The case for programme music is quite as strong as the case for opera or for the symphony. That many stupid things have been done in its name, that many fools and weaklings have fought under its banner, counts for nothing; how many symphonies, how many operas, are there that the world would willingly let die! The rightness of the form is not affected by the wrongness of the people who choose to work in it; and that the form itself is essentially right, I have, I hope, given adequate proof. Finally, to the question of how far music is justified in trying to suggest external things, we can only say that it is better not to be too dogmatic. Things that would have seemed impossible a hundred years ago are done with ease to-day. Who would believe that a windmill could be represented in music? Yet Strauss's windmill in *Don Quixote* is really extraordinarily clever and satisfying; he suggests wonderfully, too, the caracoling of the horse as the knight puts him through his paces. His pictorial faculty, indeed, is something unique in the history of music; Wagner's is only an imperfect instrument by the side of it. The representative power of music is growing day by day.

The only æsthetic fact we can be sure of is this, that no piece of representation will be tolerated unless it is at the same time *music*. That is the ultimate test ; the imitative passages that make us smile are the passages that are merely imitative, without sufficient musical charm to keep them alive for us. But here, of course, we simply get back to the position already advanced in this article—that in all poetic music there must be as thorough a satisfaction as possible not only of the literary or the pictorial but of the musical sense.

To ALFRED WILLIAMS

HERBERT SPENCER AND THE ORIGIN OF MUSiC

I

IT is now nearly fifty years since Spencer first published his celebrated essay on "The Origin and Function of Music." That essay has been elaborately assailed from many quarters; it has been objected to as insufficient from the standpoint of æsthetic psychology, and as at variance with some of the known facts of musical history. Nevertheless Spencer, in accordance with his general intellectual habit, always clung tenaciously to his theory, and, without modifying it at all, returned to the subject in later years only in order to re-asseverate his doctrine and to repel the critical assaults that were made upon it. He had no difficulty in dealing with the counter-theory of Darwin—that music sprang from the amorous rivalry of the males in the presence of the females of certain species—for Darwin's brief excursion into the alien field of musical æsthetic was as humorous and unprofitable as a discussion of bimetallism by Tchaikovski would have been. Then Spencer dealt with the redoubtable objections of the late Edmund Gurney and those of Dr. Wallaschek, undoubtedly scoring at times against them when they had needlessly overstated their own case, though not, it seems to me, removing the impression that they had successfully attacked the central point of his theory. Towards the very end of his days he returned yet again to the subject, in his *Facts and Comments*, and did me the honour to combat the brief criticism of his theory which I had put forward in my *Study of Wagner*, asserting that I exhibited a "confusion between the origin of a thing and the thing which originates from it," and that some of my criticisms "went far towards conceding" what I denied. I can only say that while I considered that Spencer passed over in silence certain of the stronger points I had urged against him, aiming at a merely dialectical victory here and there by interpreting my words in a different sense from that intended by me, I was still quite unconvinced, even by his later arguments, of the truth of his original theory. I shall try to show that that theory rests on a misunderstanding of the real nature of music, and on too ready an assumption of a causal connection between phenomena that are really only similar, and that it is helped out by unintentional misstatements as to some of the main factors of the problem. The question has an interest above and beyond Spencer's connection with it. The speech-theory of the origin of music has here and there been adopted as an established æsthetic fact, and æsthetic deductions have been made from it that must affect our views of current developments of the art. Wagner—working of course on lines of his own—contended that song is "just speech aroused to highest passion," and admiring commentators innumerable have followed him in his error. It is worth while therefore, as a contribution to a rather obscure point in musical æsthetic, to try to demonstrate the falsity of the speech-theory, and at the same time to place over against it a theory of the origin and nature of music that squares better with the facts of history and psychology ; and this is best done by examining the speech - theory in the hands of its strongest advocate.

Briefly, Spencer's theory is this : " Variations of voice are the physiological results of variations of feeling," since " all feelings . . . have this common characteristic, that they are muscular stimuli." Thus according to the intensity and the quality of the feeling, the tones in which it is expressed will vary in loudness, in *timbre*, in pitch, in width of intervals, and in rapidity. " These vocal peculiarities, which indicate ex- cited feeling, are those which especially dis- tinguish song from ordinary speech." In other words, excited speech merges into recitative, and recitative in its turn merges into song ; and song " originally diverged from emotional speech in a gradual, unobtrusive manner." Against this view I argued, in my *Study of Wagner*, that " it errs in supposing that, because song exhibits some of the characteristics of speech, the one has necessarily taken its rise from the other. The resemblances between the external characteristics of speech and those of song are only what might be expected, seeing that both are phenomena of sound, and sound can only vary in the ways indicated by Spencer. . . . The mere resemblance of song

and speech in their most external characteristics is not a proof that one is the outcome of
the other, but simply that they have certain
causal phenomena in common ; while the internal
differences between them are greater than their
resemblances." The careful reader will observe,
in fact, that Spencer unconsciously sophisticates
his argument from the very commencement. It
is quite true that "variations of voice are the
physiological results of variations of feeling" ; it
is also quite true that the "vocal peculiarities
which indicate excited feeling"—such as loudness, high pitch, increased resonance, and so on
—are more pronounced in song than in ordinary
speech. But it does not at all follow from this
that *song took these peculiarities from speech*—
that speech got them first, then developed them
into recitative, and then still further into song.
To make a symmetrical but artificial chain of this
kind is to beg the question at the outset. Spencer
never put before himself the obvious alternative
—"Could not, and would not, song have had all
these peculiarities even if speech had never been
invented? Given, that is, the capacity of men to
feel emotion in varying degrees, would not a
strong emotion naturally express itself in louder,
more varied, more resonant tones than a weak
emotion—and this even if man had as yet no
language?" Spencer, in fact, simply details the
characteristics of *tone* as the expression of feeling,
and then illegitimately appropriates them, in the
first place, to one order of tone, namely speech.
No one would dream of disputing the physio-

logical facts which he established in his essay with his usual patient and scrupulous accuracy. It is unquestionable that, on the whole, a loud tone in speaking and a loud tone in singing both indicate heightened feeling; and that in all the other respects enumerated by him, song and speech exhibit precisely the same characteristics. But this does not authorise us, in any way, to assert that song has "grown out of" speech. Spencer argued too hastily from a mere analogy to a cause. We are prepared to admit—to state the foregoing argument in another way — that in moments of emotional excitement the ordinary speech of men becomes more rhythmical, acquires a more pronounced *timbre*, and generally varies in the ways Spencer has enumerated. What we are *not* prepared to admit is that this is either a lower form of music or the stuff out of which music has grown. Our contention is that while the difference between speech and excited speech is one of degree only, *the difference between speech and music is one not merely of degree, but of kind* —we are dealing with similar physiological but widely separated psychological phenomena; and that this is true not only of modern music, as Spencer seems to admit, but of that primitive music out of which our complex modern art has grown.

Moreover, Spencer ignored the new light which modern physio-psychological research has thrown upon the question, some of which I referred to in the *Study of Wagner*. Stricker, in his *Du Langage et de la Musique* (1885), has, among a lot of statements and conclusions that need to be taken with caution, at all events made out a good case for believing that the organs of speech and the organs of song are controlled by different cerebral spheres. Wallaschek's conclusions, again, are too important to be passed over in silence by any advocate of the speech-theory. I venture to quote in full from my *Wagner* the passage in which I condensed Wallaschek's argument: "Further, it is now not only placed beyond dispute that the faculty of articulate speech has its distinct cerebral centre, but it has been localised in the third frontal convolution of the left hemisphere of the brain; and Dr. Wallaschek, in a brilliant paper, has striven to show that there must be another centre that controls musical thought and speech.[1] Without going into Dr. Wallaschek's theory in detail, it may be sufficient here to note some of his facts and conclusions: (*a*) "the forming of concepts goes on in a different part of the brain, and the concepts travel along other channels, than the expression of the feelings and the merely automatic processes;"[2] (*b*) children with aphasia (*i.e.* destruction or disturbance of the faculty of articulate speech) are yet able to sing;[3] (*c*) patients with aphasia, who cannot speak connectedly upon ordinary occasions, can sometimes articulate the words when singing a

[1] *Ueber die Bedeutung der Aphasia für den musikalischen Ausdruck* (Vierteljahrsschr für Mus-Wiss., September 1891).
[2] Article cited, p. 57.
[3] *Ibid.*, p. 60.

song—the words being brought up into consciousness by association with the melody;[1] (*d*) the third left frontal convolution (which controls articulate speech) is very small in idiots and lower races, who yet are highly susceptible to music;[2] (*e*) the faculty of musical memory may be destroyed without disturbing the other mental faculties;[3] (*f*) consequently "we express ourselves and hear in quite a different manner when we sing and when we speak."[4]   All this evidence Spencer ignored to the last.

Nor does it ever seem to have occurred to him to analyse the state of mind of a musician at the moment of composition, and to utilise the result thus obtained in order to throw light on the origin of music.   Had he done this he would have seen the force—which his criticism of me showed he had *not* seen—of M. Combarieu's remark that " Mr. Spencer neglects or ignores everything that gives to the art he is studying its special and unique character ; he does not appear to have realised what a musical composi-

---

[1] For example: "One patient, from the beginning of his disease to his death, could say nothing but *Yes* and *No*. . . . One morning a patient began to sing 'I dreamt I dwelt in marble halls.'   The speechless patient joined in and sang the first verse with the other, and then the second verse alone, articulating every word correctly."—*Ibid.*, p. 61.

[2] Article cited, p. 53, *note :* "Many idiots, who are scarcely capable of other impressions, are extraordinarily susceptible to music, and can remember a song which they have once heard."

[3] "A peasant, who as the result of a heavy blow on the head lay unconscious for three days, found, when he came to himself, that he had forgotten all the music he ever knew, though he had lost nothing else."—*Ibid.*, p. 64 (quoted from Carpenter, *Mental Physiology,* 4th edit., p. 443).

[4] *Ibid.*, p. 65.

tion is, what are the rules it obeys, what is the nature of the charm and the beauty we find in it. In short, we can bring against him a fundamental fact, in comparison with which everything else has only a quite secondary value : that is, the existence of a musical manner of thinking (*une pensée musicale*). The musician thinks with sounds, as the literary man thinks with words."[1]

Here, indeed, is the crux of the disagreement between Spencer and those who reject the speech-theory as an absolutely inadequate explanation of the origin of music. What was his criticism of this criticism ? "Here," he says, "we have a striking example of the way in which an hypothesis is made to appear untenable by representing it as being something which it does not profess to be. I gave an account of the *origin* of music, and now I am blamed because my conception of the origin of music does not include a conception of music as fully developed. What is every process of evolution but the gradual assumption of traits which were not originally possessed?" It will be seen, I think, that Spencer quite missed the true point of M. Combarieu's objection. We do not expect that from a theory of the origin of music among primitive men one should be able to forecast all the later *forms* into which music has branched ; but we do expect that, since evolution is a con-

---

[1] See Jules Combarieu, *Les rapports de la musique et de la poésie, considerées au point de vue de l'expression* (1894), wherein there is an elaborate and searching examination of Spencer's theory.

tinuous process, the theory of the earlier music should not be at variance with all the main psychological features of the later music. We say to Spencer, "Take your theory, and we are unable to work it out in detail. You assert that the expression of musical thought and emotion has taken three successive forms—excited speech, recitative, and music. Well, we find it impossible to leap to this conclusion, as you have done, merely because there are certain resemblances, due to physiological causes, between speech and song. We cannot trace such a process historically — for your own sketch of the supposed historical process is demonstrably inaccurate in evidence and hasty in inference—nor can we even *imagine* the process psychologically. To us, there is a great psychological and æsthetic gulf fixed between excited speech and song— *not only between the speech and the song of to-day, but between the ruder speech and ruder song of primitive man.* On the other hand, we have a theory that imposes no such strain, either historical or psychological, upon us. That theory is, that music arises from a peculiar set of stimuli and peculiar organs of expression of its own, with which speech not only has nothing whatever to do now, but never had anything to do, as *fons et origo.* Allowing for all the differences between our music and that of the savage who blows his reed and thumps his tam-tam, and for all the differences of general mental structure between him and us, we can still see that the same causes which incite us to music incited him. Now no one will for a moment contend that there is any but an infinitesimal resemblance between a Bach fugue or a Strauss symphonic poem and excited speech ; neither can we perceive that there was ever any but the faintest resemblance between the causes that provoked the savage to excited speech and those that impelled him to his rude kind of music. But *your* theory, while it disregards the plain fact that no demonstration could deduce a Bach fugue from excited speech, and overlooks the mental elements in primitive man from which the Bach fugue *could* develop step by step, invites us to believe that music grew out of something with which we are unable to correlate it either now or in the most primitive times."

"But," it may be objected, "all this is pure assertion. You simply take music as it is written to-day, attribute this to something which you call a 'musical faculty,' or a 'musical manner of thinking,' and then, having invented this convenient faculty, blandly assume that it is from a similar faculty that the rude music of primitive man originated. What you have to do is to prove the existence of this musical faculty, this specifically musical way of conceiving and expressing things, that, on your assumption, is innate in the human mind, and needs no help from speech even in the earliest days of the race." Well, no one, I think, will question the existence in us, at the present day, of something that may well be called, in general terms, the musical faculty. For the musician as we now know him—and, indeed, have known him for some centuries—music is a means of emotional expression that can function without the aid of poetry or even of speech. It takes its rise from its own order of feelings; it has its own self-sufficient manner of expressing them; it tells its own story to the mind of the hearer; and neither the feeling, nor its manner of expression, nor its effect on the auditor, suggests any dependence on speech. The musician, in order to begin composition, has not to receive a preliminary stimulus either from poetry, or from any concept or sentiment that could for a moment be expressed in words. (He may, of course, set poetry to music; but on the other hand he may not; and it is the self-existing order of music we are now discussing.) The musician, under the influence of an inward stimulus of some very obscure kind, may take three or four tones—say those of the opening subject of a sonata or a fugue—and build with them a structure ordered and controlled by certain laws purely its own, having for its object the susciting in our minds of a series of feelings from which all thought of speech is absent. The musician joys in building tones together in this way; we in our turn joy both in the process of building and in the finished edifice itself.

"So far, so good," the opponent may say; "this is what music now is, as the result of a long course of evolution from its original germ. But will you assert that primitive man was impelled to *his* rude music by the workings of some similar faculty—that, without any reliance, even in the earliest days, upon speech, and without any intermediate stage of recitative, he *produced music*, bearing the same relation to his emotions as the music of Bach and Beethoven did to theirs?" Well, this is precisely what we do assert; nor do I see any difficulty in the way of the theory that primitive man came to utter himself in his rude music by the same psychological processes by which we utter ourselves in ours to-day. Speech had no more to do with the impulse to his music than it has with the impulse to ours. Spencer's theory would have it that first man spoke, then he advanced to excited speech, that this became more rhythmical and more definite and thus expanded into recitative, and that from this there emerged song "in a gradual, unobtrusive manner"—so gradual and so unobtrusive, I am afraid, that we can neither trace it emerging nor imagine it doing so. Is it not more reasonable to believe that music first came into the world when the savage took delight in any tones—those of the human voice, of a reed, or of a drum—purely *as* tone, and began to take a further simple delight in the relations between tones? Need we concern ourselves at all with speech, excited or torpid? Can we not begin with mere feeling venting itself in mere sound— as we know it must have done at first—and draw a line from this straight through all the music of all the world? Why should we assume that for man to express his feelings in tone he must first have invented speech, and then have developed the emotional side of this until it was able to cut itself loose and commence life on its own account, by some process that is really unimaginable? We know that feeling vents itself in sound, and that waves of feeling vent themselves in waves of sound, as may be observed in the vague crooning of an infant over its toys, or the moaning of a man in pain. This is one fundamental fact in the origin of music. Another is the indisputable fact that men, whether civilised or savage—that many animals, indeed—are susceptible to tone *purely as tone;* and a further fact is that the primitive organism takes pleasure in the relations between tones, as may be seen in the boy who keeps on thumping two tin cans that happen to give out different sounds. There is surely no need to insist upon the point that both tones and the relations between tones *in themselves* interest and charm, in a minor degree, the savage as they do us. It is from this phenomenon, I should imagine, not from excited speech, that music took its rise; and the evidence from the music of primitive tribes, upon which Spencer drew in support of his theory, does nothing to invalidate mine. In his original essay he quoted, from his own *Descriptive Sociology*, a number of passages relating to the song-customs of various undeveloped races. I cannot, among all these quotations, see one that suggests that the music of these people was simply a hyper-excited form of speech. On the contrary, it is clear from his own citations that their delight was in music purely as music; that their feelings spontaneously flowed, as ours do, into a system of tones and relations between tones that existed in and by and for itself, with only the same kind of dependence upon the words that is exhibited in a song by Brahms or a chorus by Handel.[1] No doubt the general course of the words controls the general course of music in some degree, as it does in our own song-writing; but there is nothing whatever to contradict the view that savage music, even as our own, springs spontaneously from a non-verbal emotion, and seeks an expression either absolutely independent of speech or only remotely influenced by it. The East African, says Spencer, "in singing, contents himself with improvising a few words without sense or rhythm, and repeats them till they nauseate." If this does not betoken a state of mind fundamentally analogous to that of the absolute musician, it is hard to say what the words mean. Plainly, what sets the East African singing, what determines that one note shall follow another, what makes him so indifferent to the sense or nonsense of the words, is simply the delight in tone *as* tone, in the relations of tones *as* relations of tones, simply the need for what he feels to vent itself in precisely that way and no other—in a word, the primitive *pensée musicale*, the primitive "musical manner of thinking."[2]   Abundant evidence can be had to

[1] To say nothing of the savage music which is either purely non-verbal, or linked to an almost meaningless refrain.

[2] No importance, I take it, need be attached to such sentences as that the Malays " rehearse in a kind of recitative at their *bim-bangs* or feasts." The word recitative here affords no support for Spencer's theory. Travellers who have written of the music of primitive races have always been prone to use the term too loosely. Accustomed as they are to the highly developed music of Europe,

corroborate this, and I quoted some of it in my
Wagner. "Speaking of the Iroquois, Dr. Mor-
gan says that their war-songs are in a dead
language, or, at all events, they are unable to
interpret them. . . . Mr. Baker, too, observed
the meaninglessness of the Indian song."[1] There
is not much trace here of excited speech first
becoming recitative and then musical song.[2]

Dr. Wallaschek's conclusions, again, as to the
music of savages are as follows :—

(1) "In primitive times vocal music is not at
all a union of poetry and music. We find, on
the contrary, vocal music among tribes which,
owing to the insufficient development of language,
cannot possibly have any kind of poetry. Thus
the position of vocal music is quite independent
of any other art. (2) It is impossible that in
these cases music arose as a direct imitation
of the natural accents ready made in speech.

with its fixity of scale and its wide range of instrumental tone, they
use the term recitative as the easiest one to indicate, in a rough-
and-ready way, a kind of music much less developed than our
own in these respects. But such a use of the term is quite unscientific. There is no reason to believe that what we call their
recitative is not really their music.

[1] Wallaschek, *Primitive Music*, pp. 173, 174.

[2] Of course Spencer might have rejoined that the songs in their
present state represent the fully developed tree, which had to pass,
in remoter times, through the previous stages he mentions. Apart
from the general objections I have already urged against this
theory, however, it is evident that Spencer cannot have the music
of savage races under two categories—song *and* recitative—using
the one or the other as suits the purpose of his argument at the
time. It will be seen later that his theory rests, to a very large
extent, on the supposition that the music of savages and of Orientals
represents only the second or recitative stage of the development
from speech.

(3) Because these texts are neither themselves a language, nor could the melody *alone* have been taken from a developed language, for in such case the words would have been borrowed together with the music.   Entirely meaningless words simply serve to facilitate the vocalisation." Further, "another striking feature of these savage songs is *the liberty with which the composer treats the grammatical structure of the sentence and the logical order of words.* Thus in many of the Andamanese songs the words in their poetic form are so mutilated to suit the metre as to be hardly recognisable. . . . If negroes sing they keep strict time, and do not allow themselves to be hindered by any obstacle in the use of the words." Other evidence of the same kind might be adduced, from which it is quite clear that we are face to face with a phenomenon on which Spencer's theory throws no light at all. There seems to be no doubt that there is in the savage, though of course in a relatively undeveloped form, the same musical sense as in ourselves, something that has always flown directly, for its expression, to a mode of utterance of its own, compounded of tones, relations of tones, and rhythm, which is the natural language of this sense, and which never needed to pass through the intermediate stage of imitation or exaggeration of the accents of speech.[1]

---

[1] As Berlioz expressed it in the *Grotesques de la musique,* "Music exists by itself ; it has no need of poetry, and if every human language were to perish, it would be none the less the most poetic, the grandest, and the freest of all the arts."

Look for a moment at the two theories and their implications side by side. We know that primitive man, like the animal,[1] is susceptible to tone, sequences of tone, colour of tone, and rhythm; and that, from purely physiological causes, a number of his feelings tend to express themselves in vocal sounds. Now these are all the elements we require in order to construct modern music. The composer feels strongly, and is impelled to find an outlet for his emotions in tone. According to the line of his emotion, so to speak, is the line of his music—the pure feeling takes hold of the sounds through which alone it can utter itself, and shapes them, in form, in colour, in sequence, in intensity, after its own image. We have in primitive man, in a rude and undeveloped stage, all these elements out of which the modern music-maker builds his gorgeous palaces. According to the intensity of the emotion of the savage will be the width of the intervals of his voice, the resonance, the colour of it; according to the shade of his feeling will be the shade of his rude melody; and from the *ensemble* of the qualities of the sounds

---

[1] See the chapters entitled "Orpheus at the Zoo," in Mr. Cornish's *Life at the Zoo*. Every one who has kept dogs or snakes must have noticed how vivid their musical perceptions are. My own dog has a decided musical faculty in him. He is exceedingly susceptible to the mezzo-soprano voice in the upper part of its middle register. Tones produced there—but no others in that or any other voice—he will try to imitate. It is not a howl, but a real attempt to hit the right pitch and to shape the sound with his mouth. "Excited speech" has nothing to do with *his* musical perceptions. The excited speech usually comes later, from the singer whom he is favouring with this sincerest form of flattery.

in which he is uttering himself will his hearers be able to guess what mood it was that animated his song.   Here, then, are all the elements out of which music *could* grow, even if man had never learned to speak three connected words. Yet we are asked by Spencer to believe that these elements, *sufficient in themselves to give birth to music*, remained dormant in the human breast for untold centuries, until man had evolved a fairly elaborate system of speech—for it must be remembered that Spencer's theory presupposes not the rude and merely utilitarian speech of the man only one remove from the beast, but a comparatively highly organised language, capable of expressing connectedly a savage's thoughts about something more than his daily physical wants. Some such abstract, æsthetic, reflective form of speech we are compelled to postulate if we are to grant the probability of music arising, as Spencer says it did, from the excited speech of man.   Then, when man has slowly and painfully learned to speak, and had plenty of practice in speaking excitedly, we are invited to believe that by some mysterious process *music* arose, the expression of feeling in organised tone, the delight in tone *quâ* tone, in sequences and relations *quâ* sequences and relations.   And all this time the elements out of which this organised system of sound *could* grow, which were innate in man from the very first, by reason of the fact that he had nerves, muscles, and vocal organs, have been doing absolutely nothing!   Though they required only the stimulus of feeling to call them into being, and though they were receiving this stimulus day by day, hour by hour, they had to deny themselves for centuries upon centuries, until they could receive precisely the same kind of stimulus *after* man had learned to speak! Is this credible?

II

If Spencer's theory is æsthetically and psychologically inconceivable, he is hardly happier in the pseudo-historical evidence by which he seeks to support it. His notion seems to be that all ancient music, and the Oriental and savage music of the present day, represent the art at the second or recitative stage of development—a kind of half-way house between excited speech and full-blown song. Thus the Chinese and Hindoos "seem never to have advanced" beyond recitative. "The dance-chants of savage tribes are very monotonous, and in virtue of their monotony are more nearly allied to ordinary speech than are the *songs*[1] of civilised races"—which is surely a quite illegitimate comparison. Again, "hence it follows that the primitive (Greek) recitative was simpler than our modern recitative, and, as such, much less remote from common speech than our own singing is." These typical quotations will serve to show how blandly Spencer assumes the very thing he has to prove. The dance-chants of savages are not as highly organised as our

[1] Italics mine.

European songs ; but does this indicate that
there is not the same psychological difference
between the song and the speech of the savage
as there is between the song and the speech of
the European?   The ancient Greek music was
not so complex as ours ; but will Spencer be
bold enough to say that a man of Athens, listening to contemporary music, did not feel under
it precisely the same kind of æsthetic pleasure
as we feel when we listen to a song by Brahms
or a symphony by Beethoven—a kind of pleasure
different in essence and in temperature from any
that can be given by speech?   Did the Greek,
that is, listening to Greek music, feel as I do
when I listen to an eloquent preacher or an in-
toning Quaker, or as I do when I listen to *music*
in the real sense of the term?   Surely there
can be no doubt in the matter.   Setting aside
the difference due to the enormous development
of our art on the formal and technical side, there
can be no question that the Greek took pleasure
in his music *quâ* music, not *quâ* "recitative." [1]
And as with the Greeks, so with Orientals and
savages.   How   Spencer   can   imagine   that
Oriental   music   as   a   whole,   and   particularly

[1] It seems quite clear that the Greeks had distinct tunes like our
melodies, that were passed about from one singer or player to
another. "In later times," says Müller, "there existed tunes
written by Terpander, of the kind called *nomes*. . . . These nomes
of Terpander were arranged for singing and playing on the
cithara." They were, he goes on to say, "finished compositions,
in which a certain musical idea was systematically worked out,
as is proved by the different parts which belonged to one of them."
There were popular songs, and there were certain tunes that were
sung at festivals. Nor was the music invariably associated with

that of China and India, has for the most part remained stationary at recitative, is a mystery to me, in face of the mass of evidence that may be had from any history of music or any collection of travels. There is, indeed, in much Oriental music, that dubiety of scale (according to our notions) which has ¡misled unwary travellers into the belief that the native singing cannot be real music, because it is so different from ours. But nothing can be better established than the fact that melodies pure and simple, tunes written and sung merely to express that *pensée musicale* to which I have already referred, are common in the music of all Oriental nations. Spencer's statement "that the music of Eastern races is not only without harmony, but has more the character of recitative than of melody," and that " the chant of the early Greek poet was a recitative with accompaniment in unison on his four-stringed lyre," is a fair sample of the uncritical way in which he has assumed anything that would be likely to bear out his theory. His confusion of two or three distinct things by dubbing them all " recitative " is one of the main sources of his errors on this question. As for his attempt to limit harmonic

poetry ; there was music that was purely instrumental. Olympus (B.C. 660–620) seems to have been a musician only. "Olympus is never, like Terpander, mentioned as a poet ; he is simply a musician. His nomes, indeed, seem to have been originally executed on the flute alone, without singing." See K. O. Müller's *History of the Literature of Ancient Greece* (Eng. trans.), vol. i. chap. 12. For an expert treatment of the whole subject, see Hugo Riemann's *Handbuch der Musikgeschichte*, Erster Teil (1904), especially Book I., chap. I., § 3, § 4, § 5.

O

music to modern Europe, I will only say, with Naumann, that wherever we have, as in the old Egyptian paintings, a representation of a concert with many instruments of various shapes and sizes, it is incredible that the performers should all have been playing the same notes. The result, of course, could not have been harmony in our acceptation of the word, for this is to a large extent dependent upon theory for its development; but it was conceivably one of the roots from which harmony could grow. And as Spencer admitted that his theory contained no explanation of harmony, that theory is obviously weakened by any fact indicating that the desire for harmony is innate in the human breast, like the love of tones, sequences of tones, and relations between tones. We must dismiss from our minds all the misleading connotations of the term "harmony," as we must with the term "recitative"; and when we do this there is ample evidence to show that the harmonic sense—the joy in hearing two tones sounded together—is as innate, and as independent of the stimulus of speech, as the melodic sense. The mere sweeping of the harp-strings during singing is not what *we* would call harmony; but if it does not point to a rudimentary feeling that tones in combination are more pleasurable than single tones, it is difficult to say what it does indicate. Everywhere, in truth, we come down to the really fundamental fact, that there is even in primitive man a real *musical sense*, independent of speech in origin, and, as far as we can see, much earlier than speech in the order of time, for man certainly expressed his feelings in pure indefinite sound long before he had learned to agree with his fellows to attach certain meanings to certain stereotyped sounds.

III

The music of savage tribes is, however, the last stronghold of Spencer; and if his theory fails to find proper support in that quarter, it can hardly resist all the weight of evidence that may be brought against it from others. Here, he says, he has Sir Hubert Parry on his side, "who adopts the view I have here re-explained and defended," and who "has in his chapter on Folk-Music exemplified the early stages of musical evolution, up from the howling chants of savages —Australians, Caribs, Polynesian cannibals, etc. —to the rude melodies of our own ancestors. I do not see how any unbiassed reader, after examining the evidence placed by him in its natural order, can refuse assent to the conclusion drawn." Well, the final refutation of Spencer can be had out of the mouth of Sir Hubert Parry himself. What Sir Hubert's own theory of the origin of music may be I do not know; but certainly neither the facts nor the arguments he has adduced in his *Art of Music* give any colour to the theory that music first arose as a modification of the attributes of emotional speech. Let us examine Sir Hubert Parry's evidence.

We begin at the beginning with the descending chromatic howl of the Carib which he quotes on page 49 of his book—the "howling chant" to which Spencer refers ; and if, as the philosopher will have it, this represents "the early stages of musical evolution," his case has gone by the board at once. There could be no more conclusive testimony to the fact that music has its origin not in speech, but in the venting of mere vague emotion in mere vague sound ; for where Spencer sees the previous influence of speech in this howl of the Carib I cannot imagine. He might as well suppose that speech antedates the howl of a dog or the roar of a lion. On what grounds does he find support for his theory here ? Simply that a howl of this kind, like the song of the Omaha Indians, is distinguished by indefiniteness of intervals ! " Now this," he says, " is just one of the traits to be expected if vocal music is developed out of emotional speech ; since the intervals of speech, also, are indefinite." Was there ever a more palpable *non sequitur ?* Because A has one of the characteristics of B, therefore A must have grown out of B ! Here is a complete justification of my previous remark that Spencer has converted a mere likeness into a cause. The real reason for music exhibiting some of the traits of speech is that, music and speech being the expression of allied orders of feeling, and both finding voice through the same muscular apparatus, they simply cannot help having a great many features in common. But we really require something more than a demonstration that the intonations of music, being affected by the same physical organs, point to very much the same mental and physical phenomena as the intonations of speech, in order to convince us that music *had its origin* in speech.

Take now the further examples given by Sir Hubert Parry, and discover in them, if you can, any evidence that does not go to show that they are born directly of a primitive *pensée musicale*, without any sign of the previous intervention of speech. Written over them all, indeed, is conclusive proof that when primitive man sings, or even croons, to himself, he is unconsciously guided by a rudimentary musical sense. Savages contrive, says Sir Hubert, "little fragmentary figures of two or three notes, which they reiterate incessantly over and over again. Sometimes a single figure suffices. When they are clever enough to devise two they alternate them, but [naturally] without much sense or orderliness"; and he shows, later on, how even among savages there is a continuous growth in this primitive sense of design. Now all this is in accordance with the theory of the origin of music already advanced in this essay; and these phenomena of savage music will easily account for all the most complex modern developments of the art, which Spencer half admits his theory will *not* account for. Savage man, merely because he is a physical organism, expresses himself in sound. Again, merely because he is a physical and psychical organism, he takes pleasure in sounds, in successions of sounds, and in the co-relations of sounds; and, to complete

the list of the elements necessary to constitute all
the music that has ever been written in the world,
Sir Hubert Parry shows that, even in the savage
whose rude attempt at song is little more than a
howl, there is a rudimentary sense of form, of
balance, of design. "When little fragments of
melody[1] become stereotyped," says Sir Hubert,
"as they do in every savage community sufficiently advanced to perceive and remember,
attempts are made to alternate and contrast them
in some way ; and the excitement of sympathy
with an expressive cry is merged in a crudely
artistic pleasure derived from the contemplation of
something of the nature of a pattern." Is there
any support for the speech-theory here? Is it
not, indeed, an interloper pure and simple, obscur-
ing a trail that is perfectly clear and open if left
alone?

The one fact upon which Spencer always seems
to rely is that the intervals of speech and the
intervals of the most primitive chant are both
indefinite. Even here, however, Sir Hubert
Parry's book is unpropitious to him, for Sir
Hubert insists on the obvious fact that indefinite-

---

[1] It does not seem to have occurred to Spencer that if savages
have melodies, however tiny and primitive, it can hardly be true
that they are only in the recitative stage. The plain fact is that
his use of the term recitative was wholly unscientific. He never
saw that there is a vast æsthetic distinction between recitative in
the sense of more sonorous and more formal speech—as in the case
of an orator or a preacher—and recitative in the musical sense.
In the latter case the distinctively musical appetite comes into
play ; in the former it does not. The one is an intensification of
ordinary speech, but never becomes more than speech ; the other
is music, even though restricted music. They spring from different
faculties and appeal to different organs of enjoyment.

ness of intervals in early music is entirely a matter of lack of instruments by which to fix the various notes of a scale. "It is extremely difficult to make sure what intervals savages intend to utter, as they are very uncertain about hitting anything like exact notes till they have advanced enough to have instruments with regular relations of notes more or less indicated upon them." To pass from an indefinite howl to a definite series of notes, when an instrument has been invented that guides the voice and fixes its tones, may be the work of a day. Wherein then comes the function of speech and recitative, which are supposed to occupy the intermediate stages of evolution between the howl and the song—for I suppose Spencer would hardly contend that man learned to speak *before* he learned to howl? And at what stage appears this elementary feeling for musical design which the savage exhibits? Can this be conceived to grow out of the habit of speech? If not, if it is independent of speech, if it is something that concerns itself with pure sound alone, what was it doing in all the ages when man was making sounds, but had not yet made himself a language? "The crudest efforts of savages," says Sir Hubert Parry, "throw light upon the true nature of musical design, and upon the manner in which human beings endeavoured to grapple with it." Again, "the savage state indicates a taste for design, but an incapacity for making the designs consistent and logical; in the lowest intelligent stage, the capacity for disposing short contrasting figures in an orderly and intelligent way is shown." Once more, can speech be logically conceived as playing the leading part in this long but continuous drama of evolution?

Finally, in Sir Hubert Parry's own pages Spencer could have found evidence of yet another element of pure musical enjoyment in the savage mind—none other than an incipient desire for harmony. Speaking of the rise of harmony in the Middle Ages, and of the curious device of making two wholly different tunes go together by the process of "easing off the corners and adapting the points where the cacophony was too intolerable to be endured," Sir Hubert shows the existence of this same practice among savages. "This," he says, "may seem a very surprising and even laughable way of obtaining an artistic effect, but in reality the actual practice of combining several tunes together is by no means uncommon. Several savage and semi-civilised races adopt the practice, as, for instance, the Bushmen at the lower end of the human scale, and the Javese, Siamese, Burmese, and Moors about the middle. In these cases the process usually consists of simultaneously singing or playing short and simple musical figures, such as savages habitually reiterate, with the addition in some cases of a long sort of indefinite wailing tune which goes on independently of all the rest of the performance. The Javese carry such devices to extremes, producing a kind of reckless, incoherent, instrumental counterpoint, very much like a number of people playing various tunes at once, with just sufficient feeling for some definite central principle to accommodate the jarring elements. The practice of combining tunes seems to have become universal quite suddenly, and it led very quickly to fresh developments. And it is worth noting that one of these developments was precisely the same in principle as that adopted by the Bushmen and the Javese, and other semi-savage experimenters in such things; which was to accompany the main combination of two melodies by a short musical figure which could be incessantly reiterated as an accompaniment." Phenomena like these undermine the crude and hasty inference that Orientals and savages have no notion of harmony; they prove that, as low down in the human scale as our investigations will carry us, man tries to make harmony because it pleases his musical sense. How far he succeeds depends upon other things than his mere desire.

So that, to sum up, we can dismiss speech altogether from our hypothesis of the origin of music, seeing that, while no man can represent to us either the psychological or historical processes by which music has grown or could grow out of speech, we find innate in the human organism every element out of which music *can* grow, independently of speech—the delight in tone, the delight in successions of tones, the delight in combinations of tones, the delight in rhythm, the delight in design. Even Spencer himself, in the chapter on "Developed Music" in his *Facts and Comments*, sees that these elements are sufficient to account for certain kinds of music, though his total analysis, particularly in the distinction between merely symmetrical music and poetical music, is æsthetically incomplete and *à priori.* To Spencer's oft - reiterated question, " If my theory does not explain the origin of music, how else can its genesis be explained?" we may reply that his theory really explains nothing ; it only asserts. It points to certain resemblances between speech and song, and then dogmatically lays it down, without an atom of proof, that the one has arisen from the other. *Per contra,* an analysis of primitive music shows us that in the rudest savage we have, in embryo, every element that goes to make the most complicated music of modern times—some of these elements, indeed, appearing even in animals. If we are to believe that these in themselves could not develop into music, we must have a reason why ; and if we are to believe that an imitation of the accents of speech was necessary before primitive man could express what he felt in mere indefinite sound, we must have not only some proof that it ever occurred, but some demonstration of how the process is possible ; for to me, at least, it is psychologically inconceivable. When Spencer says that "song emerged from speech," he is, I contend, merely using a verbal formula that conveys nothing representable to us ; it is of the family of those "pseudo-ideas" upon which he himself has emptied the vials of his scorn in *First Principles.*

To BERTRAM DOBELL

MAETERLINCK AND MUSIC

ONE is always meeting with curious literary and artistic affinities where one least expects them. The human mind, of course, is really homogeneous throughout. We have all to build up our inner and outer universe out of very much the same kind of brain and sense organs : so that it is hardly surprising if here and there one feels that the work of this or that musician or artist is the counterpart of the work of this or that poet or prose writer, or *vice versâ*. One sees, for example, a good deal of Weber and the German Romanticists in the stories of Hoffmann ; of Lessing and Diderot in the work of Gluck ; of Tourgeniev and Dostoievski in the music of Tchaikovski ; of Berlioz's music— as Heine suggested—in the pictures of Martin. This phenomenon is so frequent as to excite little wonder. What is rather more curious is to find, here and there, that one of the main spiritual principles of a certain artist is implicit in the æsthetic system of another artist who works in an entirely different medium, and whose whole work, at first sight, seems to be of a diametrically opposite order. Between Wagner and Maeterlinck, for instance, who would say that there is a fundamental sympathy of soul and a community of artistic outlook — between the musician of stupendous passion and restless activity and the quiet mystic who seems to be serenely poised far above all activity and all passion, placing, in his lofty philosophising, so little store by all the things that appeared so vital, so real, to the musician? Nevertheless there is, as I shall try to show, a curious similarity between the æsthetic systems of the two men.[1] They share something of the same excellencies; they break down or find their limitations almost at the same point. Let us cursorily examine the two systems.

I

If we did not possess Maeterlinck's own dramas, we might be able to judge from his essays what his position towards the drama and fiction would be. Here we have revealed to us a manner of apprehending life and of looking out upon the world that could find expression only in some such novel dramatic form as Maeterlinck has adopted. The dramatist himself, however, has given us, in his exquisite chapters on "The Tragical in Daily Life" and "The Awakening of the Soul," in *The Treasure of the Humble*, a statement, at once explicit and impassioned, of his

---

[1] I am compelled to draw attention to the words "æsthetic *systems*" because, on the appearance of this article in *The Atlantic Monthly*, a not unkindly reviewer took me to task for asserting, as he thought, that the art-*work* of Wagner was akin to that of Maeterlinck; he pointed out, quite rightly, that César Franck's work lies closer to Maeterlinck's than does Wagner's. But of course I had never asserted that Wagner and Maeterlinck spoke to us in the same language or of the same things. I was only concerned to prove that underlying the so very different practice of the two men was a curious similarity of æsthetic theory.

creed. He advances the theory that the ordinary
tragedy of startling incident is, or ought to be, a
thing of the past, a concept of barbaric ages, when
men could be thrilled by the secret underforces
of life only by reaching towards them through
crude and violent action. In a more refined and
subtle age like this, we should be able to trace
the hand of destiny even when it does not work
through media so coarse and palpable. It is not
the primitive sensation of seeing one man act
the murder of another that is the essence of
tragedy. It is the sense of spiritual enlighten-
ment that comes to us ; the feeling that, somehow
or other, the murder itself, the passion and the
events that led up to it, the consequences that
flow from it, are all subtly interwoven threads of
the great indwelling laws of things. Most of the
action, indeed, that is associated with our current
notion of tragedy is, from a higher point of view,
both æsthetically superfluous and an evidence of
our earthiness. We should be capable of being
moved to pity, of feeling the most refined tragic
sorrow, by a play that eliminates the coarser and
more obvious facts, and relies on gentler and
more intimate suggestions of universal truth.
Our present age, he thinks, is capable, or is becoming capable, of this. "In former days," he
says in his essay on "The Awakening of the
Soul," "if there was question, for a moment, of
a presentiment, of the strange impressions produced by a chance meeting or a look, of a deci-
sion that the unknown side of human reason had
governed, of an intervention or a force, inexpli-

cable and yet understood, of the sacred laws of sympathy and antipathy, of elective and instinctive affinities, of the overwhelming influence of the thing that had not been spoken — in former days these problems would have been carelessly passed by ; and, besides, it was but seldom that they obtruded themselves upon the serenity of the thinker. They seemed to come about by the merest chance. That they are ever pressing upon life, unceasingly and with prodigious force —this was unsuspected of all ; and the philosopher hastened back to familiar studies of passion, and of incident that floated on the surface."

This is clearly part of a philosophy of life and art in which the cruder nervous strands are put aside, as useless for that spiritual illumination which the thinker desires. They are too thick to be sensitive to the finer currents that pass through them ; only the more delicate nerve-tracts, alive to every wave of feeling, can be stimulated to philosophic light and heat. The essence of all Maeterlinck's work, of course, is this supersensitiveness. He is endowed with other senses than ours, other modes of apprehending the universe. He is a mystic, and by reason of being a mystic he is at the same time out of touch with many things that the normal man calls real, and delicately sensitive to many currents in the spiritual atmosphere of the universe of whose very existence the normal man is all his life unaware. We have to remember that this world is after all only what our own senses and intellect make it for each of us. The little we can see and feel must be as nothing compared

with the immensities that we can neither see nor
feel, but that always attend our thoughts, our
footsteps, our very breathing, like silent, invisible
spectators. Even the world of the animal is not
our world, for the animal is alive to many things
that never penetrate our consciousness ; and there
are exceptionally constituted human beings on
whose nerves the universe seems to write different
messages from those that are communicated to
the ordinary soul. The mystic catches vibrations
in life to which duller natures are, except in
moments of abnormal exaltation, for the most
part insensitive. When we find fault with him
for the apparent weakness of his hold upon reality,
we need to remember that his realities are not
always ours. He frequently has difficulty in expressing himself in our ordinary speech, for the
reason that this is mainly the instrument of normal
cerebration, not of the subnormal or the super-
normal. Hence Maeterlinck's theorem—which is
not half such a paradox as it looks—that the
profounder vibrations of the soul are more easily
communicated by silence than by speech. We
are beset by intuitions that can never find adequate
expression in words. " How strangely," he says,
" do we diminish a thing as soon as we try to
express it in words ! " Speech hardly seems
necessary to him as a means of carrying on his
thoughts, which, as they lie in deeper, more
obscure places than language has ever visited,
must seek a more immediate way of passage
from his own brain to that of another. " A time
will come, perhaps, when our souls will know

P

of each other without the intermediary of the senses. . . . A spiritual epoch is perhaps upon us. . . ." Thus the favourite means of communication between the soul of the spiritual elect is not speech, but silence—silence, which is far more eloquent, far more illuminative of the profoundest depths of being, than language can ever be. " It is idle," he writes, "to think that by means of words any real communication can ever pass from one man to another. . . . It is only when life is sluggish within us that we speak." And just as the mystic despises words as instruments of communication, so he looks down upon facts as guides to illumination. As the inner life is too subtle to be expressed in ordinary language, so its interests are too refined to be spent upon crude facts. These are " nothing but the laggards, the spies and camp followers, of the great forces we cannot see." [1]

II

Here, then, is a philosophy of life which, in the hands of the artist, aims at creating a new type of "static" drama, in which speech shall give way, as far as possible, to suggestion, incident and action to the immediate revelation of soul-states. Though the drama is to deal with real life in a way that Maeterlinck would regard as most rigorously real, there is to be a progressive withdrawal from most of the points that the average man regards as the essence of reality.

[1] Compare Amiel's saying—" Action is but coarsened thought."

In the first place, naked facts and violent actions are to be passed over, as not necessary for the communication to us of the essential thing that the dramatist has to say ; in the second place, mere words are no longer to be looked upon as indispensable intermediaries between the thought and the expression.   Now all this, in its main features, finds a very close parallel in the work and the arguments of Wagner.   Let us look for a moment at his theories as they figure in actual practice, taken out of the wordy metaphysic in which he delighted to obscure them.

The drama and the novel represent an attempt to fire the reader with a certain emotion that has already flamed up in the writer.   The tragedy of *King Lear*, for example, aims at inspiring in us a sentiment of pity for an old man who is shattered by filial ingratitude.   *Othello* aims at enlisting our sympathies for an affectionate man and wife whose happiness is broken to pieces, partly by misunderstanding, partly by diabolical machinations.   There are innumerable other points in the plays, but these are the great central forces.   These are what moved Shakespeare to the composition of the dramas.   These are the ideas from which he started ; and these are the ideas that finally remain with us when we have seen or read the plays.   But owing to the clumsy, intractable nature of the material in which he works, the dramatist can stimulate this central idea or feeling in us only by a most roundabout process.   He cannot plunge at once into his subject.   He must commence at a point far distant from that to which he wishes to lead us, and then work up to it gradually.   He cannot adequately communicate an emotion without unfolding before our eyes the long and complex scenes or set of circumstances that give rise to this emotion.   He cannot confine himself to the characters and the events that make up the real drama ; he has to illustrate these—to draw sparks from them, as it were—by the impact of minor incidents and persons.   In a word, he has to fill us with a multiplicity of more or less superfluous feelings before he can communicate to us the feeling that is really essential.

In music all this is altered.   (The reader will of course remember that I am expounding Wagner.)   There being no distinction between the feeling and the expression, no bar between the emotion and the speech, the musician can plunge at once into the very heart of his subject. Further, he need never leave the heart of it ; he can devote all his energies to elucidating the really necessary factors ; he has no need to waste half his time in showing, from the description of extraneous things, how such and such a situation has come about, or how a man comes to feel in such and such a way.   It takes half-an-hour's reading of the Tristan legend, or any poem on the subject, before we feel the atmosphere of tragedy closing round us, or know precisely why it should come.   In Wagner's opera, not only is the fact that there *is* a tragedy suggested in the first bars of the music, but the very tint and spiritual quality of the tragedy are painted for us at once. All through the work, again, we live in the very centre of the metropolis of that territory of emotion—love, grief, and pity— to which the legend and the poets have to guide us by devious and frequently uninteresting paths. We see Tristan and Isolde in the first bar and in the last; we never leave them for a moment. Thus not only does the musician draw us at once to the point he wishes us to reach, but his independence of all the scaffolding necessary to the poet gives him more freedom of development. He can wring from the souls of his characters the last bitter juice of their emotions. Wagner himself was fond of pointing out the gradual growth of his art in these respects. In the *Flying Dutchman* he tried "to keep the plot to its simplest features; to exclude all useless detail, such as the intrigues one borrows from common life." The plot of *Tannhäuser* will be found "far more markedly evolving from its inner motives"; while "the whole interest of *Lohengrin* consists in an inner working within the heart of Elsa, involving every secret of the soul." Wagner's aim was to shake himself clear of the wearisome mass of detail that, in the poetical drama, is necessary to show the "whence and wherefore" of each feeling. "I too, as I have told you," he writes, "felt driven to this 'whence and wherefore'; and for long it banned me from the magic of my art. But my time of penance taught me to overcome the question. All doubt at last was taken from me, when I gave myself up to the *Tristan*. Here, in perfect trustfulness, I plunged into the inner depth of soul-events, and from out this inmost centre of the world I fearlessly built up its outer form. A glance at the *volumen* of this poem will show you at once that the exhaustive detail-work which an historical poet is obliged to devote to clearing up the outward bearing of his plot, to the detriment of a lucid exposition of its inner motives, I now trusted myself to apply to these latter alone. Life and death, the whole import and existence of the outer world, here hang on nothing but the inner movements of the soul. The whole affecting Action comes about for the reason only that the inmost soul demands it, and steps to light with the very shape foretokened in the inner shrine."

Here the analogy with Maeterlinck's theory becomes evident. Both men despise the cruder, external, historical, active facts on which the drama has felt itself till now compelled to rely ; both aim at a subtle form of drama in which the soul-states shall be the first and last thing. There is more in life, they say, than conscious reason ; it is the innermost processes of the soul that we desire to have laid bare to us in drama. This reflection led Wagner to the choice of the myth as the best material on which to work. " I therefore believed," he writes, " I must term the ' mythos' the poet's ideal Stuff—that native nameless poem of the Folk, which throughout the ages we ever meet new handled by the great poets of periods of consummate culture ; for in it *there almost vanishes the conventional form of man's relations, merely explicable to abstract reason,* to show instead the eternally intelligible, the purely human." This is not clarity itself, but what Wagner means is that in music as he conceives it you come face to face with the essential truth of things at once, without having to make a wearisome journey through a mass of unimportant detail, as you have to do in the novel and the poetical drama before you can get to the heart of the emotion. And this is quite true, so far as it goes. If you conceive life like the mystic or his soul's brother the musician, if you prefer the general to the particular, the vague to the definite, the suggested to the spoken, you will naturally seek a medium that shall allow free passage to your emotion in its broadest form. Like Wagner, you will not want to stop and explain for half-an-hour who Tristan and Isolde were, who were the people round them, what the causes were that led to their tragic end, and so on. You will want to get to the centre of your subject at once ; you abandon all attempts at demonstration and plunge at once into expression. And if, with Maeterlinck, it seems quite unimportant to know the names and histories of two or three given men and women, the scenes in which they live, the commonplace routine of their daily lives—if you only want to know how destiny is dealing with them, what bitter-sweet emotion is being distilled from their souls in some quiet hour that is pregnant with vital meaning—then you will pass over, like the musician, every detail that

seems to you unimportant, and concentrate yourself on that supremely fateful hour. You will not
depict anything happening, because it is not the
event that is the essential thing, but the soul-
states that are born of the event. To Maeterlinck, as to Wagner, the "purely human"—the
whole man, the essential man—lies deeper than
what is "merely explicable to abstract reason."
"A new, indescribable power," he says, in speaking of Ibsen's *Master Builder*, "dominates this
somnambulistic drama. All that is said therein
at once hides and reveals the source of an
unknown life. And if we are bewildered at
times, let us not forget that our soul often
appears, to our feeble eyes, to be but the
maddest of forces, and that there are in man
many regions more fertile, more profound, and
more interesting than those of his reason or his
intelligence."

For these obscure perceptions of the soul,
words alone are plainly an inadequate mode of
expression. Hence both Wagner and Maeterlinck feel that some more direct kind of utterance
is required, some more immediate means of communication between the feeling of the artist and
the feeling of the auditor. Wagner finds this in
music, which substitutes a direct appeal for the
indirect appeal of the ordinary poet. The
dramatic poem must be drafted "in such a
fashion that it may penetrate the finest fibres
of the musical tissue, and the spoken *thought*
entirely dissolves into the *feeling*." Not that
there is to be any surrender of that grip upon

the inner life that is the essence of thoughtful drama. On the contrary, Wagner maintains, after the manner of Maeterlinck, that it is only when the soul is set free from the disturbing accidents of the temporary life that it can see clearly into the movements of the universal life. Wagner holds that in the Beethoven symphony, for example, a world-view is presented, quite as philosophical, quite as logically connected, as any that can be put together in words. " In this symphony, instruments speak a language whereof the world at no previous time had any knowledge; for here, with a hitherto unknown persistence, the purely musical expression enchains the hearer in an inconceivably varied mesh of nuances; rouses his inmost being to a degree unreachable by any other art; and in all its changefulness reveals an ordering principle so free and bold that we can deem it more forcible than any logic, yet without the laws of logic entering into it in the slightest; nay, rather, the reasoning march of thought, with its track of causes and effects, here finds no sort of foothold. So that this symphony must positively appear to us a revelation from another world; and in truth it opens out a scheme of the world's phenomena quite different from the ordinary logical scheme, and whereof one foremost thing is undeniable: that it thrusts home with the most overwhelming conviction, and guides our feeling with such a sureness that the logic-mongering reason is completely routed and disarmed thereby."

Now set beside this view of the relations of the

musical drama to the poetical drama Maeterlinck's comparison of his own dramatic ideals with those of the "active" poet. The latter passes unthinkingly over many of the feelings that give to a tragic event its real significance. Why should not these feelings, the essential core of the drama, be given fuller play, and the mere incidents be looked upon as either superfluous or purely ancillary? He too, like Wagner, wants to show the heart of a tragic situation without the customary tedious cataloguing of all its limbs. He wants the spiritual essence of drama, and the essence alone, not the crude material facts from which this essence has to be distilled. The whole of Maeterlinck's magnificent passage must here be quoted : "The mysterious chant of the Infinite, the ominous silence of the soul and of God, the murmur of Eternity on the horizon, the destiny or fatality that we are conscious of within us, though by what tokens none can tell—do not all these underlie *King Lear, Macbeth, Hamlet?* And would it not be possible, by some interchanging of the *rôles*, to bring them nearer to us, and send the actor farther off? Is it beyond the mark to say that the true tragic element, normal, deep-rooted, and universal—that the true tragic element of life only begins at the moment when so-called adventures, sorrows, and dangers have disappeared? . . . When we think of it, is it not the tranquillity that is terrible, the tranquillity watched by the stars? And is it in tumult or in silence that the spirit of life quickens within us? Is it not when we are told, at the end of the

story, 'They were happy,' that the great disquiet
should intrude itself? What is taking place
while they are happy? Are there not elements
of deeper gravity and stability in happiness, in a
single moment of repose, than in the whirlwind
of passion? Is it not then that we at last
behold the march of time—ay, and of many
another on-stealing besides, more secret still—is
it not then that the hours rush forward? Are not
deeper chords set vibrating by all these things
than by the dagger-stroke of conventional drama?
Is it not at the very moment when a man believes
himself secure from bodily death that the strange
and silent tragedy of the being and the immensities does indeed raise its curtain on the stage?
Is it while I flee before a naked sword that my
existence touches its most interesting point? Is
life always at its sublimest in a kiss? Are there
not other moments, when one hears purer voices
that do not fade away so soon? Does the soul
flower only on nights of storm? Hitherto, doubt-
less, this belief has prevailed. It is only the life
of violence, the life of bygone days, that is perceived by nearly all our tragic writers; and truly
may one say that anachronism dominates the
stage, and that dramatic art dates back as many
years as the art of sculpture."

He places the spiritual purposes of painting
and music on a higher plane; "for these," he
says, "have learned to select and reproduce those
obscurer phases of daily life that are not the less
deep-rooted and amazing. They know that all
that life has lost, as regards mere superficial

ornament, has been more than counterbalanced by the depth, the intimate meaning, and the spiritual gravity it has acquired.   The true artist no longer chooses Marius triumphing over the Cimbrians, or the assassination of the Duke of Guise, as a fit subject for his art ; for he is well aware that the psychology of victory or murder is but elementary and exceptional, and that the solemn voice of men and things, the voice that issues forth so timidly and hesitatingly, cannot be heard amidst the idle uproar of acts of violence. And therefore will he place on his canvas a house lost in the heart of the country, an open door at the end of a passage, a face or hands at rest, and by these simple images will add to our consciousness of life, which is a possession that it is no longer possible to lose."

III

The excellence and the wisdom of these thoughts need no pointing out.   What is the defect in them —or, rather, wherein are they incomplete?

This may be seen, in the first place, by playing off Maeterlinck's theory against that of Wagner. It is quite true, as Wagner says, that his kind of music-drama has one great advantage over the poetical drama : that by surrendering certain outlying interests it can concentrate all its power on the central interest—giving full play, as Wagner would express it, to the inner motives of the dramatic action.   But, on the other hand, music must, from its very nature, fail to touch a score of ideas and passions that are within us, and for whose expression we are compelled to go to poetry that is unhampered by music. Thus there are certain mental states with which music can have practically no communion. The girl can sing, as Ruskin has told us, of her lost love, but the miser cannot sing of his lost money-bags. For a study of the miser, then, and of all the shades of character that resemble his, we must look, not to music, but to poetry or prose. Again, any one who has seen Verdi's *Otello* on the stage must have been struck with the relative feebleness of the character-drawing of Iago. A monster of this kind, made up entirely of cunning and deception, is a concept almost entirely foreign to the art of music, which does indeed give a heightened value to the primary emotions, but, on the other hand, has difficulty in reaching beyond these. One frequently finds it hard to believe that Wagner's Mime, who sings such pleasant music, is really a hateful character, owing to the difficulty music has in expressing the mean and despicable. It can render, mainly by physical means, the horrible and the terrible, but the contemptible, the abortive, are practically beyond its sphere.

Nor, again, even in the field where music and poetry meet, does music so far cover the ground, as Wagner would contend, as to make non-musical poetry a superfluity, a mere echo of what can be heard in fuller tones in the drama that is a blend of poetry and music. For the sheer emotional beauty of pity, for exquisite tenderness and complete consolation, nothing, in any art, could surpass certain portions of *Parsifal.* But it is essentially *emotion* here, not thought; it is wholly esoteric; it achieves its miracle by withdrawing into its own lovely atmosphere the crude, hard facts of the world, and there transforming them. If we want an expression of pity that shall bear more closely on our real life, give us the emotional balm at the same time that it allows free play to our philosophic thought, we must go to poetry. Look at the colloquy of the pots in the Rubaiyat, in which the humanist Omar empties the vials of his compassion upon the marred and broken beings of this world :—

> "Said one among them—'Surely not in vain
> My substance of the common Earth was ta'en
>   And to this Figure moulded, to be broke,
> Or trampled back to shapeless Earth again.'
>
> Then said a Second—'Ne'er a peevish Boy
> Would break the Bowl from which he drank in joy:
>   And He that with His hand the Vessel made
> Will surely not in after Wrath destroy.'
>
> After a momentary silence spake
> Some Vessel of a more ungainly Make;
>   'They sneer at me for leaning all awry :
> What! did the Hand then of the Potter shake ?'"

There is not here the sensuous anodyne of Wagner's music, but there is something equally precious; the thought is farther flung; it brings more elements of reality back with it to be bathed and softened in emotion; it stirs the more vital philosophic depths. As one reads the verses, one thinks sadly of all the bruised

and broken beings of the world, the poor mis-
shapen souls who carry within them, from no
fault of their own, the seeds of the things that
are to blight or slay them—the men afflicted
with incurable vices of body or mind or will, the
criminals, often more sinned against than sin-
ning, upon whom society wreaks its legalised
vengeance. We have not merely a warm wave
of pity passing through us, as in the case of
Parsifal; the exquisite art of the thing is
strengthened by the closeness of its association
with innumerable problems of theology, of philosophy, and of social science. So, again, with
the line Maeterlinck himself places in the mouth
of old Arkel, after one of the most terrible scenes
in *Pelleas and Melisanda:* "If I were God, how
I should pity the heart of men!" Music, in its
grave, wise speech after a dire catastrophe, may
almost compass some such wealth of ethical significance as this; but there is in Maeterlinck's
line a peculiar fulness of divination that can
be conveyed to us only in words. Numberless
other instances might be cited, all proving this
existence of a philosophic sphere to which even
the greatest music can, by reason of its indefiniteness, never have access. Matthew Arnold may
have been a prejudiced witness, being a poet
himself; yet one feels that he has the right with
him in that passage, in his *Epilogue to Lessing's
Laocöon*, in which he points out how the painter
and the musician excel respectively in expressing
"the aspect of the moment" and "the feeling of
the moment," but that the poet deals more philo-

sophically with the total life and interlacement of
things :—

> " He must life's movement tell !
> The thread which binds it all in one,
> And not its separate parts alone.
> The movement he must tell of life,
> Its pain and pleasure, rest and strife ;
> His eye must travel down, at full,
> The long, unpausing spectacle ;
> With faithful unrelaxing force
> Attend it from its primal source,
> From change to change and year to year,
> Attend it of its mid career,
> Attend it to the last repose,
> And solemn silence of its close."

Arnold's expression might perhaps have been
a little more artistic, but there is no controverting
the general truth he voices—that poetry looks
before and after in a way that music cannot
possibly do ; is wider in its philosophic sweep
than music, clearer in its vision, making up for
its weaker idealism by its sympathetic evocation
of a hundred notes that are denied to music.

IV

And just as we pass from music to poetry to
reach certain emotions that are not to be found
in the more generalised art, so we pass from
Maeterlinck's æsthetic world to that of the cruder
realist, in the search for certain further artistic
satisfactions.   Mysticism has this in common
with music—that it gives voice to the broader,
more generalised feelings of mankind, and hesi-
tates to come into contact with the less ecstatic

faculties that are exercised upon the harder facts of life. Maeterlinck, like Wagner, tries to lay hold upon the universal in art; but he does so simply because, again like Wagner, he is comparatively insensitive to other stimuli. And as Wagner's æsthetic holds good for the most part only of those who, like him, apprehend the world through music, so Maeterlinck's theory of drama is completely valid only for those who share his general attitude toward life and knowledge. If it is really the mystics who have the key to the knowledge of things; if, as Maeterlinck himself says in his introduction to Ruysbroeck's *L'Orne-ment des Noces Spirituelles*, "toute certitude est en eux seuls," and that "les vérités mystiques ont sur les vérités ordinaires un privilège étrange —elles ne peuvent ni vieillir ni mourir "; if in the hypnotic semi-swoon of the faculties before the abyss of the universal we come closest to the real secret of things, then is there nothing to be added to or taken from Maeterlinck's statement of the essence of drama. If, on the other hand, the evolution of the more acutely specialised perceptions in us points to man's need of a mental system that shall embrace ever more and more of the phenomena of the world, then must we have an art that can shape these perceptions too into a beauty of their own. Did we all apprehend the universe as Maeterlinck and the mystics do— through a kind of sixth sense that is an instantaneous blend of the ordinary five; could we all arrive at his serenely philosophical outlook, and be content with so much understanding of the

Q

world as came to us in immediate intuitions—we
should then see in his kind of art a mode of
expression coextensive with all that we could
know or feel. But since we do not all look at
life with the semi-Oriental fatalism of Maeterlinck, in whose soul the passive elements seem
to outweigh the active, we have to turn to other
types of dramatic art for the satisfaction of our
cravings. "The poet," he says in one place,
"adds to ordinary life something—I know not
what—which is the poet's secret: and there
comes to us a sudden revelation of life in its
stupendous grandeur, in its submissiveness to the
unknown powers, in its endless affinities, in its
awe-inspiring misery." Well, for a great many
of us there are moments when "submissiveness
to the unknown powers" does not express the
be-all and the end-all of life — more vivid
moments of revolt, of struggle with uncertainties,
of passionate assertions of personality, that have
little kinship with the grey resignation of the
mystic. If life is ugly and bitter, there is an
art that can interest us deeply in this bitterness
and ugliness, because it ministers to that deep-
seated need of ours to leave no corner of life and
nature unexplored. This art of the mercilessly
real may not be so "philosophical" as Maeterlinck's; it may not speak to us so clearly of the
"mysterious chant of the infinite, the ominous
silence of the soul and of God, the murmur of
Eternity on the horizon," for these voices can
make themselves heard only in a wider, serener,
less turbid space than ours. But just as the poet

foregoes some of the formal perfection of the
musician, finding his compensation in his power
to touch a wider range of things, so the realist
finds in the bracing, ever-interesting contact with
the cruder facts of life something that compen-
sates him for missing the broader peace of the
mystic — a sense of energetic personality, of
struggle with and dominion over inimical forces,
that the languor of mysticism cannot provide.
"No human reason," says Maeterlinck, in our
actions, "no human reason ; nothing but destiny."
Well, thought and action, to the mystic, may be
only the children of illusion ; but may there not
be as much illusion in passivity, in the ecstatic
collapse of the intellect under the pressure of an
incomprehensible world ?   In the Maeterlinck
drama, beautiful as it is, we cannot all of us find
complete satisfaction.   To quote the words that
he himself has used in another context : "Here
we are no longer in the well-known valleys of
human and psychic life.   We find ourselves at
the door of the third enclosure—that of the
divine life of the mystics.   We have to grope
timidly, and make sure of every footstep, as we
cross the threshold."   And when we *have* crossed
the threshold, we find ourselves hungering and
thirsting for the more troubled but at any rate
broader life we have left behind us ; just as the
Wagnerian drama, mighty as it is, brings home
to us the fact that there are needs of our nature
that music cannot satisfy.   Formal perfection,
absolute homogeneity, are obtainable in an art
only when we abstract it from outer incident and

long reflection. Music comes before poetry in this respect, poetry before the drama, the drama before fiction. Take, from a master of reticence, an example of apparent dissipation of artistic force that Wagner would have held to prove his own theories. It is the scene in *Madame Bovary* where Léon, expecting to see Emma, is detained at dinner by Homais. "At two o'clock they were still at table, opposite each other. The large room was emptying; the stovepipe, in the shape of a palm tree, spread its gilt leaves over the white ceiling, and near them, outside the window, in the bright sunshine, a little fountain gurgled in a white basin, where, in the midst of watercress and asparagus, three torpid lobsters stretched across to some quails that lay heaped up in a pile on their sides." "Watercress! asparagus! quails! three torpid lobsters!" Wagner would have said, "what have these to do with art? Music's manner of describing the impatience of two separated lovers is that of the mad prelude to the duet in *Tristan*. Here we have all the essential soul-states, without the admixture of crude external realities." Yet there is something in Léon's impatience that music cannot express—the dreary boredom inflicted by his companion, the helpless wandering of the mind over the insignificant uglinesses of his surroundings. This also is part of human psychology, and a part that can find expression only in words. In consideration of the wider sweep of the artistic net, we gladly abate our demands for perfection of quality in the yield;

for the phenomena of the extensive and the intensive are meant to be compensatory, the one taking the burden upon itself where the strength of the other fails. Wagner erred in thinking that the union of all the arts in music-drama could render each separate art superfluous ; Maeterlinck errs in thinking that the mystic, in his withdrawal to the centre of consciousness, can tell us all we desire to know of the outer circle.[1]

[1] It is interesting to note that many things in Maeterlinck either move us, by their very vagueness, just in the way that music does, or else seem like a fragment from a libretto, needing to be set to music before they can attain their full significance. Of the former class the reader will remember such things as the conclusion of *Alladine and Palomides.* To the latter class belong many of those curious scenes in which the characters keep on reiterating apparently insignificant words, to the intense annoyance of the Man in the Street, who cannot see the meaning of it all. In *Aglavaine and Selysette* there are many passages that seem, without music, to be only the skeleton, the scaffolding, of an emotional effect. There is a salient example of the same thing in *Joyzelle :*

Joyzelle. Je t'embrassais la nuit, quand j'embrassais mes rêves ..
Lancéor. Je n'ai pas eu de doute . . .
Joyzelle. Je n'ai pas eu de crainte . . .
Lancéor. Et tout m'est accordé . . .
Joyzelle. Et tout me rend heureuse ! . . .
Lancéor. Que tes yeux sont profonds et pleins de confiance ! . . .
Joyzelle. Et que les tiens sont purs et pleins de certitudes ! . . .
Lancéor. Comme je les reconnais ! . . .
Joyzelle. Et comme je les retrouve ! . . .
Lancéor. Tes mains sur mes épaules ont le geste qu'elles avaient quand je les attendais sans oser m'eveiller . . .
Joyzelle. Et ton bras sur mon cou reprend la même place . . .
Lancéor. C'est ainsi qu'autrefois tes paupières se fermaient au souffle de l'amour.
Joyzelle. Et c'est de même aussi que les larmes montaient dans tes yeux qui s'ouvraient . . .
Lancéor. Quand le bonheur est tel . . .
Joyzelle. Le malheur ne vient pas tant que l'amour l'enchaine .
Lancéor. Tu m'aimes ? . . .
Joyzelle. Oui . . .

It reads almost exactly like a libretto without its music.

To SIR *EDWARD* *ELGAR*

RICHARD STRAUSS AND THE MUSIC OF THE FUTURE

I

TWO or three years ago Richard Strauss was practically unknown in this country. A few people had heard works of his abroad; a few more had bought his complex scores and worried through them as best they could, mostly deriving from them only the impression that Strauss was getting madder and madder every year. From other and happier climes, where the demand for music is almost as great as the supply, there came weird stories of this new art. One thing was universally admitted as being beyond dispute—that Strauss was a master of orchestral effect such as the world had never seen; but all the rest was pure legend. In 1897 *Also sprach Zarathustra* was played at the Crystal Palace; old Sir George Grove, in a private letter, expressed what was probably the opinion of most of the people who sat it out: "What can have happened to drag down music from the high level of beauty, interest, sense, force, grace, coherence and any other good quality, which it rises to in Beethoven and also (not so high) in Mendelssohn, down to the low level of ugliness and want of interest that we had in Strauss's absurd farrago . . . ? *Noise* and *effect* seems to be so much the aim now." It was the old, old story. The man who listens to a new art and is momentarily revolted by it never thinks that the deficiencies may be not in the art but in himself; with sublime arrogance he disposes in half-an-hour of a work that perhaps took a brain three times the weight of his own half a decade to write. There was some excuse for Grove; he was nearly eighty years old, and *Also sprach Zarathustra* may well have sounded to his venerable ears like chaos come again. Other people had not the same excuse. In any case, an isolated performance of so complex a work as this was hardly the way to educate the musical masses up to the new evangel. The Strauss-flower languished decidedly for some time after in England. It is true that one could occasionally hear, either in London or in the provinces, *Till Eulenspiegel, Don Juan, Tod und Verklärung*, and a song or two, but this was all. Now and then there was a little wrangle in the press over the merits and tendencies of Strauss. One courageous group of critics dared to say that here was a composer likely to be the next big figure in musical history after Wagner; another group, equally courageous, was steadily occupied in laying up material for the laughter of future generations. Some of these latter gentlemen had already firmly secured their place in history by their opposition, two or three decades ago, to Wagner. Now, with undiminished zeal and energy, anxious to achieve a plural immortality, they industriously plied their mops against the oceanic tide of Strauss. A third group followed the banner of the ingenious gentleman who "hedged" by declaring that Strauss's music was still *sub judice*—as if *all* musicians were not continually *sub judice*. But while it was very gratifying to behold this contest—all fighting being a testimony to life—what was all the strife about? Merely, for the most part over *Don Juan*, a comparatively early work of Strauss, in no way representative of the possibilities of his methods or of the stage of evolution at which he had even then arrived. The real Strauss was to be seen not in *Don Juan* but in *Don Quixote*, *Also sprach Zarathustra*, and *Ein Heldenleben*. Yet the flower of the intelligence of England was wrangling noisily over three works of the composer's youth—*Till Eulenspiegel*, *Tod und Verklärung*, and *Don Juan!* It was as if, in 1881, just before the production of *Parsifal*, the English champions of the rival schools had been slaying each other over the question as to whether Wagner had not gone a little too far in *Tannhäuser* and *Lohengrin*. Verily England was asleep.

Then Strauss himself came twice to the metropolis, first to conduct some miscellaneous works, then to produce his latest tone-poem *Ein Heldenleben*, for the first time in England. Now the interest, or at any rate the curiosity, of London was stirred a little. An abstract, disinterested passion for music itself, a cultivated desire for new things as distinguished from the merely circus interest in new performers, seems beyond the powers of all but a few souls in that vast population. Organised discussion of a new composer only comes into being when he himself happens to be in the city. As Sir Thomas Browne has it, " Some believe the better for seeing Christ's sepulchre ; and when they have seen the Red Sea, doubt not of the miracle." As it was, it is questionable whether so large an audience would have flocked to hear—or to see—Strauss on the *Heldenleben* occasion, if that concert had not also happened to be the first at which Mr. Henry Wood appeared after a long illness. When, some six months later, a three days' Strauss Festival was given at St. James's Hall, with the fine Amsterdam orchestra that plays him so intelligently, and with Mengelberg and Strauss himself as conductors, but this time without a convalescent Mr. Wood, the general public showed disgracefully little interest in the thing. However, the seed had been sown, and its growth has been fairly rapid. We have not yet heard in England the latest work of Strauss—the *Symphonia domestica* — and *Don Quixote*[1] has not been repeated since it was given its solitary English performance at the Festival. But *Ein Heldenleben*—the terrible *Ein Heldenleben*, the bugbear, the bogey of a couple of years ago—has become astonishingly popular. It is played quite frequently ; young ladies barely out of their teens study the score and discuss the love-music appreciatively. *Till Eulenspiegel, Tod und Verklärung, Don Juan,*—these we hear so often that one no longer gets a shock when one sees them on the bills ; even *Also sprach Zarathustra* is occasionally given. *Aus Italien* has had several

[1] It is put down for a performance in London this spring.

performances, and the youthful Symphony in F minor (op. 12) has been played once at least. The violin concerto, the violin sonata, the 'cello sonata, and the piano quartett may all be heard from time to time. So that at last the reproach of total ignorance of Strauss is taken away from us, even if we do not hear so much of him, especially of his very latest works, as we would like.

It is a pity we cannot get more performances of his bigger works, for the amateur who does not hear him often on the orchestra, and who tries to get a knowledge of him from the easier things that can be played at home, is likely to get a very false impression of him. He has passed through so many stages of artistic development that we have only to pick up an early work of his here and there to be capable of a dogmatism concerning him that is ludicrously wrong. I can recall no example in musical history of a man with such native strength and such pronounced individuality suggesting, in his youthful works, so many other musicians of note who have gone before him. You will find in the earlier Strauss abundant traces of Mozart, of Haydn, of Beethoven, of Wagner, of Schumann, of Brahms, of Liszt. Yet the curious thing is that nowhere do we feel that Strauss has been, even for a little time, wholly under the influence of any one of these; he is always himself, though he unaccountably lapses at times into the most distinct reminiscences of the manner of other men. No one but he could have penned the vigorous Piano Sonata (op. 5); in the first movement, for example, not only the *mâle tristesse* of the mood, but the firm and flexible handling is indubitably his. Yet in this same movement, with its modern atmosphere, its modern force, and its modern audacity, he must needs insert passages here and there that go right back to the eighteenth century, in their form, their speech, and their psychology. Something of the same phenomenon meets us again in his Symphony in F minor (op. 12). The singular thing is that he has never had a real Beethoven epoch, or a real Schumann epoch, or a real Wagner epoch ; but that he seemed to fall quite naturally, at times, into bygone modes of feeling and utterance, like a man whose prose style had an unaccountable tendency to lapse, every now and then, into reminiscences of the authors he read most in his youth. The *Guntram* (op. 25) may have looked very Wagnerian when it first appeared ; but as we read it now, in the light of Strauss's later work, it is clear that Wagner does not enter into a twentieth part of the opera. People could pick out the passages that resembled Wagner—particularly that extraordinary reminiscence of *Tristan* which Strauss seems to use so unconsciously—and sum the whole opera up as the work of a mere disciple of Wagner. It was hard in those days to grasp the significance of the more individual parts of *Guntram,* or to frame to oneself a connected scheme of what the composer's psychological processes were. But we can see it all now, after *Also sprach Zarathustra, Don Quixote, Enoch Arden* and the songs ; and it is evident that *Guntram* never owed its origin to

Wagner, but to a mind of quite a different type from his. It is not Wagner's texture, it is above all not Wagner's world-view; it comes from a brain of a different outlook, making its own terminology for itself as it goes along, and only occasionally dropping into the idiom of Strauss's great forerunner. So again with the much-cited influence of Liszt upon him. That the flower of Strauss's achievement has grown up from the soil Liszt watered is unquestionable. But no one work, no section of one work, can be quoted that sounds as if it came direct from Liszt. With the exception of some half-dozen of the juvenile writings, there is nothing of Strauss that does not, in spite of its suggestions of this or that predecessor, belong as completely to him as *Orfeo* does to Gluck or *Lohengrin* to Wagner; while in the work of the last few years, the years of attained maturity and full self-consciousness, he stands proudly, loftily alone, unique among musicians long before he had reached his fortieth year. Yet the tradition that he is merely an artificial blend of Wagner and Liszt will probably hold the field for a long time to come.

So great, again, is the distance between his earlier and his later work that one who only knows him from the efforts of his adolescence is certain to misconceive him. The present Strauss commands respect even from those who think he is merely using his great gifts to achieve perversity and ugliness; but we may go through page after page of his earliest work and yet hardly once come across anything that would make us believe we were face to face with genius. Some of it, like the *Fünf Clavierstücke* (op. 3) and the *Stimmungsbilder* (op. 9), is quite mediocre at times, commonplace in rhythm, weak in structure, and decidedly cheap in melody. Even where his early work was most excellent—and some of it was admirable—it was impossible to say from it that the composer was one of the predestined spirits of music, fated to remove landmarks, to explore undiscovered countries. Clearly it was not a common talent; even in those days it was generally vigorous, audacious, self-confident; but it rarely flamed up into incandescence. In those years of apprenticeship Strauss was quietly and almost unconsciously evolving a musical bias that was to re-mould the æsthetics of music — doubtful yet as to whither his own ideals were drawing him, and no doubt puzzled at times at his failure to get precisely the picture he would have liked, but still remaining autonomous, a new and vigorous force aiming at an idiom of its own. We see now how hopelessly absurd it is to judge the composer of *Also sprach Zarathustra* by any of the standards of the past—that the man's whole mind is unique, seeing things in music that no one ever saw before, and taking the most direct, even if most perilous, path to the expression of them. It took him a long time to learn that he had no great faculty for abstract beauty, for weaving the impalpable stuff of a vision into something that lives and shall be immortal, like the sculptor's work, by virtue of the sheer harmony of every element of its being. The

great test of the existence of this order of beauty
in a musician is to be had in his slow movements.
Mere vigour of rhythm and intensity of colour
here go for less than anywhere else : in this ideal,
abstracted world, where the soul listens darkling,
brooding upon the mystery of things like the
dove upon the waters, the musician's sense of
sheer self-existent beauty must be at its finest ;
and the complete absorption in pure tone that
such a mood demands is the quality of the
absolute rather than of the poetic musician. I
am not for a moment, of course, denying that
Strauss has written some slow passages which
are surcharged with emotional beauty—such as
the " Redemption " theme at the end of *Tod und
Verklärung*, the noble *mit Andacht* section at
the beginning of *Also sprach Zarathustra*, the
pathetic death-music in *Don Quixote*, or the end
of *Ein Heldenleben*. What I mean is that his
is not the order of musical mind to which the
extended formalism of the symphony, with its
intentness on architectonic effect, is the most
propitious. His genius is for the literary rather
than for the architectural or sculpturesque.

Look, for example, at his songs. If his gift
were for sheer musical beauty, the melody that
sings from pure joy in itself, it would certainly
appear here if anywhere. Yet among all his
songs I cannot recall more than one or two
that seem to be written out of the mere heart
of lyrism itself; while in all the really great
ones the magic and the power come not from
pure melodic or harmonic loveliness, but from

R

the sense they give us of absolute emotional veracity—as it were a man speaking upon a lofty subject very gravely and with intense conviction, and so attaining, not the rapturous abandonment of poetry, but an eloquent, impassioned, heart-searching prose.

Strauss is perhaps not a great melodist, if we restrict that term to the meaning it has acquired in the absolute music of the past. Only once, I think—in the slow movement of the Piano Quartett (op. 13)—does he sing himself into that ideal world of ecstasy and enchantment in which the older musicians spent their most golden hours. Here, indeed, he loses sight of that real world of men and things which it has been his glory to make musical for us in his later work; here, indeed, he is content to sing in rapt absorption, content to pour out a flood of tone that shall be all it is meant to be if it is divine, merely "a wonder and a wild desire." This movement stands unique among Strauss's work, both in its pure beauty and in its æsthetic purpose. For once in his life, at all events, the great realist has had his honeyed hour of idealism. But the very qualities of alertness, of quick interest in life, which have gone to make Strauss, in his later music, the symbol of a new era of æsthetics, have prevented him from falling often into that ecstatic, clairvoyant swoon from which the music of the great dreamers has been born. A melody, with him, is not something irresponsibly beautiful, as sheer a delight to the ear as the flight of a bird or the play of sunlight on the water are to the eye, but a commentary upon a character or a situation, aiming at veracity in the first place rather than at self-existent beauty. Hence that impression of tortuous, huddled drawing which we get at times in a work like *Guntram*, where his hand has not yet learned to follow the inward vision with complete fidelity. Hence also the feeling given us occasionally, by some of his melodies, that they are bordering perilously on the commonplace or the obvious—as in the cadence of the charming little folk-song with which *Till Eulenspiegel* ends, or in one or two portions of the finale of *Tod und Verklärung*. The closer a musician comes to pure simplicity the more difficult is it to achieve verisimilitude without dropping into bathos. If Strauss has now and again made us feel that it is only a step from the sublime to the ridiculous, it behoves us to remember also that no musician has ever been so triumphant in his handling of the simplest material—as in some passages of *Also sprach Zarathustra*, the ending of *Ein Heldenleben*, the Sancho Panza music in *Don Quixote*, or the music of the children in *Feuersnot*. If Tchai-kovski brought the last new shudder into music, Strauss has endowed it with a new simplicity. It is this, indeed, that makes him Strauss; for paradoxical as it may seem, this builder of colossal tone-poems, this wielder of the mightiest orchestral language ever yet spoken, this Mad Mullah of harmony, is what he is because he has dared to throw over almost all the conventions that have clustered round the art in the last two hundred years. He is complex because he is simple; he appears so wildly artificial because he is absolutely natural; he is called sophisticated because he casts aside all artifice and speaks like the natural musical man. To establish which position, let us digress for a moment into a discussion of æsthetics.

II

Of all the arts, music is the one whose ideal of form is the loftiest, the most exacting, the most imperative; the art in which we are least willing to tolerate any defection from the highest we can conceive. This, indeed, has been the cause both of the rapid development of music in comparison with the other arts, and of the frenetic warfare of the schools in one generation after another. The intensity of the great musician's desire for ideal perfection in his art leads to his carrying it, within a few years, over a curve of evolution that it takes a century for the other arts to describe. This æsthetic concentration gave us the Beethoven symphony and the Wagner music-drama—each the most perfect thing of its kind, each the most perfect expression of the musical needs of the generation that brought it into life. At the same time this principle of evolution has caused the world, when it discovered how absolutely complete was the musician's achievement of the particular thing he had aimed at, to desire to rest permanently in that form, to regard it as the final word in music. It was so with the symphony according to Beethoven, and with the opera according to Wagner. Now what we have to recognise in the case of Richard Strauss is that he is the destroyer — or at any rate, the symbol of destruction—of all previous values, as Nietzsche would say, and the creator at once of a new expression and a new form.

Music could no more stop at Wagner than it could stop at Bach, Gluck, or Beethoven. The expansion of manner which music underwent at the hands of each of these men, be it noted, was the fruit of a correlative expansion of the mental world of the musician—not the individual musician, but the type. The great interest of Wagner for many of us is that with him, for the first time, music aimed at becoming co-extensive with human life. (So much, I think, may be broadly postulated without entering on very contentious grounds, if we complete the proposition by saying that Berlioz and Liszt — the Liszt of the twelve symphonic poems, the *Dante* symphony and the *Faust* symphony—are to be understood as subsumed under Wagner.) But the very element in his work that made Wagner an unquestionable evolution from Beethoven — the clear perception that in the symphony pure and simple you could never, do what you would, advance entirely out of the decorative into the human, that to concern herself more pointedly with man and the world, music must call in the aid of poetry, with its wider and deeper associations with human life—this was at the same time, curiously enough, the element that marked the limits of the opera and foretold its ultimate passing away.   Opera, it is now evident, is *not* the form of either the present or the future.   It was once the revolutionary form, and under its red banner men imbrued their hands with the gore of their fellow-men ; now it is a classic, and in twenty years we shall have a school that quotes its Wagner against the new troublers of our musical conventions as a former school quoted Mozart and Beethoven against Wagner.   And why is the opera now beginning to be recognised as a limited form, instead of the universal form which Wagner fondly hoped to make it ?   Simply because it has now become clear to us that the admixture of the human voice in music really limits the range of the art as much as the absence of it formerly limited the symphony.   What the old music needed was fertilisation by speech, as Wagner never wearied of telling us ; what music at present needs is emancipation from the tyranny of speech.   A glance at the æsthetic of the art will make this seem less paradoxical than it sounds at first.

As I have tried to show in another essay in this volume, the people who despise programme music as a derogation from the high nature and pure origin of the art are labouring under a delusion.   Music, they say, ought to be able to stand alone, in splendid isolation as it were ; and they regard it as a sign of musical weakness when a composer, associating himself with the literary element of poetry, "calls in to his aid a foreign art," as they express it. All this is based upon a misunderstanding of the real essence of music, and a faulty analysis of the psychological states from which it has sprung. From the very infancy of the art, there have been two main impulses stimulating the musician—the abstract and the human, the decorative and the poetic. The fact that these two are almost always interblended, in one proportion or another, in the actual music we know, does not in any way upset the analysis. Broadly speaking, the revolution effected by Wagner was precisely an infusion of a greater human pre-occupation into an art that had previously been over-intent on the architectural or decorative. He saw that it was impossible for a modern man to say all he wanted to say in a form that attributed relatively too much importance to the propriety of the pattern, and left too little opportunity for the sleuth-like tracking of thoughts as fluid, as complex, as evasive as life itself. On the one hand the transition had to be made from inarticulate to articulate tone, from music as a generalised expression to music as a particularised expression of life ; and this could only be done by conquering for her, by means of speech, a new territory of human interests in which she was to be supreme. On the other hand, there had to be a general break-up of the older official form, and a general discarding of useless garments in order that the limbs of this fresh young art might move more freely. What Wagner's achievement was we know. Apart from his stupendous musical gifts, he will live by the closeness of the bearing of his thought upon actual life ; for he was searchingly real, albeit in his own semi-romantic way.

But the impetus given to music by Wagner could not end where he desired it to end. Already, in his own lifetime, Berlioz and Liszt had hit upon a form of symphonic poem, which, had it not been for the overwhelming vogue of Wagner's operas, would probably have come to be recognised as the pre-eminent form of the nineteenth century. It must always be remembered that Liszt was no mere imitator of Wagner, but that they worked separately for many years on much the same general æsthetic lines — Liszt being, if anything, the one of the twain who saw first the new possibilities of modern music. Now that Wagner's work is done and become a thing of the past — the art-form which he perfected having died with him, so far as we can see at present — the long-submerged trail of Liszt is making its reappearance. Despised as a composer in his own epoch, he is now having a posthumous and vicarious justification in Richard Strauss. Like the river Arethusa, that was lost in one place and came to light again in another, the peculiar psychology of the symphonic poem according to Liszt re-emerges in *Tod und Verklärung* and *Also sprach Zarathustra*, after having been hidden for half a century by the more lyrical, less "representative" art of *Tristan* and the *Meistersinger*. The strong point of Strauss is just that he has shown how often speech can

with the greatest advantage be discarded in
music, because speech, while a fertilising element
up to a certain point, becomes a positive ob-
struction when once that point has been passed.
Where there are words there is necessarily a
human voice, and where there is a voice you are
necessarily bound by the limitations of the voice,
and shut out from one-half of the circle of life.
You can, of course, accept these limitations as
far as the voice itself is concerned, and leave to
the orchestra the portrayal of things that are too
vast, too mysterious, or too terrible to be sung—
which was the method of Wagner. But the
success of this system depends upon the quality
of your subject; and when you come to the big
modern material, and desire to look through music
at the life and the philosophy of your own day,
you will find that the voice is, as often as not, a
hindrance. A subject like *Also sprach Zarathustra*, for example, neither demands nor would
tolerate the human voice in a musical setting of
it. Nietzsche's book is not lyrical, not dramatic;
it is—or purports to be—a piece of philosophy,
a reflection upon the cosmos as it appears to a
bitter, disillusioned modern man. In weaving
music into a gigantic scheme like this, the tiny
egoistic tinkle of the human voice would be a
ludicrous descent into bathos.[1] We have only to

---

[1] It is worth noting how Berlioz justified his own setting of some
passages in *Roméo et Juliette* orchestrally instead of vocally. "If,"
he says, "in the celebrated scenes of the garden and the ceme-
tery, the dialogue of the two lovers, the *a parte* of Juliet and the
passionate outbursts of Romeo are not vocalised, if, in short, the
duets of love and despair are confided to the orchestra, the reasons

look round at the music of the past hundred years to see that, as its psychology extended, it first of all required speech to gain it access to one new territory, and then had to throw over speech in order to secure entrance into a territory still more remote and more mysterious. This is the environment towards which Strauss has had to feel his way through one experiment after another.

Now just as Wagner's music, though more complex than the old art in certain respects, was simpler than the old in that it substituted a natural for a stilted form of operatic speech—a revolution similar to that effected in English poetry by the lyrical writers of the end of the eighteenth and beginning of the nineteenth centuries—so Strauss represents yet another movement towards naturalness, when compared with contemporary music-makers like Brahms or even Tchaikovski. The proof of this is writ large over almost all his music, from opus 5 onwards ; it is visible everywhere, in his melodies, his rhythms, his harmonies, his *facture*. Now and again, of course, there is a lapse into the polite formalities which come so fatally easy to the

for this are numerous and easy to grasp. First, because we are dealing with a symphony, not with an opera. Secondly, duets of this nature having been treated vocally a thousand times, and by the greatest masters, there was both prudence and curiosity in trying another mode of expression. It is, moreover, because the very sublimity of this love made the painting of it so dangerous for the musician, that he had to give his imagination a latitude which the positive connotations of chanted words would not have permitted him, by resorting to the instrumental language—a language richer, more varied, less restricted, and by its very indefiniteness incomparably more powerful in cases of this kind."

musician of all artists. But on the whole Strauss gives one the impression of a singularly fresh and unconventional temperament, whose new mode of vision spontaneously generates its own new manner of utterance. The peculiar quality of his mature style is its absolute *Selbstständigkeit*—its entire independence, throughout its whole texture, of any laws but its own. I need not speak of his marvellous orchestration, for his overlordship there is unquestionable. But we need only look at his harmonies—those harmonies which are the horror of a great many people who are by no means academics—to see how supremely natural, how infinitely remote from the mere desire to stagger humanity,[1] is the style of Strauss even in its most defiant moments.[2] What was said of old of the harmonies of Wagner is now being said of the

[1] The reader will, of course, remember that I am here speaking only of the *tissue* of Strauss's work. In the intellectual part of it, as I shall show later, he sometimes does things with the deliberate intention of startling us. See Section IV. of this essay.

[2] Perhaps I ought to except such things as the passage in *Ein Heldenleben* (page 50 of the full score), where the strings and oboe run up in sevenths, instead of the sixths we expect—an agonising thing that always sounds as if somebody in the orchestra had made a mistake. Either Strauss wrote it so out of pure devilment, with his tongue in his cheek all the time, or it may answer to some subtle harmony in his brain that ours are incompetent to grasp. There can be no doubt that his ear must be vastly more acute than the normal organ. As Mr. James Huneker puts it in a brilliant article in his *Overtones*: " His is the most marvellous agglomeration of cortical cells that science has ever recorded. So acute are his powers of acoustical differentiation that he must hear, not alone tones beyond the base and the top of the normal scale unheard of by ordinary humans, but he must also hear, or rather overhear, the vibratory waves from all individual sounds. His music gives us the impression of new over-tones, of scales that violate the well-tempered, of tonalities that approximate to the quarter-tones of Oriental music."

harmonies of his successor. I will frankly admit that there are certain things among them which are a cruel laceration of our ears—things at which we can only cross ourselves piously, as at the profanity of the natural man at the street corner, and hurry on our way. These deviations from the normal are mostly to be seen in his songs, where he permits himself a much broader license than in any of his other works. For the rest, it will be found that, a few eccentricities apart, our first prejudice against most of his novel harmonies and progressions is due simply to their unexpectedness, and that as soon as we have grown accustomed to them they seem quite logical and inevitable. Undoubtedly our palate for harmony has been cloyed by too much of the saccharine ; the tonic, astringent quality of the discord has not yet been sufficiently appreciated by any musician but Strauss. Like all other superstitions, the harmonic superstition cannot survive the bold experimenter. One's faith in the malign powers that dog the footsteps of him who walks under a ladder, or spills the salt at table, receives a rude shock when we find a man tempting Providence in this way and coming to no particular harm ; and many things in music that we would *à priori* pronounce impossible look quite simple and natural when they are actually done. To end a big orchestral work with reiterated successions of the chord of B natural followed by the tonic of C natural seems like a device of Colney Hatch ; but it is strangely suggestive and hugely impressive in *Also sprach Zarathustra*.

Of course the invention and elaboration of a new technique are very difficult matters; and it is only to be expected that here and there Strauss should give us the impression of not being quite at home even in his own territory. Nothing could be more audacious, or, as a rule, more successful, than his bland persistence in a certain figure or a certain sequence when the chances are all in favour of the thing toppling down like a house of cards long before he can reach the summit; there is something positively grim and eerie, at times, in the *nonchalant* way Strauss steers his bark through all the dangers of the musical deep. In the lovely song *Ich schwebe* (op. 48, No. 2), for example, one is alternately astonished and amused at the freedom of the harmonic sequences; one hardly knows whether to be angry at the cool unconventionality with which we are being treated, or to chuckle with delight at the sheer impudence of the performance. Strauss seems to think it a fallacy to look upon chords as being built up from a certain base. In a way, his system is a reversion to the view of the old contrapuntists, that music is a matter of a series of horizontal lines, not of the vertical lines into which the thoughts of the modern harmonist have come to flow. Substitute horizontal figures or groups for horizontal lines, and we have the distinction between the harmonic Strauss in his more daring moments, and, say, the harmonic Tchaikovski. A certain sequence of chords has to be carried through, willy-nilly, in one part of the piano or of the orchestra;

another and quite independent sequence has to be carried through, willy-nilly, in another part. They are heard against each other at every point of their career. If they blend, according to the current notions of harmony, well and good; if they do not, equally well and good. You are only shocked for the moment, says Strauss, because your ear has become sophisticated, artificialised, by dwelling too long in the conventional harmonic atmosphere that has been manufactured for you; you must learn to breathe a new atmosphere, to take delight in a new type of musical sequence, wherein opposing notes or opposing chords go each to its own appointed end, regardless of isolated harmonic effects, or of certain cramping formalities known as "resolutions." We have to learn to think horizontally. In musical matters, however, it takes even the most advanced of us a little time to readjust our point of view; and whether it is that we are not yet quite worthy of the light of the new dispensation, or whether the voice of the prophet fails him at times and his speech becomes a little thick and his thought a trifle incoherent, it is certain that Strauss now and again tries our patience somewhat. Here and there in *Ein Heldenleben* and some of the maddest of the songs we feel that no amount of familiarity with the music will ever make us like certain effects—or defects—of harmony; and even in a great song like the *Traum durch die Dämmerung* (op. 29, No. 1) we have an uneasy feeling, at more than one point, that instead of Strauss being the master he has become

the servant of his material. There is just a
suspicion, here and there, that he is working his
pre-ordained sequence a shade too rigidly, and
that he would have gained by relaxing it a little.
In any case, as I have already remarked, it is
generally in his songs—which, beautiful as they
are, are not the most important part of his work
—that his harmonic system is most apt to take our
breath away ; though I cannot agree with a recent
writer that the harmonies are merely " wild ex-
perimentation." In ninety-nine cases out of a
hundred they seem to me perfectly spontaneous,
even when they are most trying ; I think Strauss
writes precisely as he feels, without any mere
attempt, in cold blood, to achieve the unexpected
or the impossible. One frequent cause of the
novelty of his harmonic progressions is that he
resolves the constituent tones of his chords in
any part of the gamut he chooses. This, of
course, is only a continuance of a tendency that
has been going on in music for the last hundred
years ; and Wagner and Liszt have made certain
resolutions of this kind so familiar to us that they
now excite no comment. In another half-century
the majority of the new harmonies and new
resolutions of Strauss will probably be part
of the common vocabulary of every musical
penny-a-liner.

Whatever may be thought, however, of the
sincerity or artificiality of his harmonies, there
can be no question that in his melodies and his
rhythms he is pre-eminently natural and unforced.
Once he had got rid of the suspicion of medio-

crity that hung about him in his earlier works, owing to his having momentarily taken up with the wrong artistic company, he made rapid progress along a line that was peculiarly his own. No one can listen to *Don Juan*, for example (op. 20), without feeling how exquisitely fresh is the work, how absolutely adolescent in the best sense. Here for the first time we have a revelation of what the future Strauss was to be—the writer of a new music, in which the expression and the technique shall follow the poetic idea with an unquestioning, unswerving fidelity. He is now acquiring an instrument of speech that, in its power to bite into the essentials of an object, reminds us of the consummate style of Flaubert or Maupassant; the realist Strauss is coming into view. All the previous works of any importance—the Symphony in F minor (op. 12), the String Quartett (op. 13), the *Wanderers Sturmlied* (op. 14), *Aus Italien* (op. 16), and the Violin Sonata (op. 18)—had been preliminary studies for this. In these works we see Strauss finally emerging from the slough of polite acquiescence in the manners of his forerunners which had been now and then painfully evident in the *Fünf Klavierstücke* (op. 3) and the *Stimmungsbilder* (op. 9), and even at times in the virile, breezy Piano Sonata (op. 5). He gradually forms a musical style of his own, in which the idiom is extraordinarily spontaneous and forceful. The melody becomes more serpentiform, more flexibly articulated, more and more independent, in its rhythm, of the four or eight-bar props upon which composers generally find it so convenient to lean. I do not refer so much to the mere crossing or interlocking of rhythms which the *Wanderers Sturmlied* and *Also sprach Zarathustra* exhibit here and there, for this is more or less an affair of merely conscious technique, which may, as is frequently the case in Brahms, exist rather on paper than in actuality, and make more impression on the eye than on the ear. The rhythmical interest of the juvenile works of Strauss lies rather in the growing sense of perfect freedom and naturalness in the trajectory of the melodies. All the new qualities of the works that lie between opus 12 and opus 18 come to their fine fruition in *Don Juan*, which is the first work of Strauss that shows in something like its entirety the true psychology, æsthetic and moral, of the man.

III

Upon some features of that psychology—its sincerity, its originality, its artistic fearlessness— I have already touched. Strauss, however, is an epoch-making man not only in virtue of his expression and his technique, but in virtue of the range and the quality of his subjects. He is the first complete realist in music. The Romantic movement came to a somewhat belated head in Wagner, who had been the chief master of the ceremonies at the prolonged funeral of the classical spirit. The Romantic movement persisted longer in music than in any of the other arts ; and even

in our own day it still makes an occasional ineffectual effort to raise its old head, ludicrous now
with its faded garlands of flowers overhanging
the wrinkled cheeks. But it has done its work,
and the future is with the men who live not in
that old and somewhat artificial world of gloomy
forests, enchanted castles, men that are like gods
and gods that are like men, impossible maidens,
and superannuated professors of magic,[1] but in a
world recognisably similar to that in which we
ourselves move from day to day. We like our
art to have a rather more acrid taste, and to
come to closer quarters with reality. Even the
apparatus of the Wagnerian opera seems to us a
trifle *vieux-jeu* in these days. Strauss has wisely
recognised that the operatic form, at its worst a
ludicrous parody on life, is at its best only a compromise, limited in its choice of subjects no less
than in its structure. Much greater freedom is
to be had in the symphonic poem, or in other
purely instrumental modern forms, because here
we have at once a wider range of subjects open
to us, and a medium of expression into which the
voice, with its limiting associations, does not enter.
Nothing but the freest, most expansive of forms
could be suited to the peculiar temperament of a

---

[1] In *Feuersnot*, it may be said, Strauss himself goes back for a
moment to something like that old world. But he does not take
it seriously ; the quaint mediæval story is only a background
against which he can display his passion, his humour, his irony.
Wagner would have made a portentous thing of the *Feuersnot*
subject ; he would have discovered the profoundest philosophy
and ethic in it. Strauss behaves towards it like a graceless,
irreverent urchin in a cathedral.

realist like Strauss, and fine as his own opera work is, bubbling over, as *Feuersnot* is, with life and humour, it is not there that we see the essential Strauss.

For it is as a realist that he is most remarkable. He is not a dreamer, nor a philosopher, except in so far as philosophy—in Mr. Meredith's sense of the term—is at the centre of every great artist's vision of life. He is at his best in studies of character in action, as in *Till Eulenspiegel* and *Don Quixote ;* and he follows his trail with the most cheerful disregard as to whether his work is or is not formal music in the older acceptations of the word. Further, his interest is in human life as a whole, not in the one wearisome episode of the eternal masculine and the eternal feminine. Strauss's is the cleanest, most sexless, most athletic music I know. Just as it is the easiest thing in the world to make love, so is the making of love-music the easiest part of the musician's trade. It is one other sign of the death of the Romantic spirit and the revival of realism in Strauss that he should have thrown over almost all the old erotic tags of the musician —though he can be passionate enough upon occasion—in order to tell the story, in the true modern spirit, of other elements in human life that also have their poetry and their pathos. One refreshing characteristic of the earlier works—such as the Piano Sonata, the Violin Sonata, and the Piano Quartett — was their unclouded virility, their total freedom from those phantasms of sex that have been hovering over so much of our

music during the past century.　The adolescent
work of Strauss is proud, vigorous, uncontami-
nated, Greek in quality.　Even in the *Don Juan*,
it may be noted, his interest is in another aspect
of the story than the blatantly erotic; and the
music itself is plainly not the work of a Romanticist
but of a realist and humanist.　The love-themes
in *Don Juan* are not sexual in the way that
Wagner or Tchaikovski, for example, would have
made them.　Even in his songs his love-making
is grave and philosophical, with none of the feline
sex-element showing through it that is so pro-
minent in Wagner; Strauss is untroubled by the
hysterica passio of the tiles.　For this generation,
at all events, the last word in mere sex-music has
been said in *Tristan and Isolde*; and instead of
imitating his weaker brethren, who occupy themselves energetically in vending the spilth of
Wagner's wine, Strauss has turned his eyes
upon other elements than the erotic in the
human composition.　Hence the cosmic magnificence of conception of *Also sprach Zarathustra*,
the graphic humour of *Till Eulenspiegel*, and
the supreme humanity of his greatest work, *Don
Quixote*.

I call this his greatest work, because it is the
one in which his qualities of realist and humanist
come to their finest flower.　It has all the fervour
of *Don Juan*, and all the humour of *Till Eulenspiegel*, with a technique still more amazing than
that of either of these works, and that riper feeling
that could only come to him with the process of
the years.　I would rank the *Don Quixote* higher

even than *Also sprach Zarathustra*, because of this sensation that it gives us of the enormous fund of sincere emotion that underlies all Strauss's audacity and cleverness, and that never leaves him even in his moments of most reckless humour. Certainly *Also sprach Zarathustra* is a marvellous work ; no such overwhelming picture of man and the universe has ever before been unfolded to our eyes in music ; it almost makes the world-philosophy of Wagner seem, in comparison, like the bleat of evangelical orthodoxy. But it is in the *Don Quixote* that Strauss is most really and truly himself and most thoroughly human. It is here also that every trace of other men's style has definitely disappeared, for even in *Also sprach Zarathustra* we seem at times to catch the voice of Liszt. The *Don Quixote* marks the final rupture of the realist and the romantic schools in music. I say nothing here of its technique, though that alone is sufficient to make one ask oneself whether it is possible for music to develop further than this. Nowhere, outside the work of glorious old Bach, is there such a combination in music of inexhaustible fertility of imagination and the most rigid austerity in the choice of material. Description would avail nothing for these aspects of *Don Quixote;* every student must revel in the riches of the work on his own account. But when we consider its more human qualities, the *Don Quixote* must be pronounced an epoch-making work, both in its form and its psychology. It is not a symphonic poem, but a series of variations upon practically three themes—Don Quixote, Sancho Panza, and Dulcinea ; and for wit, humour, pathos, and humanism there is nothing like it in the whole library of music.   Certainly to any one who knows Strauss's music of *Don Quixote*, the story of Cervantes is henceforth inconceivable without it ; the story itself, indeed, has not half the humour and the profound sadness which is infused into it by Strauss.   What he has done in this work is to inaugurate the period of the novel in music.   We have had our immortal lyrists, our sculptors, our dramatists, our builders of exquisite temples ; we now come to the writers of fiction, to our Flaubert and Tourgeniev and Dostoievski.   And here we see the subtle fitness of things that has deprived Strauss of those purely lyrical qualities, whose absence, as I have previously argued, makes it impossible for him to be an absolute creator of shapes of pure self-sustained beauty.   His type of melody is now seen to be not a failing but a magnificent gift.   It is the prose of music—a grave, flexible, eloquent prose, the one instrument in the world that is suitable for the prose fiction in music that it is Strauss's destiny to develop.   His style is nervous, compact, sinuous, as good prose should be, which, as it is related, through its subject-matter, more responsibly to life than is poetry, must relinquish some of the fine abandonment of song, and find its compensation in a perfect blend, a perfect compromise, of logic and rapture, truth and ideality.   "I can conceive," says Flaubert in one of his letters, "a style which should be beautiful ; which some one

will write one of these days, in ten years or in
ten centuries; which shall be rhythmical as verse,
precise as the language of science, and with un-
dulations, modulations as of a violoncello, flashes
of fire; a style which would enter into the idea
like the stroke of a stiletto; a style on which our
thoughts would sail over gleaming surfaces, as it
were, in a boat with a good wind aft.   It must
be said that prose is born of yesterday; verse is
the form *par excellence* of the ancient literatures.
All the prosodic combinations have been made;
but those of prose are still to make."

No better description, it seems to me, could
be had of the musical style of Strauss, with
its constant adaptation to the emotional and
intellectual atmosphere of the moment, and its
appropriateness to the realistic suggestion of
character and *milieu* which is his mission in
music.   His qualities are homogeneous; he is
not a Wagner *manqué* nor an illegitimate son
of Liszt, but the creator of a new order of things
in music, the founder of a new type of art.   The
only test of a literature being alive is, as Dr.
Georg Brandes says, whether it gives rise to
new problems, new questionings.   Judged by
this test, the art of Strauss is the main sign of
new and independent life in music since Wagner;
for it perpetually spurs us on to fresh problems
of æsthetics, of psychology, and of form.

IV

It is not difficult to understand the attitude of musical purists towards Strauss, and of many others who are not altogether purists. There is something provocative, defiant, almost repellent, in the power of the man's genius. He is so enormously strong, so proudly self-confident, that he joys in flouting the world in the face as it has never been flouted before. His whole career is a testimony to how far courage and resource can carry a man. According to all known precedents, he ought to have struggled for years, vainly endeavouring to get a bare hearing; when he was actually performed he should have been crushed under critical ridicule and poisoned with critical venom; he should have had a ceaseless fight with singers, with players, with opera-houses, with publishers, with concert-givers, and have perished miserably, a martyr to an impossible ideal. For sheer indifference to other people's opinion, for sheer determination to go his own way without regard for all the time-honoured conventions, there is simply nothing like him in the history of music. Yet his career has been one of unbroken triumph. At the age of forty he is not only recognised as the most astonishing of European musicians, but there is no demand of his, no matter how imperious, that people do not gladly hasten to fulfil. In *Zarathustra* he apparently reaches the limits of what can be demanded from a human orchestra; yet in *Don Quixote*, and again in *Ein Heldenleben*, he strains their breaking sinews to a still higher tension; while in the *Symphonia domestica* he treats them and us with a superb, tyrannic insolence. Never before has an orchestra of sixty-two strings, two harps, a piccolo, three flutes, two oboes, an oboe d'amore, a cor anglais, five clarinets, five bassoons, four saxophones, eight horns, four trumpets, three trombones, a bass tuba, four kettledrums, a triangle, a tambourine, a glockenspiel, cymbals, and a big drum, been required to describe a day in the life of a baby; never before have the energies of over a hundred able-bodied men been bent to such a task. He tunes his strings below the normal limit just as he likes; he employs obsolete instruments, and others that are never used in concert-orchestras; he multiplies difficulties, and, by reason of the many rehearsals required, makes performances of his works enormously expensive affairs. Yet he does it all with sublime impunity. An Oriental potentate riding his horse contemptuously over the prostrate bodies of a half-adoring, half-resentful populace, is the only image that will justly describe him in his forceful, irresistible career. The gods have indeed smiled on Strauss. Much of his success, or of his power to command success, may no doubt be due to financial causes; he has never had to fight the world with an empty purse and empty stomach. But still he is the most remarkable phenomenon the musical world has ever seen; no composer ever insulted

us one quarter so much without having the life
drubbed out of him.

He is evidently a man of enormous nervous
energy. You can see it, for one thing, in the style
of his melodies. They are remarkable for their
huge leaps, the great arcs they traverse, the
wide distances between their parts—all pointing
to great waves of nervous energy that cannot
be confined within the narrow bounds of the
ordinary melody. Occasionally it does him
rather a disservice; it becomes his master
instead of his servant. There is really no need
for this incessant piling-up of more and more
sound in the orchestra; its one sufficient condemnation is that frequently no result comes
out commensurate with the huge means that
have to be employed. Thousands of pages of
our modern music would be equally great, equally
moving, with a vastly smaller expenditure of
effort. A man like Strauss takes an exuberant
joy, the joy of a healthy athlete doing difficult
feats, in weaving a musical texture that is a
marvel of ingenious technique. It looks, and
really is, wonderful on paper; but there is no
gainsaying that precisely the same effect could
often be achieved by much simpler means. Now
and again we find ourselves saying that line after
line might have been struck out of the score
without any of the final effect being lost. Nay,
Strauss's absorption in the pure joy of scoring
occasionally leads him into errors of technique
that a smaller man would have escaped. In the
dance in *Zarathustra*, for example, his excessive

subdivision of the strings merely results in the waltz-theme coming out far too feebly. His own specification at the beginning of the score is for sixteen first violins (to consider this section alone). In the waltz he divides them into (1) first desk, (2) second, third, fourth, and fifth desks. Then he divides the first desk again, giving part of them an arpeggio figure, and the remainder a theme in two parts, involving a further subdivision of this small remainder. The result is that the melody is shorn of all its power. He has marked it *forte*, but a *forte* is impossible, even with the proper toning down of the rest of the strings. There is no earthly need for such a page as this. The whole strength of the strings is frittered away upon things that do not come out, and would be quite unimportant if they did come out; and the really important theme is shorn of all its impressiveness. There is really no necessity for a great deal of the orchestral complexity in which Strauss now and then delights. It is not essential to the proper presentation of his ideas; it puts an unnecessary strain on the time and the nerves of the orchestra; and it tempts young admirers to go and do likewise, with results absolutely fatal to their chance of getting a performance from any conductor.

It may be that we are only beating the air in calling Strauss's attention to facts like these; it may be that without his defects we should not have his qualities, that the turbulent flood of energy that leads him into occasional extravagances of scoring is only part of the greater flood

that makes his inspiration the colossal, overwhelming thing it is. All through the man's
brain there is a touch of disorder, a strain of
something or other abnormal, that makes it hard
for him to work at anything for ten minutes without an irresistible desire surging up in him to
deface it. He works at the picture like the soul
of inspiration itself; then suddenly a saturnine
whim shoots along his nerves, and he makes a
long erratic stroke with the brush that comes
perilously near to destroying the harmony of the
whole thing. An able critic once expressed it to
me, after a performance of *Ein Heldenleben*, that
Strauss as a composer was something like Rubinstein as a pianist—he cannot go through anything
of any length without doing at least one foolish
thing in it. Roughly speaking he was right.
Shall we say that in every great musician there is
a flaw in the mental structure that has to show in
one way or another, and that those are lucky in
whom it does not show in their music? So much
folly, that is, is given to each of them, and it has
to come out somewhere. In Wagner it came
out in the prose works; they were a beneficent
scheme of Providence for sweeping the brain free
of its cobwebs, and leaving the purified instrument in all the better condition for its music.
Beethoven's madness came out in his private life,
again leaving the brain working in music in perfect ease and balance. Strauss does not write
prose works like Wagner, and does not, like Beethoven, pour the water all over himself when he
is washing his hands, or use a lady's candle-

snuffers as a tooth-pick. He is distressingly normal in these respects; and lacking such safety valves for the little bit of folly there is in him, it unfortunately comes out in his music. In the earlier days he could give full rein to his humour, his power of characterisation, with the minimum of desire to irritate his hearer for the pure love of the thing; in *Till Eulenspiegel*, for example, it is almost all pure delight, a flow of wit and humour that only for a moment or two is interrupted by the antics of the mischievous schoolboy. But after that the tendency grew seriously on Strauss to mar his picture by some piece of malicious folly, to thrust his head through the canvas and grin at the public, or to place his thumb to his nose and extend his fingers at them in a derisive flourish.

It is in *Ein Heldenleben* that this tendency is seen at its worst. With all its great beauties and its titanic powers, it remains finally less satisfactory than it easily might have been. It is not all bathed in the one light; the picture has been seen disconnectedly; it is an attempt at the marriage of contrarieties. The great question is, What does *Ein Heldenleben* purport to represent? Is it meant for a purely objective painting of a hero — a representation, as it were, of the hero, *per se*—or is it intended, in parts at least, to draw the hearer's attention to the personality of Strauss himself? The official explanation of the work—authorised, we are told, by the composer — is that *Ein Heldenleben* is meant as a kind of pendant to *Don Quixote*. There he had sketched an individual figure, "whose vain search after heroism leads to insanity." Here he was concerned to present "not a single poetic or historical figure, but rather a more general and free ideal of great and manly heroism"; and the idea that the hero of the poem is anywhere Strauss himself is scouted vigorously.

Now, as regards the general handling of the music, it is, I think, because Strauss has had this generalised picture in his mind that he has here come to grief. *Don Quixote* is such a masterpiece of humanism precisely because Strauss has confined himself to a strictly human figure. You can psychologise both broadly and minutely about a human character, but it is extremely difficult to make a pure abstraction interesting. At every step you are likely to fall into either the bombastic or the commonplace. Especially in music should an abstraction be treated as broadly as possible ; the only hope of salvation lies in avoiding an absurd contrast between the particular and the general. This is precisely what Strauss, with all his genius, has not succeeded in avoiding ; and when we come to examine his scheme a little more closely, we have every reason to be dissatisfied with the authorised version of its purport. In the first place, this hero in the abstract, this representative of "a more general and free ideal of great and manly heroism," becomes less and less a generalised type as the work goes on, and at last—in spite of what the inspired commentators may say—strikes a great many of us as being nothing more nor less than a musician—

rather a singular narrowing, surely, of the conception of a hero ; and this musician has a curious resemblance to Strauss himself. No official disclaimers can get rid of those twenty or twenty-five quotations from Strauss's own earlier works which figure as " the Hero's Works of Peace " in the authorised analysis. The ingenious remark of the analyst, that " quoting salient features from his most important works, he lets us see that the experiences of the hero have also been his own," is really the idlest trifling. When a man sets out to describe a typical hero, a " general and free ideal of great and manly heroism," he does not, as a rule, give as samples of that universal hero's activity a bunch of quotations from almost every work he himself has already written. To have done this seriously would have argued a ludicrous egoism in Strauss ; and, in spite of the official story, I prefer to believe that he was not quite so absurd as this. We are here face to face with that curious muddling of the purpose, that perverse desire to stick his own head through the canvas, that is occasionally so characteristic of him. He cannot resist the impulse at once to exhibit his marvellous technique, and to fling a pot of paint in the public's face, as Ruskin said of Whistler ; and the result is this wonderfully clever but psychologically unjustifiable rhapsody upon himself, inserted in the middle of what is meant to be a purely objective portrait of a hero. It is not easy, again, to understand the significance or see the appropriateness of the section entitled " The Hero's Battlefield." If ever there was anything in music that could be said to aim at suggesting, crudely and melodramatically, the horror and the nervous excitement of a physical conflict between armed hosts, it is this section, with its appalling and hideous racket, that sounds like strenuous boiler-riveting. But *musicians* do not fight battles of this kind, surely ; and a scheme that represents a hero whose " works of peace " are purely intellectual becomes nonsense when it depicts him fighting like a Hooligan among Hooligans, bludgeoning and being bludgeoned.

It is all due, of course, to this muddling up of the two plans—that of a very definite hero whom Strauss knows very well, and that of a generalised and indefinite hero whom he finds himself compelled to describe in the biggest superlatives. The two conceptions will not equate, will not blend ; the one is always trying to destroy the other. All through the work one is dimly conscious of an absence of homogeneity, of failure to make the general scheme as coherent and convincing as it might be ; though the man's genius is so titanic that it almost kills our criticism while we are listening to the work. It is a pity, too, that he should sacrifice for a moment the nobility of the general scheme in order to turn aside for a trifling *jeu d'esprit*, in the notorious section that treats of the hero's antagonists. There is cleverness in the characterisation ; Strauss is painting the portraits of individual critics who have annoyed him, and those who have seen him, at rehearsal, suggest to the eyes of the players the different types he is satirising,

must needs laugh even against their own will.
But the section as a whole is a monstrosity ; and
it is lamentable to see a great genius turn aside
from that mighty statue that he has just begun
to carve, in order to vent his personal feeling
against his personal antagonists.   It is simply a
crime against art.

V

It is in *Ein Heldenleben*, more than anywhere
else, that we have the defects of Strauss's qualities.
He is of the type that, masterly as its self-control
generally is, cannot refrain at times from becoming defiantly extravagant.   It all goes along with
his enormous vital energy, that energy which is
met with in only one or two men in every century,
and that invariably prompts its possessor now
and then to the commission of something or
other we would rather have had left undone.
There is in Strauss something of the *déborde-
ment* of Rabelais, a lust of existence and of
apprehension too big to be kept within normal
bounds.   There is something in him, too, of
Hokusai—that colossal genius whose eager spirit
seemed to try to fill every corner, every crevice,
of the visible world ; something of the Japanese
artist's interest in all forms of life, something too
of the same occasional corruption of the imagination—as in the unfinished series of prints entitled
The Hundred Tales, where the artist, out of the
very excess of his power and ardour, turns life

T

into a hideous, terrifying mockery of itself. Strauss is cosmic in his understanding and his sympathies, but not as men like Goethe and Leonardo are, whose vision is always clear, and whose energies are always held in check by another energy higher than themselves; like Rabelais, like Hokusai, like Goya, there come to him moments when the flood of life within him overflows, and he is hardly master of the strange shapes that issue from his brain. A positive artistic rage seizes him, and he embraces life with an ardour that is cruel, brutal—a passion that has a touch of Sadism in it.

If this enormous sensitiveness to everything that goes on in the world, and this quickness of reaction of the imagination upon it all, are answerable for Strauss's occasional lapses from good taste, they account also for the profounder and more vital qualities of his art—his humour and his humanism, the qualities that make *Feuersnot* so delightful and *Don Quixote* so exceedingly great. London treated the latter work unkindly at its solitary hearing of it; it is, indeed, too vast, too many-sided, to be understood at first acquaintance. One critic called it "ugly, laboured, and eccentric"; another wrote that it "contains more sheer ugliness than any other score written by any responsible person of whom we have ever heard, or whose work we have ever studied. . . . Everything seems in *Don Quixote* to be discordant for the sheer sake of discord. . . . We condemn that work from every musicianly point of view; the thing is an artistic arrogance, an attempt to make the best out of the worst, . . . utterly and completely a failure ; it has no recommendation of beauty, not even the recommendation of fine construction ; it is a hopeless piece of exaggerated and intentional cleverness." Well, a significant thing happened on the very night on which *Don Quixote* created such heartburning. This frightfully complex work, which was absolutely unknown to more than perhaps ten people in the audience, and was consequently misunderstood almost from first to last, was followed by the much earlier *Tod und Verklärung*, a work which itself, a few years ago, was looked upon as perilously near folly and ugliness. Anyone who now thinks *Tod und Verklärung* a tough nut to crack is looked upon as a hopeless Conservative in music, so very quickly does the world move in these matters. Even the *Times* said that after *Don Quixote* the *Tod und Verklärung* sounded quite sane and normal, or words to that effect. We know how *Also sprach Zarathustra* was received in 1897, and how accustomed we have grown to it since then, on the strength of some three or four per-formances ; we know how many people who shied nervously at the first performance of *Ein Heldenleben* now take it as easily as a cat laps milk. In the face of facts like these, is it not somewhat hasty to bespatter the *Don Quixote* with opprobious epithets on the strength of just one performance? People have blundered over Strauss before, and been compelled to eat their words when they came to know him better ; they have run away from the ogre like frightened children, only to discover long after that the supposed ogre was a kindly and well-disposed person, of something more than ordinary human build perhaps, but still on the plane of normal, not sub-normal nor super-normal, humanity. I say with confidence that they will in time admit that they have gone grievously astray over *Don Quixote.* It lies on the mere surface of the matter that some parts of it are ravishingly beautiful ; you have only to play for yourself on the piano the death music, or the Don's long eulogy of the knightly life, to feel the very heart leap within you. If this is not surpassingly great music there is no music in the world worthy of the name. Of other parts the beauty will be perceived when the work is better known ; and the *Don Quixote* will then be recognised to be in some ways the profoundest, noblest thing Strauss has ever done. It is, of course, extraordinarily realistic in its imitations at times, and I can imagine how the sheep and the wind-machine jar on the nerves of ordinarily sensitive people. But you must just laugh at these things and pass them by, take them as a piece of deliberate musical impertinence, and laugh with the composer, not at him. It is really a gratuitous assumption that Strauss is a fool because he has given free wing to his *diablerie* here and there ; he knows as well as any one the precise value of all this kind of thing, but he apparently claims that once or twice in a lifetime it is worth doing for the pure fun of it. We must first of all get

the right point of view if we are to understand
Don Quixote. It is all set in a strange, mad
atmosphere; the folly that hovers round it is
part of the psychology of the piece; and it is the
perfect transmutation of the mental processes of
Quixote into tone that makes the work so
wonderful, so unique. If a man is not smitten
through and through by the pathos of section
after section of the piece, I can only say, for my
part, that he has not grasped the real significance
of the work. Frequent hearing of it will make
the extraordinarily original musical tissue quite
familiar to men's ears, and when this has been
done there will be no bar to the comprehension
of the profoundly human psychology of a masterpiece that only Strauss could have written. The
score is a treasure-house of true and noble things,
which only come to you in full force when you
have steeped yourself in its strange atmosphere.
Take, for example, the variation immediately
preceding the Finale, representing the weary
homeward ride of Quixote and Sancho after the
Don's defeat by the Knight of the White Moon.
In these long descending wails of the orchestra
you have all the anguish, all the disillusionment
of the poor knight painted with an expressiveness, a fidelity, that sets one thinking of visual
as well as auditory things. He illustrates the
scene as consummately as a pictorial artist could
do, and at the same time throws over it the melt-
ing melancholy that music alone among the arts
can express. You can see these poor broken
creatures, with bowed heads, pacing wearily along

on steeds no less sorry, no less bruised than themselves. The whole thing breathes physical and mental fatigue and moral despair. The score of *Don Quixote* is full of a human quality that we rarely get to such perfection anywhere else, even in Strauss ; and London lost a golden opportunity in not taking the work to its heart at once. As it was, the more obvious bits of realism in it revolted a good many people, and left them with insufficient patience to seek beneath the better kind of humour for the pathos that under-lies it ; while the extraordinary complexity of the musical tissue was all against a comprehension of ,the work at a first hearing.

What makes the *Don Quixote* so great a work is, in a word, the wise and tender humanity of its humour. We can put aside, if we like, all the wonderful witchery of its technique, its extra-ordinary graphic power, its exhilarating and amusing imitations of reality—for there is here a descriptive sense surpassing in its manifestations *Till Eulenspiegel* and *Ein Heldenleben* at their best. The wise man, who accepts with thankful-ness all that music can give him, will not reject all this with a sneer and a condescending remark about music "confining itself to its proper pro-vince." The day has gone by for primitive academic æsthetics of that kind. But I do not want to lay stress upon this side of *Don Quixote*, simply because there is infinitely more in the work than this. It represents musical character-sketching brought to a finer point of perfection than can be met with anywhere outside the magic world of Wagner. But it differs from Wagner's drawing in that it is less opulent, more concise, more sharply conceived; it is wholly appropriate to the sketching block upon which the characters are drawn, just as Wagner's heroic figures depend upon and are justified by the huge canvas and the gorgeous range of colour that he is able to devote to them. The *Don Quixote* puts us in mind of first-rate book-illustration; we could hardly see the characters more distinctly, both in themselves and in relation to their surroundings, if they were set before us in black and white.

And how tender the drawing is, how exquisitely human is the feeling for these two poor tragic-comic actors! It is this that finally makes the work so precious—its unfailing pity, its intuitive avoidance of anything that would make it simply unthinking comedy. Strauss's Sancho is very humorous, but your laughter at him is always softened with tears; while the portrait of Quixote has an added touch of pathos in that it invariably suggests the spare, worn frame of the poor, middle-aged knight. It is true in this as in every other respect. His love-singing is that of a middle-aged man; the pitiful sorrow that envelops the ride homeward after his defeat is that of middle-age; the knight is broken, disillusioned, as only men can be whose physical as well as mental forces have passed their prime. For my part, I can no longer think of Cervantes's story without Strauss's music, just as I cannot think of Goethe's *Erl King* without the music of Schubert, or of the *Lorelei* without the music of Liszt.

"The German literary laugh," says Mr. Meredith, in his *Essay on Comedy*, "like the timed awakenings of their Barbarossa in the hollows of the Untersberg, is infrequent, and rather monstrous—never a laugh of men and women in concert. It comes of unrefined abstract fancy, grotesque or grim, or gross, like the peculiar humours of their little earthmen. Spiritual laughter they have not yet attained to." So much may be said, I think, of some of Strauss's laughter. Here and there—in *Ein Heldenleben*, for example—it seems to come from the dry and wizened throat of the "little earthman"; it is not yet broadly and deeply human, not yet cosmopolitan in its appeal. His humour on occasions like this is very like Jean Paul's; you hardly know whether he is laughing with you or at you—perhaps he does not quite know himself. But in *Don Quixote* you have the philosophic laughter of the great humanist. It is not to be found there only among Strauss's works. It gave warmth and pathos to *Till Eulenspiegel*—for wonderful humoresque as that is, its informing spirit is something much more complex and much more pity-moving than the idly humorous. We have assimilated only half of *Till Eulenspiegel* if we see nothing but *diablerie* in it. But it is in *Don Quixote* that the blending of tears and laughter is most perfect; and I, for my part, would gladly sacrifice *Ein Heldenleben* for this, were I compelled to make the choice, just as I would relinquish the epic and dramatic grandeur of *Die Götterdämmerung* if I might have left to me *Die Meistersinger*, with its perpetual truth, its perpetual sanity, its perpetual appeal to real men and women in a real world.

●　　●　　●　　●　　●　　●

It will be seen from page 252 that the foregoing essay was set up in type before the *Symphonia domestica* was produced in London in February last. That performance threw a new light on Strauss and his art, and calls for some few words of comment. We need not here go very deeply into the question of how much or how little programme there is in the work. There is a strain of foolishness in Strauss that always prompts him to go through the heavy farce of mystifying his hearers at first. He tells them he prefers not to give them the clue to his literary scheme, but wants them to accept the work as absolute music; this was his tactic, for example, with *Till Eulenspiegel.* All the while he gives one clue after another to his personal friends, till at length sufficient information is gathered to reconstruct the story that he had worked upon; this gradually gets into all the programme books, and then we are able to listen to the work in the only way it *can* be listened to with any comprehension—with a full knowledge of the programme. So it is now with the *Symphonia domestica.* He has told us that " he wished the work to be judged as absolute music"; he has also told us that "he had in his mind a very definite programme when composing the symphony." Some of his admirers, with a canine fidelity that is positively touching, have tried to reconcile these contradictory positions by ingenious dialectic. That, however, is taking Strauss's whimsies just a little too seriously; it suggests the Shakesperologists of the George Dawson type, who used to tell us that even "if there is anything you do not understand or which you think is wrong in Shakespere, you may safely conclude that he is right and you are wrong." We need not discuss Strauss's self-contradictions as if they were æsthetic antinomies that could be resolved by an Hegelian dialectic in a more profound harmony; the real explanation is simply that we are dealing with a man of erratic nerves, a musician not very well used to consistent thinking, whose sense of humour sometimes skittishly takes a turning along which it is hardly worth our while to follow it. There is not the faintest doubt that the whole symphony is founded on a very definite programme, and that we shall know it all one of these days, as we now know the minutest details of the programmes of *Till Eulenspiegel* and *Ein Heldenleben*.

Then the question arises, is the programme of the *Symphonia domestica* intrinsically interesting? It avowedly illustrates a day in the composer's family life, " and we are told "—to quote Messrs. Pitt and Kalisch, the authors of the admirable Queen's Hall analytical book—"that it illustrates such every-day incidents as a Walk in the Country, the Baby's Evening and Morning Bath, the Striking of the Clock, the Yawns of the Parents when awakened by the Child, and so on." They will have it, however, that there is more in the work than this, and that underneath this "trivial subject" there is "one of far deeper and wider import"—*i.e.* "not so much a day in the life of a particular family as a realisation of the joys and griefs of motherhood and paternity, the gradual growth of the child-soul, and the mutual relationship of children and parents. . . ." But this exalted theory soon comes to grief. It is quite clear that the striking of seven in the evening and again in the morning confines the time of the drama within twelve hours ; and on these lines indeed there is some sense in the programme. That is, we see in the first section the parents and child ; in the second (the *scherzo*) the joys and diversions of the group, the lullaby, the striking of 7 P.M., and the putting of the child to bed ; in the third (the *adagio*), the parents' love-scene and the striking of 7 A.M. ; in the fourth (the *finale*) the morning wakening, and—in the double fugue—the dispute between the parents as to the future of the child. This is not a very great scheme, but it is at least comprehensible ; mix Teutonic moonshine up with it and it becomes nonsense. Thus Messrs. Pitt and Kalisch, trying to put the best face possible on that stupid noise that is meant to illustrate "the energetic protests of the child when it is first brought into contact with the

alien element of cold water" (by the way, *are*
babies usually dumped into cold water?) remark
that "if the more idealistic method of interpretation be adopted, it may be taken as a very
uncompromising musical picture of the earliest
struggles of a new-born soul." But this "idealistic method" will not work. The episode in
question occurs just before the clock strikes
7 P.M. It occurs again just before the clock
strikes 7 A.M. Are we to understand, then,
that the "new-born soul" is born once in the
evening and again next morning? This is
being "born again" with a vengeance—quick
work even in these days of Welsh revivals and
Torrey-Alexander missions! No, we must reject
the "idealistic method of interpretation," and
just settle down to the plain fact that Strauss
is painting nothing more ideal than the baby
squalling in its bath (hot or cold), just as in
other works he has painted Till's death-rattle,
the dying shudder of Don Juan, the wind-mill
and the sheep of Don Quixote, and the bray-
ing of Sancho Panza's donkey—all frankly realistic things, which we do not attempt to gild
with idealistic interpretations.

I lay stress upon these trivial points because
it is important that we should know exactly
what Strauss's intentions were, for only with a
knowledge of them can we judge his symphony
as a work of art. It is quite clear then that
he has thought it worth while to put about a
hundred people to a great deal of trouble and
expense in order to suggest the imbecile spec-

tacle of a baby shrieking in its bath; and I think it is time the world protested against so much of its leisure and its funds being taken up with sheer inanities of this kind. In Strauss's previous works there are at most only two or three passages of realism at which I would shy; they have generally been saved for us by some touch of beauty, or humour, or technical cleverness. But the baby episodes in the *Symphonia domestica* are too great a demand on our indulgence, and one is bound to say that there is something physically wrong with a brain that can fall so low as this. I hold him to be a man of enormous gifts, a magician, a wonder-worker of the first rank. But he can do nothing now on a large scale without deliberately spoiling it at some point or other out of pure freakishness—a freakishness that has ceased to be humour, and is merely the temporary lapse into silliness of a very clever man.

It goes without saying that if there is this degeneration—temporary or permanent—of the artistic sense that I suppose to be now going on in Strauss, it will show in other departments; and I think it shows pretty evidently in the music of the symphony as a whole. To my mind there is not a memorable theme in it; neither the theme of the husband, of the wife, nor of the child has anything like the quality that will entitle it to rank with the pregnant melodies of Strauss's other work. Think of the countless felicities of *Ein Heldenleben*, and you will realise at once the comparative poverty of the *Symphonia domestica.* Further, he is getting too fond of working upon mere snippets of phrases, instead of the great soaring, sweeping melodies of his earlier days ; these tiny figures will of course go contrapuntally with almost any-thing—which is probably one reason for his using them—but for that same reason their perpetual chattering in the orchestra becomes in the end rather tiresome. I am not denying, of course, that at times the music rises to great heights ; the scene of the parents playing with the child is exquisitely beautiful ; there are fine moments in the love-music; and the fugue simply picks one up and carries one away, so broad and healthy is its heartiness. There is again much of that old technical mastery that makes slaves of us even where our soul revolts against the actual message of the composer. But on the whole I do not see how the new work can stand comparison with *Ein Heldenleben* in any way. It looks far more impressive on paper than it actually sounds ; it is grossly overscored, a good third of the notes being perfectly superfluous, as anyone can dis-cover for himself by following it with the score. The mania is growing on Strauss for filling the music-paper with something or other, it matters not what ; he has a lust for ink ; it positively afflicts him to see an empty bar for any instru-ment. Master of orchestration as he is, there is page after page in the *Symphonia domestica* containing the grossest of miscalculations ; time after time we can see what his intention has been and how completely it has been frustrated by his own extravagance. He wants to wear all the clothes in his wardrobe at once. The same tendency is noticeable in his thematic work. When he has a good theme now he cannot leave it alone; he must fumble and fuss all round it till he has blurred its outline and stifled half its expression; the pleasant little lullaby, for example, would have been three times as effective without that jerky counterpoint against it in the oboe d'amore, bassoon, and viola, which simply gives the impression that somebody or other is always coming in at the wrong place, and quite disturbs the atmosphere of the lullaby itself. Altogether I am inclined to think that the new work as a whole shows a decided falling-off. And the reason? Well, is it not very likely that there has at last happened what some of us prophesied some two or three years ago? No artist can put so great a physical and mental strain upon himself as Strauss does and still keep his brain at its best. With all his many duties and occupations, his conducting and his constant travelling, it is a wonder he has any strength left to compose. For years he has been wearing his sensitive nervous system down to the very edge; and I should not be surprised to find that in doing so he has injured a good deal the delicacy of its tissue. It is said that he lives the busy life he does in order to make enough money to give up all public work and devote himself entirely to composition; but before that time comes he will probably, if he is not careful, have lost more of the divine fire than he can ever replace. The *Symphonia domestica* I take to be the work of an enormously clever man who was once a genius.

APPENDIX

WAGNER, BERLIOZ, LISZT, AND MR. ASHTON ELLIS

THE passage on page 6 seems to have roused the ire of Mr. Ashton Ellis, who devotes some seven and a half strenuous pages of the fifth volume of his "Life of Wagner" partly to childish personal abuse of myself, partly to an attempt to discredit my arguments. Over Mr. Ellis's mixture of clumsy rudeness and heavy Teutonic facetiousness we need not linger; these things have no novelty for Wagner students who have sojourned long in the Ellisian fields of controversy. Nor need we turn aside to follow Mr. Ellis in his wild attempt to make it appear that I had relied solely on a passage in Tiersot's *Berlioz et la société de son temps*, when my remarks on Hueffer's translation of Wagner's word "Geschmacklosigkeiten," as applied to *Faust*, might have shown him that I knew both Hueffer's volumes and the German original. These things are entertaining but irrelevant. Let us rather get to the real business—the guilt or innocence of Wagner.

Let me, for clearness' sake, summarise the main facts again.

(1) In 1848, Liszt, having become all-powerful at Weimar, began to make valiant efforts on behalf of modern composers. He did much for Wagner, especially by his performances of *Lohengrin*. He also revived Berlioz's opera, *Benvenuto Cellini*. Wagner fully agreed with *Lohengrin* being given, but not so fully with the revival of *Benvenuto Cellini*. He told Liszt he did not see what great good could come from this, though all the time anxiously protesting that his feeling towards Berlioz was of the kindest.

U

(2) Writing to Liszt on 8th September 1852, disparaging Berlioz's *Cellini* and his *Faust*, he speaks of the latter as the "Faust Symphony."

(3) The use of the term "symphony" is *à priori* evidence of Wagner's ignorance of the work.

(4) No evidence can be brought to show that he knew either *Cellini* or *Faust*, while everything indicates that he could not know them. Wagner was not in Paris in 1838 and 1846, when they were respectively given; nor could he have known them from the scores, which were not published till after 1852—the date of the letter to Liszt.

(5) In Hueffer's translation of the Wagner-Liszt correspondence, of which the second edition is "revised and furnished with an index by W. Ashton Ellis," the word "symphony" is deliberately omitted, thus hiding from the reader the one word that might set him doubting whether Wagner really knew the work he disparaged.

(6) In the third volume of Mr. Ellis's "Life of Wagner," which deals with this correspondence of 1852, the whole sentence referring to the "Faust Symphony" is omitted. Wagner is thus made to appear a perfect angel of goodwill towards Berlioz, without any such qualification as the letter as a whole suggests.

Mr. Ellis is first of all very angry with me for dragging him into the matter at all. Then he gets more angry with me for failing to see what is clear enough to him, that Wagner was invariably and inevitably right in everything he did or said—as it were the "Archibald the All-right" of music. Finally, he produces what he takes to be conclusive evidence in Wagner's favour. Let us look into these matters in a calm and friendly way.

(1) It cannot be disputed that Hueffer's omission of the word "symphony" from his translation of Wagner's letter to Liszt of 8th September 1852 was deliberate. Now in his preface to the volumes he goes out of his way to plume himself on the perfect fidelity of his translation to the original. "There are things in the letters," he says, "which are of comparatively little interest to the

English reader." "There is no doubt that judicious
omissions might have made these pages more readable
and more amusing." But the book "is almost of a
monumental character, and his deep respect for this
character has induced the translator to produce its every
feature. . . . Not a line has been omitted." And again:
"To sum up, this translation of the correspondence is
intended to be an exact facsimile of the German
original." As we have seen, these statements are not
true; Hueffer suppressed a vital word. The only reason
we can imagine for his doing so was the knowledge that
the inclusion of the word might make people suspect
that Wagner did not know the work he miscalled a
"Faust Symphony."

(2) A second edition of Hueffer's translation was
brought out, "revised, and furnished with an index, by
W. Ashton Ellis." Mr. Ellis now indignantly points
out that in his preface he distinctly stated that "in
view of the admirable nature of Dr. Hueffer's work,
revision was unnecessary save in the case of a few mis-
printed words and dates." Very good. Did Mr. Ellis
compare Hueffer's translation with the original? Then
he should have detected and rectified Hueffer's sup-
pression of the word "symphony." Did he not compare
the two? Then he had no right to certify Hueffer's
work as so "admirable" that "revision was unnecessary." In this one point, at any rate, it was decidedly
not admirable; it evidently stood more in need of Mr.
Ellis's revision than Mr. Ellis's certificate.

(3) Mr. Ellis can say nothing better in defence of his
own omission of the whole passage from the third volume
of his "Life" than that, as he was writing a life not of
Berlioz but of Wagner, he had no space for "a dissertation on so entirely distinct a theme as the *Faust* of
Berlioz." No one expected from him a dissertation on
Faust. All he was expected to do was to find space, in
a voluminous biography that takes about 1800 pages to
tell the story of the first forty-two years of Wagner's life,

for five or six lines of a letter that threw an important light on Wagner, especially as Mr. Ellis was actually quoting from the letter in question.

Here is the passage in the original :—

" Glaub mir—ich liebe Berlioz, mag er sich auch misstrauisch und eigensinnig von mir entfernt halten : er kennt mich nicht ; aber ich kenne ihn. Wenn ich mir von Einem etwas erwarte, so ist dies von Berlioz : nicht aber auf dem Wege, auf dem er bis zu den Geschmacklosigkeiten seiner Faust-symphonie gelangte—denn geht er dort weiter, so kann er nur noch vollständig lächerlich werden. Gebraucht ein Musiker den Dichter, so ist diess Berlioz, und sein Unglück ist, dass er sich diesen Dichter immer nach seiner musikalischen Laune zurechtlegt, bald Shakespeare, bald Goethe, sich nach seinem Belieben zurichtet. Er braucht den Dichter, der ihn durch und durch erfüllt, der ihn vor Entzücken zwingt, der ihm das ist, was der Mann dem Weibe ist."

Hueffer's translation of it as follows :—

" Believe me, I *love* Berlioz, although he keeps apart from me in his distrust and obstinacy ; he does not know me, but I know him. If I have expectations of any one it is of Berlioz, but not in the direction in which he has arrived at the absurdities of his *Faust.* If he proceeds further in that direction he must become perfectly ridiculous. If ever a musician wanted the poet it is Berlioz, and his misfortune is that he always prepares this poet for himself, according to his musical whim, arbitrarily handling now Shakespeare, now Goethe. He wants a poet who would completely penetrate him," &c.

Mr. Ellis, in his " Life " (vol. iii. pp. 336, 337), deals with the passage thus :—

" Believe me,—I *love* Berlioz, however mistrustfully and obstinately he holds aloof from me ; he does not know me,—but I know him. If there is one man I expect something of, it is Berlioz. . . . But he needs a poet who shall fill him through and through," &c.

Mr. Ellis, it will be observed, is not using Hueffer's

translation; and as the passage does not occur in Glasenapp's "Life of Wagner" at all (which puts out of the question any translation from a mutilated version), it is clear that Mr. Ellis has translated direct from the German original. When he tells us that he had no design of concealment in omitting the phrases about the "Faust Symphony" we are, of course, bound to believe him. But it is unfortunate that in his sudden and most unusual passion for economy of space he should stop just short of the word that is so awkward for Wagner. And one would rather he had not given a factitious air of sequence to the clauses of his quotation by removing the "but" from its proper position (after "If there is one man I expect something of, it is Berlioz"), endowing it with a capital letter, and making it the commencement of a new sentence. The English reader will see what has happened by looking at Hueffer's version: everything from "not in the direction" to "now Goethe" has been omitted, and the "but" carried down from its proper place after "it is of Berlioz," and improperly made to begin another sentence. The German reader will see that the "nicht aber" (not however) of the sentence "nicht aber auf dem Wege, auf dem er bis zu den Geschmacklosigkeiten seiner Faust-symphonie gelangte" has been shelved, and a fresh "Aber" called from the void and made to preface the sentence "Er gebraucht den Dichter," &c.

Let us now examine the *Benvenuto Cellini* case. The passage in Wagner's letters to Liszt of 13th April and 8th September 1852 run thus (Hueffer's translation):—

"What is this you have heard about me in connection with your performance of *Cellini*? You seem to suppose that I am hostile to it. Of this error I want you to get rid. . . . In the consequences which, as I am told, you expect from the performance of *Cellini* I cannot believe, that is all."—"B. (Bülow) has shewn quite correctly where the failure of *Cellini* lies, viz., in the poem and in the unnatural position in which the musician was forcibly placed by being expected to disguise by purely musical intentions a want which the poet alone could have made good."

Unable to give a jot of evidence that Wagner could possibly have known *Cellini*, Mr. Ellis guesses that he was condemning the work not on the score of the music, but on the basis of "a libretto or second-hand report." Even if this were so, it would not justify Wagner's remarks. What would *he* have said of any one who ran down *Tristan* without knowing any more of it than "a libretto or a second-hand report," and on the strength of this threw cold water on a theatrical manager's scheme for performing it? But there is no reason to believe that Wagner had even so much as a libretto. Liszt's tone to Wagner throughout the correspondence is that of a man fully acquainted with *Cellini* at first hand to a man who is only repeating current tittle-tattle about it. The reason Wagner gave for objecting to the revival of the opera was that he had heard that Berlioz was "recasting" it, and that it would become him much better to write a new work than to touch-up an old one. On the 7th October 1852 Liszt, after agreeing that "the weakness of Berlioz's mode of working" comes from his poem, goes on to say, "but you have been erroneously *led to believe* that Berlioz is writing his *Cellini*. This is not the case; the question at issue is simply as to a very considerable cut—nearly a whole tableau—which I have proposed to Berlioz, and which he has approved of. . . . If it interests you *I will send you the new libretto together with the old one*, and I think you will approve of the change. . . ." Is it not clear that Liszt assumes as a matter of fact Wagner's complete ignorance of the work? In an earlier letter, dated 23rd August, Liszt tells him that in November he is expecting Berlioz, "whose *Cellini* (with a considerable cut) must not be shelved, for *in spite of all the stupid things that have been set going about it, 'Cellini'* is and remains a remarkable and highly estimable work. *I am sure you would*

like many things in it." The latter of the two
passages I have here italicised shows once more that
Liszt speaks to Wagner as to a man who does
not know the opera; and the former passage indicates that there was a good deal of stupid and
malevolent gossip afloat concerning it among people
who also were ignorant of it. Moreover, on the 31st
October 1853, Liszt again assumes Wagner's ignorance :
" For this work I retain my great predilection, which
you will not think uncalled for when you know it better."
Mr. Ellis, indeed, practically admits that all Wagner had
to go upon was a report of Bülow's in the *Neue Zeit-
schrift* of April 1852. (See, above, Wagner's letter to
Liszt of 8th September 1852 : " B. (*i.e.* Bülow) has
shewn quite correctly where the failure of ' *Cellini* ' lies,
viz., in the poem," &c. It will be noticed that the letter
in which Wagner first sniffs at *Cellini* is dated the 13th
of this same month of April.) What would Mr. Ellis
say of any anti-Wagnerian who should criticise *Tristan*
not even from the libretto, but from the second-hand
idea of it derived from some one else's article on it ?

Mr. Ellis's plea that Wagner was talking of *Cellini* not
publicly, but in a private letter, is irrelevant. A public
article would have been read by a few curious people
and forgotten ; in throwing cold water on Liszt's revival
of the opera, Wagner was in danger of doing Berlioz a
serious injury. For about fourteen years after its first
failure *Cellini* had not had a performance anywhere.
There was only one man in Europe who combined the
qualifications of knowing the opera, admiring it, being
able to conduct it, and having at his own disposal an
opera house where the work could be given. That man
was Liszt; upon him, and him alone, it depended whether
Berlioz should have a chance of showing that *Cellini* had
been unjustly condemned in 1838. Had Liszt been weak
enough to have been privately influenced by Wagner,
Berlioz would have undoubtedly suffered far more than
he could have done from a public article.

Now for the *Faust* affair. Wagner was not in Paris in 1846, when *Faust* received its two performances. Mr. Ellis, however, sagely opines that "it is not absolutely impossible (!) that Wagner should have heard fragments (!) either of the earlier *Huit Scènes* (*i.e.* the eight numbers referred to on p. 95 of the present volume), or the *Damnation* itself." This invocation of the aid of the "not-absolutely-impossible" does not help us very much, I am afraid. "But for argument's sake," continues our intrepid apologist, "let us say he had not; about the work he must have heard, or he could not know of its existence." (Here, at any rate, Mr. Ellis's penetrating intelligence has struck home. Even *I* am compelled to admit that Wagner must have heard about the work, or he could not have known of its existence.) "And if about it, why should the general outline of common artistic repute (Wagner still maintaining desultory correspondence with old Paris friends of good art-judgment, as we know) not be enough to furnish him with grounds for deploring its scheme in a private letter?" I have already dealt with the contention that Wagner was justified in running down works he did not know so long as the running-down was done privately. For the rest, the argument is just our old friend the "not-absolutely-impossible" again. It is not absolutely impossible that Wagner should have known some one who heard the work in Paris six years previously; it is not absolutely impossible that Wagner should have corresponded with this friend on the subject of *Faust*; it is not absolutely impossible that this friend should have been a man "of good art-judgment." Such a string of "may-have-beens" may be confidently left to its fate. But once more, if any one had disparaged a work of Wagner's on the strength of such dubious information, what would Wagner have said of him then, and what would Mr. Ellis say of him now?

But even Mr. Ellis, I imagine, does not take these phantom speculations of his very seriously. From his own point of view, indeed, there was never any need for him to indulge in them, so confident is he that in his closing paragraph he has a piece of evidence that is shattering in its conclusiveness. He will not have it that to call *The Damnation of Faust* a symphony is to betray ignorance of it. Was not Berlioz's *Romeo and Juliet* a "dramatic symphony"? It was indeed; but in the first place, Berlioz himself called *Romeo and Juliet* a symphony, whereas he never applied that title to *Faust;* and in the second place, *Romeo and Juliet* really *is* a symphony, in the sense that time after time the work is carried on by means of orchestral movements pure and simple—while *Faust* is not a symphony in any sense, and could hardly have been called one by any one who knew it. Mr. Ellis is "credibly informed" that it was called a symphony "in Paris at the time." I take leave to doubt it; but in any case, Mr. Ellis's credible informant might have given him some evidence that it was so called by any one who had heard it. Adolphe Adam, for example, writing about it to a friend on the morrow of its performance, calls it "a kind of opera in four parts" (see J. G. Prodhomme's *Hector Berlioz*, p. 278). Berlioz himself, as Mr. Ellis notes, styled it a "Legend" or "Dramatic Legend." Uninformed gossip no doubt gave it the title of "symphony," in the years after 1846, from a vague idea that it must necessarily have been of the same type of structure as *Romeo and Juliet*. Gossip may have had something else to go upon too. In 1829 Berlioz had really thought (as we see from a letter to Humbert Ferrand quoted in Adolphe Jullien's *Hector Berlioz*, p. 182) of writing a "symphonie descriptive de *Faust*." Shortly before that he had tried to get a commission from the Opera for a ballet on the same subject. These facts may have lingered in the air for years, and in the general vagueness upon the matter after 1846 it may well be that Berlioz's name was often associated with a *Faust* "symphony." It was apparently this ill-informed gossip that Wagner was repeating.

Fragments of *Faust*, by the way, were given at some of Berlioz's Russian and German concerts, and there was a complete performance of it at Berlin in 1847. Wagner, of course, was in Dresden at that time. There is hardly the slightest likelihood, again, that he had a score of the *Huit Scènes*, a few copies of which Berlioz had rashly had engraved at his own expense in 1829, and published at 30 francs; and even if Wagner *did* know these eight fragments, that would not justify him in criticising *The Damnation of Faust* without knowing it. I repeat that the only conclusion we can come to is that he called it a symphony because he was ignorant of it.

But now Mr. Ellis's great discovery comes in. He quotes from a letter of Liszt to Breitkopf and Härtel, the music publishers, of 30th October 1852: "I am expecting M. Berlioz here . . . and on the 21st the symphonies of *Romeo and Juliet* and *Faust* will be performed, which I proposed to you to publish." Here Mr. Ellis imagines me crying out, "It is all that wretched Wagner's fault; he had put the word into Liszt's innocent head six weeks before." "But Berlioz," Mr. Ellis goes on to say, "arrives at Weimar, conducts 'les 2 premiers actes' of his *Faust* at one concert with his *Romeo*, and behold —no longer innocent, Liszt writes Professor Christian Lobe, editor of the *Fliegende Blätter für Musik*, May 1st 1853: 'The German public is still unacquainted with the greater part of Berlioz's works, and after many enquiries that have been addressed me in the past few months, I believe a German translation of the catalogue might have a good effect; perhaps with division into categories, *e.g.* OVERTURES, *Francs Juges*, &c. . . . SYMPHONIES, (1) *Episode*, (2) *Harold*, (3) *Romeo and Juliet*, (4) *Damnation of Faust;* VOCAL PIECES, &c. &c.'"

Alas! Mr. Ellis is no happier here than in his other attempts to get out of the difficulty. It is not clear, to begin with, why he should suppose that Liszt's or any one else's knowledge of *Faust* should prove Wagner to have known it. But putting that aside, what seems to have shaped itself in Mr. Ellis's mind is some such ramshackle syllogism as this: "If Liszt, who knew the *Faust* so well, wrongly calls it a symphony, the use of the erroneous title by Wagner makes it possible that he too may have known it." It all looks promising enough; but it has one fatal flaw, one point upon which Mr. Ellis, in his hurry to whoop, forgot to make quite sure. His confident assumption that Liszt *did* know *Faust* is unjustified.

My previous point that people who did not know the work had got into the habit of calling it a symphony is proved by other letters of Liszt in which he thus speaks of it. On the 4th September 1852, for example, he writes to Cornelius: "On the 12th November I expect a visit from Berlioz, who will spend a week at Weimar. Then we shall have *Cellini*, the symphony of *Romeo and Juliet*, and some pieces from the *Faust* symphony." Mr. Ellis may think this confirms his own theory. But it is worth while looking again at the above-quoted letter of Liszt of 30th October 1852 to Breitkopf and Härtel, and the circumstances that called it forth. On the 7th June Berlioz had written to Liszt that he was going to give a concert in Paris, at which he would perform some fragments of *Faust*. "*I am truly sorry*," he says, "*that you do not know this work.* I cannot get a publisher to take it; they find it too big to engrave (*trop riche de planches*). I must apply to Ricordi of Milan. . . . In any case, if you were to find a daring German publisher capable of undertaking this rash act, you can tell him that *Faust* has been well translated into German." It is evident that after receiving this letter, Liszt wrote to Breitkopf and Härtel recommending them to publish the work; this is the proposal he refers to in his letter of 30th October 1852. So that the very letter of Liszt's which Mr. Ellis quotes triumphantly for its use of the term "Faust Symphony" was prompted by a letter from Berlioz, in which he distinctly says that Liszt does not know the work!

Bearing this in mind, let us follow up the subsequent course of events, and see whether Liszt knew it *after* Berlioz's visit to Weimar—whether, that is, he was not still in much the same state of ignorance about it when he wrote the letter of 1st May 1853 to Lobe. It can be shown that Liszt had nothing to do with the performance of the first two acts of *Faust* at Weimar; that Berlioz brought the score and parts with him from Paris and took the rehearsals and the concert himself, whereas Liszt himself took charge of *Cellini*. On the 10th October 1852 Berlioz writes to Liszt in terms that once more place the latter's complete ignorance of the work beyond dispute. Berlioz has actually to tell him the number and quality of soloists to engage. "I will leave here for Weimar on the 12th November, certain. I will arrive on the 15th, and can stay in your neighbourhood eight days, but no more. . . . Now tell me by the next post if it is necessary for me to send you the vocal parts of *Faust*, or if it will suffice that I should bring them with me. The soloists and chorus would in that case have to learn in four or five days the fragments to be given at the concert. Only a tenor and a bass (*soli*) are needed for these fragments of *Faust*, Marguerite appearing only in the last two acts." Berlioz would not tell an elementary fact like that to a man who already knew the work.

Then, on the 6th November, he writes : "I send you to-day the parcel containing the *Faust* vocal parts, the choruses, the rôles, and a German libretto . . . and the vocal score (for sixty-three people). The orchestral parcel is too large ; I will bring it myself. It would be of no use to you before my arrival." Clearly Liszt was not even going to conduct the rehearsals, which would not be begun until Berlioz arrived at Weimar. (The *Faust* fragments were evidently rehearsed hurriedly ; there is a letter of Frau Pohl's extant describing the success of the performances, and saying how amazing it was that so much should have been accomplished in so short a time.) Berlioz's further remarks once more show

that he assumes Liszt's complete ignorance of the work :
" It is not difficult; only the chorus and the principal
parts are dangerous. We will announce for the concert
the first two parts only, for which no Marguerite is
required. You will need a tenor (Faust), a deep bass
(Mephisto), and another bass (Brander). It will last an
hour." All this, pointing conclusively to Liszt's total
ignorance of the work, is in the identical letter which
Mr. Ellis actually cites in another connection !

Even after the Weimar concert, which took place about
the 20th November 1852, Liszt knew no more of *Faust*
than what he had heard there. It is clear from a letter
of his to Radecke of 9th December 1852, and one of 27th
February 1853 to Schmidt, that the parcel containing the
score and the parts was sent on to Berlioz in Paris a few
days after the concert. Liszt, in fact, though he looked
after *Cellini* and the other works, had practically nothing
to do with *Faust*. Berlioz brought the score and parts
with him, conducted the rehearsals, conducted the
concert, and then on his departure left the parcel with
Liszt, to be forwarded to him in Paris. Moreover, we
may be pretty sure that all he took with him was the
score of the first two parts—all that were given at the
concert. The bulky manuscript score, now in the
Conservatoire library at Paris, is bound up in three (or
four) volumes—I forget which at the moment. If any one
should conjecture that Berlioz might have taken with him
the score of the whole work to show to Liszt, that supposition is disposed of by a letter of Berlioz, dated Dresden,
22nd April 1854. The complete *Faust* had just been
given there. Berlioz wishes Liszt had been present : " I
regret that you could not have heard the last two acts,
which you do not know." Everything points to the fact
that even Liszt's knowledge of *Faust* was limited to a
hearing of the first two acts at the Weimar concert.
There is plenty of subsequent correspondence with
Berlioz, but it is all about *Cellini*, which Liszt had produced and knew thoroughly. In after years people used

to write to him—people who were compiling books on Berlioz, or trying to get hold of his correspondence, or investigating the history of the Weimar theatre—and ask Liszt to tell them something of his relations with Berlioz. Liszt's reply is always the same; he is proud of having refloated *Cellini*, but he does not mention *Faust*. Even when he tells the Grand Duke Carl Alexander that Berlioz gave three concerts in Weimar, there is still no mention of the *Faust* fragments, which apparently had been no affair of his.

In 1853 and 1854 he still calls the work a symphony, knowing no better, having neither seen the score nor heard a complete performance of it. But in 1854 the score is published, and a copy sent to Liszt. In December of that year he writes two letters on the same day. In one of them, to Mason, the old habit is still too strong for him, and he speaks of the " dramatic symphony of *Faust* " ;[1] in the other, to Wasielewski, he refers to it as *Faust* only. Thereafter, so far as I can discover, he never speaks of it as a symphony. See, for example, his letters of 9th February 1856 to Edward Liszt, 19th February 1856 to Brendel, 3rd January 1857 to Turanyi, 16th September 1861 to Brendel, March 1883 to Vicomte Henri Delaborde, 12th September 1884 to Pohl, 1st January 1855 (" Do you know the score of his *Damnation de Faust?* "), and 24th December 1855 to Wagner.

So much for the question of Liszt and *Faust*, which Mr. Ellis dragged in so gleefully to help his own case and Wagner's. In the absence of any new facts, I contend that it is abundantly clear that Liszt too called *Faust* a symphony only because he did not know it. If Wagner

---

[1] It should be borne in mind that Liszt himself was writing a " Faust Symphony " during the period covered by this controversy. He speaks of having finished it, in fact, in the letter to Wasielewski of this very date, 14th December. His constant use of the term to describe his own work might easily account for his transferring it unconsciously to that of Berlioz.

is to be whitewashed at all, it must be by a less brittle brush than this. As regards his disparagement of both *Cellini* and *Faust*, the defence seems to me to have broken down completely; he knew nothing of either of them.

E. N.

THE END